INTERVIEWED
BY GOD

PuddleDancer
PRESS

2240 Encinitas Blvd., Ste. D-911, Encinitas, CA 92024
email@PuddleDancer.com • www.PuddleDancer.com

INTERVIEWED
BY GOD

A Journey to Freedom

BETH BANNING

"*Every lesson is a widening and deepening of consciousness. It is a stretch-*
ing of the mind beyond its conceptual limits and a stretching of the heart
beyond its emotional boundaries. It is a bringing of unconscious material
into consciousness, a healing of past wounds, and a discovery of new faith
and trust."—PAUL FERRINI

Interviewed by God
A Journey to Freedom

© 2014 Beth Banning
A PuddleDancer Press Book

Requests for permission should be addressed to:
PuddleDancer Press, Permissions Dept.
2240 Encinitas Blvd. Ste D-911, Encinitas, CA 92024
Tel: 1-760-652-5754 Fax: 1- 760-274-6400 Rights@PuddleDancer.com

Ordering Information
Please contact Independent Publishers Group,
Tel: 312-337-0747; Fax: 312-337-5985;
Email: frontdesk@ipgbook.com or visit www.IPGbook.com for other contact information and details about ordering online

Author: Beth Banning
Editor: Cher Johnson

Manufactured in the United States of America

1st Printing, September, 2014

10 9 8 7 6 5 4 3 2 1

ISBN 10: 1-934336-95-5

ISBN 13: 978-1-934336-95-3

Library of Congress Control Number: 2014943268

Publisher's Cataloging-in-Publication
(Provided by Quality Books, Inc.)

Banning, Beth.
    Interviewed by God : a journey to freedom / by Beth Banning.
    pages cm
    Includes bibliographical references.
    LCCN 2014943268
    ISBN 978-1-934336-95-3
    ISBN 978-1-934336-96-0
    ISBN 978-1-934336-97-7
    ISBN 978-1-934336-99-1

    1. Banning, Beth. 2. Spiritual biography.
    3. Meditation.   I. Title.

BL73.B364A3 2014   204'.092
                               QBI14-600111

ENDORSEMENTS

"This book will inspire you to have the confidence and desire to develop your own relationship with your personal God and thus help you to receive guidance and knowledge that is just for you."

— **Terry Cole-Whittaker**, DD, Author of, *What You Think of Me is None of My Business*

"Interview by God is a tremendous work that combines the beauty and power that can only be captured through a true personal story, and a wonderful and comprehensive format that walks the reader through the steps of transformation. Reading the book is an incredible journey, an experience of much more than words."

— **Jonathan Ellerby, PhD**, International Author of, *Return to the Sacred*

"Real consciousness comes when you realize that you are that individualized point of God, not an individual seeking God. Beth Banning's new book, *Interviewed by God: A Journey to Freedom*, demonstrates the power of God expressing itself through each of us. Her passionate and intensely personal account is an inner adventure of self-discovery that awakens us to the aliveness and flow of Spirit animating and directing us. In our search for what it is we are, she helps us to realize that we have taken a journey to a place we have never left. Great and enlightened reading!"

— **Ernest D. Chu**, Author of, *Soul Currency*, and personal development counselor

"I am often asked for an endorsement. On a few rare occasions I have been hard pushed to find honest words of recommendation, but with this book, *Interviewed by God*... no such problem! Beth Banning easily connects with her readers, allowing them to become involved with, and immersed in, her extraordinary story of spiritual growth and deep spiritual insights. I highly recommend this special book. Happy assimilation!"

~ **Michael J. Roads** - Author of, *Through the Eyes of Love trilogy* and *Stepping Between Realities*

"*Interviewed by God* is a beautifully written story about Beth's journey to transform her internal landscape leading to living a joyful life. She writes from her heart inspiring us to find what is hidden within us so we can connect with our own spiritual knowing and inner authority. Her story helps us all open to our greatest potential and move past our limitations. This book is deeply moving to read and transformative!"

~ **Sandra Ingerman**, MA, Author of, *Awakening to the Spirit World* and *Shamanic Journeying*

"*Interviewed by God* is a lovely story about an ordinary woman who has experienced some extraordinary events in her life. It is a delightful rendition about awakening and embracing the interconnectivity of spirit. If you are searching to find joy in all things great and small, then this book is a wonderful read."

~ **Lillie Leonardi**, Lecturer & Author of, *In the Shadow of a Badge*

"There can be no substitute for our own direct experience in our inner journey of self-discovery. But when someone's transformational experiences of heart and mind are shared, they offer us inspiration and insights into how we might continue on our own journey. Beth's book clearly and engagingly confirms a fundamental truth: that we are all ordinary in our humanity and extraordinary in our divinity. Her own spiritual odyssey of awakening, whilst unique to her, is universal for us all – and her book a beautiful way-shower and compassionate companion on our collective journey into wholeness."

~ **Dr. Jude Currivan**, Author of, *The 8th Chakra* and *HOPE*

"From the moment I began reading this book, it felt different. It was as though Beth's fears were my own, that her words were one's I spoke and the lifelong misunderstanding of who she REALLY is resonated with me.

I am inspired by the amazing power that she embodies in this book, her pure vulnerability and courage to put it all out there for everyone to read. I now feel that the messages I hear within me are true, the words in my head are actually from God and this has allowed me to strengthen and deepen my spiritual relationship with the truth that has always been speaking within me.

Personally I feel this book is going to change the way women perceive themselves. It's raw, it's real and it's like nothing I've ever experienced while reading a book before."

~ **Melissa Risdon** - Radio Show Host and International Speaker

"This book was written directly from the heart and spirit with such refreshing openness and vulnerability. It is obvious that the purpose is not to convince the reader of anything, but only to share the incredible experiences that have shaped her and guided her to a lovely, peaceful existence.

What is distinctive about this book is that there is no hint of "ego" in the writing. It comes from a place beneath and beyond ego - a place we all long to connect with. Anyone who is struggling to find balance and peace of mind and searching for a connection with something deeper and more meaningful in their lives will love this book."

~ **Bob Uslander**, MD, Associate Medical Director, Palliative Care
Services, LightBridge Hospice

"*Interviewed by God* is the true story of an ordinary woman experiencing an ordinary life until she learned to become still, to live in the present moment, and to look within. What unfolds is a soul awakening of an amazing magnitude. The interview format reminds us that we all have an inner source of knowledge; all we need to do is sit in stillness and be open to receive guidance from our Higher Self.

Interviewed by God is not only a story of one woman's experiences but also an opportunity for self-reflection and acceptance of ourselves as the powerful human beings we are. This is a must read for anyone on a spiritual path who may be feeling alone in their quest to understanding their true purpose in life."

~ **Sandy Levin** - Retired Professor of Education, Artist, and Yoga Instructor

DEDICATION

I dedicate this book to the love of my life, my best friend, confidant, sacred partner, and biggest supporter, Neill Gibson, whose strength, integrity and unconditional love helped make this book a reality. His caring, tenderness, encouragement and confidence in me lifted me up and guided me forward. When I think of his dedication and tireless efforts in making this book a reality I am moved to tears. Thank you, Neill, from the bottom of my heart.

CONTENTS

ACKNOWLEDGMENTS

I DID NOT BIRTH THIS BOOK ALONE; it took a community to write it, get it to print, and move it out into the hands of the people it was meant for. Creating this book has been an intense challenge, and it would not have been possible without the support, partnership, cooperation and generosity of a great many wonderful people.

First I want to acknowledge my interviewer, my pillar of strength, my foundation and my constant, compassionate and loving companion, God. For without this relationship none of this would have been possible.

I also wish to express my deep appreciation for my gifted editor and friend Cher Johnson, who patiently guided me through this 18 month editing process. Her years of experience, her keen intelligence, and passion for the written word shine through on each and every page of this book.

And for my other soul sisters and dear friends:

Ann Convery, who generously enriched the editing process with her engaging sense of humor and colorful brilliance that helped capture the lightness of heart and carefree spirit of God I felt during my conversations, but needed help to fully express.

Terry Whitaker, Laura Pedro, Elizabeth Powers, Michele Nowak-Sharkey, Judith Balian, Sandy Levin, Lynn Pollock, Lizz Huerta, Maribel Jimenez, Kim Warner, and Brandi

Atwell, who were early readers and gave me encouragement and invaluable feedback.

Jennifer Lamprey, Wendy Whitelaw, Dale Bach, Talyn Khanbabyan, Tanya Paluso, Lisa Reynaldo, Julie Freeman and Lesley Wirth, all of my local mastermind group, whose constant support, creativity and wisdom helped me to move this book out in the world and into your hands.

To my teachers and dear friends Tom and Trisha Kelly, who have been and continue to be an inspiration in my life. Their example of devotion to God and their willingness to speak about spirituality boldly and openly has supported this book more than I can say.

To the people in the book whose names I've changed to protect their anonymity, I thank you for the gifts you have given me.

I also wish to express my gratitude for my friend and supporter Meiji Stewart, owner of PuddleDancer Press, for his generosity and enthusiasm in bringing this book into print.

And finally for my son Spenser, who has been my greatest teacher and whom I love dearly.

INTRODUCTION

MY GUESS IS THAT YOUR LIFE is as full and as busy as mine, so each time I pick up a book I wonder whether it's going to be worth my time and energy. But lately I've learned that time and energy (and even matter) aren't remotely what I thought they were.

Everything has an energetic signature, and when something is created consciously, its signature becomes bold, bright and easier to feel. I've been guided to write this book about my recent adventures, and was told that even more important than the words I use is the energy that they're infused with. My intention is that the energy of these words creates a mirror that will help you reflect on your own life story.

This book is for you if:

» You have a sense that there is more to life than you've experienced up till now.
» You have a deep longing for awakening to the truth of who you are.
» You feel an unexplained restless tension rising within you.
» You've been experiencing things that you don't understand or are afraid to talk about.

To be clear, this book is not about a tragic existence, a life-threatening illness, or dangerous escapades. It's about an inner journey: my journey of awakening. I have traveled my innermost landscapes and have discovered new possibilities for living with more joy, peace, and freedom than I knew were available to me. It didn't happen because I'm in any way extraordinary. On the contrary, I'm really quite ordinary. I'm not highly educated, nor do I have exceptional intelligence. I wasn't born with a lot of money or into special circumstances, nor have I spent much of my life searching for spiritual truths.

My adventure began with an unexplainable internal pressure that was seeking release. I suspect many other people on the planet are also experiencing this. Are you one of them? If so, it's time for a radical change in how we perceive ourselves as human beings. However, this change is not one that will happen outside of us. The change we feel coming is one that is bubbling up inside, and for those of us who feel it, it can no longer be ignored.

You have not picked up this book by accident – there is an energetic signature to it. You are on the brink of a great adventure; one in which you are not alone. We know that what has been can no longer be. It is time to move beyond the "truths" that have been handed down to us and begin relying on the truth that we know inside. This book is about learning to trust yourself – this inner knowing will not mislead you. It is the one and only thing that will take you where you have always been trying to go.

The words in this book may act as signposts along your path, but they are not meant to be your ultimate guide. The most important thing you should know while reading this book is that for most of us, including me, awakening is a gradual process, not an instant manifestation. You can experience extraordinary adventures as well, and you can be directly guided from your own highest source of knowing. It doesn't matter what you call this source. These are all names for the same thing – God, All That Is, the universe, your higher self, or whatever name resonates most for you. What you call it doesn't matter; what's important is that you have a deep desire and commitment to discover the truth for yourself.

My sincere hope is that while reading this book you reflect on your own life, ask your own questions, and allow these words to work through your body, heart, and soul so that you may get the answers that are most meaningful to you.

You will gain the most benefit from this book by consciously allowing the energy imbued in these words to have their way with you. You can do this most effectively by quieting your mind as much as possible before you start reading, and then again when you put the book down.

That being said, there are two ways you can use this book:

» If you've come to this book and you're just embarking on your spiritual journey, I suggest that you start at the beginning and read it through. As you do, stop when you feel inspired to and allow the energy of what you have just read work through you, and then continue.

» If you are drawn to this book but you already have a comprehensive spiritual background, you may also want to start at the beginning and read all the way through to the end. Or you may want to get into a more meditative state and open the book randomly to that part where you are meant to start reading.

Whichever method you choose, my desire is that you use this book to help guide you to your own answers, use it for inspiration, or use it as a reminder of what you already know.

Use and share this book in any way you see fit.

However you choose to use this book, start now, don't wait. There is a great adventure waiting for you and it begins right here and right now.

CHAPTER 1

The Message

May 2011

I OPENED THE DOOR OF MY ROOM just as the sun was peeking its head up over the horizon, knowing this was our last day in Bimini. The clear turquoise water reflected the pink and gold, silver-edged clouds. I sat on the dock to meditate. My new mantra, "relax and receive," washed through me and with every wave my body felt clearer, fresher and more vibrant.

A few minutes later Sukuma touched my shoulder, letting me know it was time for my massage. As I walked to the massage room, my enjoyment of this magical world dimmed as I remembered that close to this restful compound there was a population of people on this tiny island struggling with poverty, alcoholism, and AIDS. *How could life be so peaceful and beautiful for me when there were so many people around me just barely surviving?* I thought to myself. What a paradox. How could anyone be happy in the face of such suffering? It wasn't just here that I encountered poverty and suffering, it was everywhere. At home in California, too, homeless people often stand at intersections with their handmade signs pleading for help. Where does our responsibility to help others begin and end? Can I fully enjoy this rare and wonderful trip while people around me suffer?

It was a long while before I could relax, but eventually the gentle pressure of Sukuma's hands pushed these thoughts from my mind and I drifted in and out of sleep. Towards the end of the massage – beneath my closed eyelids – I began seeing spots – hundreds of curious, sparkling dancing little blue spots. I felt so peaceful that I didn't concern myself with them. After the massage, the memory of the blue dots faded as I got my gear together for our final boat trip to swim with dolphins.

When we boarded the boat later that morning, even though I had improved with my snorkel gear, being confined on a 40-foot catamaran with 30 people was still stressful for me. Thank God for the natural beauty of this place. The sun's rays cast glistening streaks of light onto the ocean. As the boat glided out of the bay, seagulls swooped around us, their white bodies reflecting the blue of the ocean beneath them. Along the way we were escorted by flying fish, sea turtles, and barracudas.

We sailed for some time and then a wave of energy rippled through the passengers. "Over there," one person yelled. "Behind us, look!" another squealed. One scream of excitement after another popped from their mouths. All of a sudden, out of nowhere, they were all around us. "Oh my God," someone yelled, "There are so many of them!" Over 50 dolphins surrounded the boat, jumping, playing, and enjoying themselves. Then I remembered why I was willing to get on this boat; it was the most enchanting sight I've ever seen.

Amlas, the head of the WildQuest crew, cautiously

observed the dolphins to see if they wanted to stay and play with us. Standing on the bow of the boat with her blonde hair blowing in the wind, she watched closely as the dolphins swam away and then swam back. You could see how much she loved them in every bone of her thin, athletic body. When she gave us the signal to get ready, we all rushed to get our snorkeling gear on, eager to get in the water. The two best swimmers lowered themselves in first to see if the dolphins would stay. Yes, they wanted to play!

When it was my turn I grabbed the ladder and sank into the water. I wasn't quite strong enough to keep up with the other swimmers, so I decided just to stay near the boat as it sailed slowly towards the dolphins. Suddenly I felt someone grab my wrist. It was Nipun, one of the crew members that I had become very attached to. His dark hair was dripping water down the sides of his round face. I could tell by his sparkling brown eyes that he was up to something. He started to drag me toward the dolphins, swimming faster than I believed possible. My snorkel vibrated from the pressure of the water hitting it and I could hardly see through my goggles. Then suddenly I saw dolphins everywhere as he released me in the middle of the huge pod. I looked up and he stuck his thumb up in the air with a big grin.

All I could see were dolphins. Tears came to my eyes, and a wave of joy rippled through me as I watched them frolic with the swimmers. All too soon they were moving further and further away. But by then I'd had such an incredible experience I didn't care that I couldn't keep up.

When I reached the boat, almost everybody was already on board. I grabbed the ladder and hoisted myself out of the water. Everybody was squealing, giggling and telling their dolphin encounter stories as the boat moved on. And then we caught up with the dolphins, a second time! Again we stopped and played with them until they moved on. Then, as we were about to head home, a third pod appeared. Once again Amlas encouraged us into the water.

By this time I was very tired physically and emotionally, but it was my last opportunity to swim with the dolphins before we returned home. So I got my gear back on and once more slipped into the water. The others were far away, so I decided to let go of any expectations and just do my "relax and receive" meditation. I floated, face down in the water. After a little while I lifted my head and without warning a dolphin appeared right in front of me. I had a sense that she was female, and she must've been very old because she was covered with spots, a sign of age in spotted dolphins.

As I faced her in the water she scanned me with her sonar and I could feel the vibration move through my body. Then it was as if time stopped. As we floated – eye to eye – it was as though she were trying to tell me something. All of a sudden she closed her eyes and then almost brushed my shoulder as she swam away. It was one of the most magical experiences I've ever had.

The boat was close by, and as I climbed up out of the water for the last time I heard the buzz of excited conversation. Then Amlas said, "I have a suggestion. You just had quite a remarkable encounter and I suggest that you all sit quietly and really take it in." A wave of relief came over me as I realized how much I wanted to be quiet and let the experience sink in.

We all sat down silently. I closed my eyes, and the blue dots from the morning began to reappear in the blackness of my closed eyelids. I had forgotten about those blue dots from this morning's massage, but here they were again. They began to move, change shape and create patterns as they danced around.

Suddenly I recognized them: they were bubbles! It was as though I was back in the water with the dolphins – with bubbles everywhere. Out from the middle of these bubbles swam the same old spotted dolphin that I had connected with moments before. Once again she came to me, eye to eye, as though she wanted to say something. I held very still and opened my mind to hers. Feelings of both joy and deep sadness rippled through me as my mind spun with visual images of both wondrous and devastating world events. Memories of this island's poverty and pain, and my magical experiences here tumbled into the mix. And then it came – I sensed the dolphin was sending me a message. I knew something important was about to happen.

But how did I get here? What did it all mean, and how in the world was I able to receive a message from a dolphin in the first place? It all began when I started accepting, trusting, and following my internal guidance. You may or may not believe what you are about to read in this book, and that's okay. But these seemingly crazy stories are now part of my "normal" life. Over the last few years I've learned to relax enough to receive some extraordinary gifts – gifts that are there for all of us if we're open to them. This has been a miraculous journey that's brought me to a place of extraordinary peace and happiness, and to a joy I didn't know was possible. I promise this peace and joy is also available to you. Let me tell you my story…

CHAPTER 2
What is REALLY Real

"Our deepest fear is not that we are inadequate. Our deepest fear is that we are powerful beyond measure. It is our light, not our darkness that most frightens us. We ask ourselves, who am I to be brilliant, gorgeous, talented, fabulous? Actually, who are you not to be? You are a child of God. Your playing small does not serve the world. There is nothing enlightened about shrinking so that other people won't feel insecure around you. We are all meant to shine, as children do. We were born to make manifest the glory of God that is within us. It's not just in some of us; it's in everyone. And as we let our own light shine, we unconsciously give other people permission to do the same. As we are liberated from our own fear, our presence automatically liberates others."
— *Marianne Williamson*

HOUNDED BY DOUBT

January, 2011

I WOKE UP WITH A POWERFUL SURGE of kundalini energy running up and down my spine. It shot like an electric current up from my tailbone through my spine, up and out of the top of my head, and then back in and down. A minute or so later it subsided and I glanced over at the clock. It was exactly 5:30 in the morning. I never get up that early. *You've got to be kidding me*, I thought to myself. Then I turned over and went back to sleep. The same thing happened again the next morning – I woke at 5:30 AM with the same intense energy moving through my body, but once again my doubt whether this was all just my imagination had me close my eyes and go back to sleep. Then it all stopped. Nothing happened the next day or the day after that; everything went back to normal. But this strange coincidence haunted me.

You see, I had asked God to help me embody the truth of who I am, to be useful in the world, and to give me clear signs about how to do this. In one of our conversations, God suggested that I start waking up at 5:30 in the morning, meditate, and then write about my experiences. Was it really God waking me up? Or was it my mind – my imagination – wishing for something to happen? I decided to go with the idea it was God and see what would come of it, but doubt still hounded me.

Now I said to God, "I need to know if it's really you. Wake me up again and I promise I will get up. I will meditate and then I will go to the beach, as you ask, and start writing." Presto! The next day my eyes opened with a start; I looked at the clock and there were the numbers: 5:24. "*I get it, and I won't argue about six minutes*," I said to myself. It was dark in my bedroom. Neill and the dog were sound asleep. I grabbed my clothes and went downstairs.

Funny, even now after all the strange experiences I have had, I continue to doubt that they are anything more than just my imagination. But as I continue to follow God's guidance, the more they become part of my reality – part of my everyday life.

So here I am, sitting at the beach on a chilly Pacific morning, and I'm watching the pale pink dawn shoot fingers of light over the receding tide. The bench under me is cold, and, I'm clutching a mug of rapidly cooling coffee. A pelican flies overhead. I open my laptop, wondering if I should have grabbed my gloves on the way out of the house.

But what led me to follow God's directions at 5:30 in the morning? I got here one step, one thought, one feeling at a time. Each time I say YES it brings me closer to God. Each time I turn my attention from fear to love it brings me closer to who I really am, and closer to what is REALLY real. Running through me is an emotion – not quite joy, not sorrow, not contentment, not fear – but all of them combined. It's the emotion of truth – knowing that I'm one with All That Is. As the clouds turn shades of golden white, I sit here, thinking instead of writing. My hope is that the questions explored in the interviews that lie ahead in this book, and the responses that emerged from my personal experience will touch you, open you to your own questions, and help you notice and explore your own experiences of awakening.

Who Am I to Talk to God?

Day after day I did as I thought God suggested. I got up at 5:30 AM, meditated, and then went to write my story. I sat at my computer staring at a blank page. My frustration grew and my confusion intensified. It's not as though I didn't have any experience writing – I did. Before God asked me to tell you my story, I was quite a prolific writer; I wrote articles, blog posts, e-books, and self-help programs. So why was I having such a hard time?

Finally, one day as I was again staring at the empty screen, I screamed out loud as though God was sitting right in front of me. "I can't do this by myself." I said. "Why did you ask me to do this if you're not going to help me?"

You see, during this last year my life has become serene and joyful. My days were spent meditating, taking baths, walking and enjoying nature. One quiet, overcast day I was sitting on the beach when a flock of hundreds of pigeons flew in. For a long time I sat watching them take off and land in unison, making perfect patterns in the sand. As they whirled around me, all the flapping wings created such a rush of air on my skin that I could feel their intensity. I felt so connected to the movement of these birds that it brought tears to my eyes.

And it wasn't just birds or animals that moved me so deeply; it was also people. During this time I was able to experience their kindness in a new way. I watched people interact, noticed their deep desire to love one another. I saw this in the way a mother put her arm around a crying child, the special glance between two lovers, the way a person would happily give directions to another person who was lost. Kindness and caring were everywhere, and I was now not only able to see it, but I actually felt as though these acts of kindness lived within me.

But at this point I was being guided to go beyond this serene existence, to move back out into the world and at the same time somehow maintain the peace I've come to know. So when I received the guidance to write this book I assumed it would flow easily, that I would be guided through it, or it would be channeled through me. And my peace and joy, my love of life would easily be maintained. But no, that wasn't my experience. And I've come to learn over time that this – these kinds of difficulties, these kinds of challenges – are part of the reason I was asked to get back out into the world. I am to be a bridge of sorts. I am meant to learn how to maintain what I've come to know as the TRUTH in the face of what appears to be the reality of my day-to-day life out in the "normal" world, to learn how to embody this TRUTH and still play full out on the playground of life.

The next day, as I once again got up at 5:30 in the morning, I wondered whether I should just give up and go back to my peaceful life. If writing my story wasn't going to flow the way I knew everything could, then what was the point? I decided to have a little conversation with God about all this. So I asked God, "Why did you ask me to do something that wasn't going to flow? Do you just want me to sit in front of my computer typing and then erasing words hour after hour?" Nothing came. I got nothing back from God. As I sat there my frustration grew. "I need help!" I shouted out loud. And then my body started to tingle and I heard, "How can I help you?" I was shocked because I didn't usually hear God this way. It was like somebody was actually talking to me in words that I could hear with my physical ears. I usually sense, or feel, the words, but this time I actually heard them. So, thinking of a writing technique I'd used in the past, I said, "I don't know how to write a book like this; send me somebody to interview me."

And then I heard, "I'll interview you."

"You'll interview me? What does that mean?"

To which God replied, "I'll ask and you answer."

At first I couldn't wrap my brain around how this was going to work. *I mean, who am I to be interviewed by God?* As that thought ran through my head I felt my whole body tingle and a line from the famous quote by Marianne Williamson popped into my head.

"Who are you not to be?"

As soon as that line came into my mind it was as though all the experiences that I've had over the last few years rushed in, and in that moment I was back to remembering who I am. I am not only a child of God, but I am one with everything and everyone. There is no one more or less deserving of God's attention or love than I am. We all have God's love all the time – it is our essence – it is who we are. We just have to stop, remember, and be present to it. The idea of being interviewed by God struck me as more and more exciting, and my whole body continued to tingle. From that moment on, this story flowed onto the page easily and effortlessly.

THE INTERVIEW BEGINS

God: Are you ready to get going?

Beth: I'm not sure why I'm writing about any of this. Who's going to care?

God: There are many people who are having experiences similar to yours and they're embarrassed, or think it's all their imagination, and are not allowing these experiences to blossom. There are others who are right at the precipice of these extraordinary, life-changing experiences, but they are pushing them away. These people need to know they're not alone and what they're experiencing is actually more real than what they thought was true.

Beth: They need to know that there is more to life than they have been told about, is that it? They need to know that the world is much richer and more wonderful than they ever imagined.

God: Yes, it's time for people to know just how much more there is to life. You've already begun the process of transformation, and your experiences can help to guide them. I've heard you say you have had many unusual experiences. What do you mean by this?

Beth: Over the last four years, many things have happened to me that are outside the realm of ordinary human life. They come in different forms. I may feel them, hear them, or see them, but they are nothing like my previous day-to-day existence. Research has showed me that these types of experiences are not completely uncommon. On one hand, knowing that others have had similar experiences helped me at times when I thought I was going crazy. On the other hand, I mostly found that saints, eccentric geniuses or gurus in India were the ones having these experiences. There were only a few stories involving ordinary people like me.

God: So what has changed in your life over the last few years?

Beth: In short, I have gone from wanting to know everything, understand everything and control everything in my life, to a place of peacefulness and acceptance to a degree that I've never known. I don't mind now when plans change, or someone else thinks they have a better idea about how to do things. And I don't have to agree with or understand exactly what someone is talking about in order to hear what they're saying and be able to empathize with them. My whole being has shifted. As I continue to have these unique experiences, they change me and how I perceive the world in incredible ways. I've gone from an almost compulsive need to "know" everything to an acceptance of just what's going on in the moment, and a sense of calm trusting about the future.

God: If you only had one word to use in relation to what's happening, what would it be?

Beth: Awareness.

God: Why awareness?

Beth: I have become aware of beautiful things that I had little knowledge of in my former reality; for example, the remarkable gift of my physical form. Just living in my body became a joy – seeing the glistening black feathers of a crow in the sun, hearing the waves shush through the sand, touching the velvet petals of a rose. Each moment became incredibly expansive. When I'm willing to be present and allow a moment to just be, it's bigger, bolder and more magnificent than I ever imagined. My desire to know the future kept me from everything that's right here in this moment. I know this might sound 'new age' and simplistic, but it's created an experience that allows me to enjoy my day-to-day life in a way that I'd never thought possible.

Often when people wake up to the beauty of living in awareness, it's because they've had a major trauma, or hit rock bottom, or had an awful childhood, but not me. I had a good life and have been quite happy, so when I realized what was possible – the extent of love and joy and satisfaction that I could actually have, I was blown away. Lately I have come to feel peaceful and relaxed in a way that I've never known.

But like most of us, I've always felt this strange underlying sense of tension. Now that's completely gone. I know that everyone can experience this expansive peace, relaxation, and joy, and I wish that for them.

CHAPTER 3
Glimmers of Awakening

"If I had influence with the good fairy who is supposed to preside over the christening of all children, I should ask that her gift to each child in the world be a sense of wonder so indestructible that it would last throughout life..."

~ Rachel Carson

THE "OVERLY SENSITIVE" CHILD

God: I'm curious about how it all started – what triggered this transformation of awareness?

Beth: I believe it started when I was a child, then became repressed, and has now re-awakened in my adult life. My impression is that we all come into this life very open, with that sense of peace and connection I'm now feeling. And then we can quickly lose it. Even when I was first writing this book and experiencing the frustration, I could feel it trying to slip away. It's a very delicate connection, one that needs to be nurtured. When I first experienced it as a child, the adults around me didn't understand what was happening to me. My fear and confusion led me to suppress it, and then, with the

constant reinforcement from school and society, this connection slowly faded into a dark corner of my being.

God: What's your first memory about this connection?

Beth: When I was very young, several events occurred
that foreshadowed what's happening now in this realm of
awakening, or my connection to you.

In 1964, when I was six years old, my mom, dad, brothers and I lived in a shabby apartment building in Spanish
Harlem in New York City, far from the posh neighborhoods
and Broadway shows of Manhattan. I was a petite little girl
with big blue-green eyes, and to the outside world I probably
looked quite average. But inside, where many children would
be growing in imagination, joy and wonder, I was filled with
doubt, confusion, and fear.

We had been invited over to my great aunt's apartment
on the Upper West Side, right across the street from Cen-
tral Park, for Thanksgiving. Aunt Ada lived in a big beautiful apartment and out her front window you could see the
Macy's Day Parade with all the big floats coming right down
the avenue. That morning I got all dressed up, put on my
patent leather shoes, and ran back and forth from the living
room to my mom's room, checking to see whether she was
ready to go yet.

At last we all jumped in a cab and off we went to my aunt's.
As we drove, the streets got wider and the architecture more
imposing. Her building had a doorman with a black coat and
white gloves to open the door for us, and I remember feeling
very special, like Cinderella at the ball. We took the elevator
up to her apartment, but as soon as the door opened I felt
something wrong. A prickly wave of energy washed through
me. The further into the room we went the stronger the feeling became. I got quiet and grabbed onto my mother's dress.
She put her arm around me, leaned down and asked me what

was wrong. "I don't feel good," I whispered.

As we walked farther in and a forest of adult legs pressed around me, the intense energy became so strong I grabbed onto my mother's legs and hid my face against her. She tried to pry me off of her, but I began to cry and clutched her even harder. People were staring by now, and my father leaned down and covered me like a blanket with his body. My hands slowly let go and he guided me over to a chair by the window so I could watch the parade. All my former excitement was gone. I didn't understand why I felt this mass of incoherent, unpleasant feelings. Now I understand that I was actually sensing the tangle of emotions from all the other people in the room. But at the time I thought they were my feelings, and so I felt confused and disturbed.

This happened over and over, whenever I walked into a room with people, whether in large groups or small ones. I would get very quiet and try to hide. Or if the energy was too overwhelming, I might start screaming. My parents and relatives labeled me as depressed, overly sensitive, and angry, and that year they started taking me to a psychologist. Just being able to talk about my feelings helped a little, but it didn't solve the issue. I continued to pick up random feelings when I was around people, and my life at home was stressful as well. My parents were loving and well-meaning, but they didn't understand what was going on with me, and had problems of their own.

We were a typical lower middle class family in many ways. As far back as I can remember my parents argued about money. They were polar opposites when it came to spending habits. My dad spent money like it grew on trees and he owned a whole grove of them. But my mother had grown up in poverty during the depression, and had so much fear about money that she was very tight with it. Living in New York

City was always expensive, even living where we did, so you can imagine the kinds of arguments they had.

Both my parents were arty creative types and neither of them liked working for other people. My mom jumped from one retail job to another and took art classes on the side. My father did his best, but he struggled with his acting career and so started a series of side businesses to make ends meet. At that time he had a New York City tour company and used his actor friends as the tour guides. But still, there was never enough money.

EXPLODING FROM THE INSIDE OUT

A few years later when I was about eight, something happened that haunted me for years. I was lying in bed at night about to fall asleep when this intense sensation spontaneously erupted in my groin area. It was as though I was exploding from the inside out, as if there was a strong burst of energy pouring out of me. There was a pressure like I was urinating, but no liquid was coming out. I became so scared I ran to the bathroom and got a roll of toilet paper and stuffed wads of it down my underwear to stop whatever it was that was happening to me. My mother heard the noise, came in, turned on the light and saw me frantically stuffing toilet paper down my pants.

She looked horrified, and so I felt ashamed and even more scared than I was before. She yelled at me, "What in the world are you doing?" Then she grabbed the toilet paper roll out of my hand and began pulling the toilet paper from my underwear. Once again she screamed "Oh my God! What are you doing?" This incident led to another trip to the psychologist. The doctor at the time eased my mother's concerns by telling her I was just developing sexual feelings and there was nothing to worry about. But as I grew older, memories of this experience stayed with me. And when I began to have normal sexual feelings, I remembered that childhood incident and wondered if the psychologist had been right. After my adult awakening, I knew for sure that this hadn't been a sexual experience. It was much, much more.

A third strange phenomenon started around the same time as the toilet paper incident. I began having peculiar feelings at night when I was going to sleep. I'd be lying there and suddenly I would experience a tingling sensation that made my hands feel very small and at the same time very thick. It felt as if I was being covered with a syrupy dense liquid. I then felt this sensation move into every part of my body. Whenever this happened I would get scared and would frantically try to rub it off myself by moving my hands back and forth quickly against my skin. This helped bring my skin back to feeling normal, but it was still strange and disturbing.

I tried to explain this feeling to my mother, but all I could say is that I felt very small and thick and icky and it scared me. Once again, this was interpreted as my troubled imagination and resulted in another trip to the psychologist.

As you can imagine, having all these unusual experiences as a child and no one to help me understand what was going on left me feeling quite confused, unhappy and apprehensive.

SHE MIGHT HAVE BEEN AN ANGEL

God: It must've been very difficult for you to deal with all this. Was there anyone you could relate to?

Beth: Yes. Around 1970, when I was 12, things changed when I met a wonderful woman named Phoebe. Phoebe floated quickly in and out of my life. We had just moved from Manhattan to Newburgh, New York, a small town on the Hudson River. At the time my father was running a 'rock and roll' newspaper in Manhattan and commuting back and forth by train.

That summer, my parents decided to have a big party for everyone who worked on the paper. We lived in 100-year-old Victorian house that looked as if it had gone through a war. My mother, the handyman of the family, spent much of her time painting, stripping wallpaper, and repairing the house so that it would be presentable for the upcoming party. I remember her climbing up and down ladders with her tool belt on, and my father sitting in the living room watching a ballgame and occasionally looking up and asking if she needed any help.

They were quite an odd couple, these two, but they were getting along better now and this division of labor seemed to work for them. My mom worked and worked on the house and as the party date grew closer the house began to look quite charming, in contrast to the wreck it was when we moved in. The party day finally arrived and the guests started showing up, one after the other. It was the early '70s, so people were dressed up in very colorful outfits with bellbottoms, tie-dyed tops, and long flowing skirts with flowers. It was fun just watching them come through the door. By 3:00 PM the party was in full swing. There were people eating and talking, and in one corner a group of musicians was jamming.

I sat quietly in the corner of the living room by myself, feeling overwhelmed, as usual. Then a beautiful woman with long black hair and a flowing white outfit caught my eye from across the room. She looked like something out of a movie, and I couldn't take my eyes off her. She walked towards me, closer and closer, until she knelt down in front of me and asked if she could sit next to me. I didn't know what to say, but she was already sitting down, so I didn't really have to answer.

She looked at me and said, "I'm Phoebe. You don't feel good, do you?"

"No, but I just have to sit quietly and breath in and out." I said this because that's what psychologists told me.

"Breathing's good," she said and then went on to ask whether I wanted to know why I didn't feel good.

"It's because I'm too sensitive," I said.

"Yes, you're sensitive all right, but you're not too much of anything," she said, and then started laughing. Her laugh was contagious and I couldn't help but laugh as well. We sat there for quite a while, just giggling and laughing as she pretended to tickle me.

Then she said, "You just feel things very deeply and pick up other people's feelings and emotions. A lot of what you're feeling isn't really you; it's what other people in the room are feeling." She then gave me some advice for the future. She said I was to pay attention to how I was feeling when I was with other people. If suddenly I felt different, this was a clue that I might be picking up other people's emotions. All I had to do is remind myself that those feelings weren't mine and let them flow through me. Then she said she needed to mingle, gave me a hug goodbye, and walked off.

I never saw Phoebe again after that day. I wanted to – I was hoping to see her often – so I asked my mom who she was and if we could invite her back sometime soon, but my mother had no idea who I was talking about. For all I know she could have been an angel, just stopping by to help a little girl. No matter who she was, what I know for sure is that meeting Phoebe was an important event in my life; she helped me understand that all these other feelings weren't mine and I didn't have to take them on.

God: Didn't Phoebe tell you about the bubble?

Beth: Oh yes. I forgot, thanks. The ability to sense the emotions of others increased as I grew older. Phoebe had also introduced the bubble idea, which allowed me to separate myself from other people's feelings. She suggested that when I felt overwhelmed, I was to imagine myself surrounded by a large, clear bubble that could keep the foreign feelings out. After meeting her I was able to relax and have more fun as a child, but it had its price. The strategy helped me to create a shield of sorts between my feelings and those of other people, but it also created a feeling of separation between them and me. She didn't actually tell me to create a shield, but that's how I ended up interpreting it, and eventually the shield grew from being just an energetic barrier to an emotional and interpersonal one. And as I created this shield, I also developed a feeling of insecurity and the belief that I was unsafe in the world and needed to protect myself. This affected me deeply and colored my whole life. I learned to be very skeptical and hyper-aware of what was going on around me in order to keep from picking up energy that wasn't mine. I had integrated the idea that Phoebe gave me about separating my feelings from those of other people and not taking on their energy, but then I unconsciously took this one step further and began separating myself from people in many other ways.

God: Then did this strategy work for you or not?

Beth: It worked to some degree. I wasn't completely overwhelmed anymore. Nevertheless, I still could feel the suffering that was all around me. I wanted to know and understand all the "rules" of my world, the spoken and unspoken, because if I knew what was going to happen, then I could be ready for it.

I began asking people lots of questions until it became a compulsion. Over and over, I'd ask things like, "How are you? Are you okay? Is everything all right?" This strategy sometimes backfired because people would become annoyed with me, which ironically led to the unpleasant feelings I was trying to avoid. A friend's mother told me if I didn't stop asking her if she was all right she would send me home, and my friends at school avoided me at lunchtime.

So I learned not to ask so many questions. I'd look for subtler clues, such as body language, conversational tone and facial expressions. Even though I became skillful at this I still was not able to fully protect myself from the feelings of pain, anger, and sadness that surrounded me. Eventually I turned my attention to figuring out why people felt the way they did and trying to help them feel better.

God, do you really think that people are going to care about all these childhood stories?

God: There will be people who will benefit from your stories. Have you any idea how many people are suffering deep down inside because they've pushed these kinds of things out of their awareness?

Beth: I've never really thought about it that way.

God: You are like a mirror that would allow them to see and remember what they have forgotten. You reveal yourself so that they may see themselves. They do not need to have had the same experiences as you for them to remember what has happened in their own lives, and consequently have a sense of permission to remember and talk about their own stories.

WHEN PEOPLE FEEL SCARED
AND HOPELESS

In 1972, when I was 14 and in junior high school, we were still living in Newburgh, New York. My parents had originally moved there to protect us from the crime and the drugs in New York City. Little did they know that per capita, Newburgh had more drugs and crime than the city did. The early 1970s were the days of racial tension and race riots, and Newburgh had its share. I was sitting in class one day when an announcement came over the loudspeaker: "Students and faculty, the school will be closing until further notice. Please gather your belongings and exit the building calmly and quietly."

A race riot had just broken out in the school. There was panic in the hallways, and people were running and crying. Some kids were breaking windows and throwing furniture around. I'd never been so scared. Black and white kids who had been friendly with each other the day before changed in an instant; it was as if we had never known each other, or as if suddenly someone said there was a war and we were on opposite sides.

I had to find my younger brother, Adam, and get the hell out of there. I ran frantically up and down the halls, in and out of classrooms until finally I looked up and saw his dirty blond head of hair by the top of the stairwell. I watched in horror as a boy ran up behind him and deliberately shoved him down the stairs. I saw my little brother tumble head over heels, his head hitting step after step, as if in slow motion. I was terrified. When he hit the ground I raced over and I grabbed his hand, crying with relief as I saw he was able to stand up. I remember feeling all the intense pain and anger radiating from the people around me and I wondered what was happening. Why did that boy hurt my brother?

A teacher saw what happened and ran over to us. He guided us to one of the exits and we started running the ten blocks home. It was all like a strange nightmare. All the way home the feelings of fear, anger, and confusion kept circling through me and questions kept running over and over in my mind.

As we ran up to our house I saw my mother standing outside, looking scared and relieved at the same time. She ran towards us, grabbed us and hurried us inside. A few minutes later when we knew we were safe, I looked at her and asked, "What's going on, and why is everybody so angry?"

She looked at me and said, "When people feel scared and hopeless and no one listens to them, they get angry."

In that moment I felt more love and compassion for people than I ever had before. My heart opened and I let the feelings of those people in. A deep sadness took me over and I cried, and I knew I was crying for all the people in the world that felt scared and hopeless and that weren't being heard about their pain.

God: So now do you know why you're writing this book?

Beth: When I think of that moment, it's all so clear. There are so many people in pain who don't feel heard, who live their lives in fear and despair.

God: To be disconnected from the source of love and

peace, is the seed of all pain. There are so many people who have had, or will have experiences like yours, experiences that they can't explain, and who have no one to tell them they're normal, and loved. Your book will let them know they're not alone.

Beth: Yes, now I get it.

God: How else did these childhood experiences affect your life?

Beth: I developed all sorts of limiting beliefs. I developed them around my picking up other people's energies, around the toilet paper incident, and about the experience of feeling very small and thick and then being told it was my imagination. In fact, once these beliefs became the truth to me they more or less created my life.

This became a pattern. When something happened, such as being told that those sensations I felt were just my imagination, I made that explanation mean that I can't trust myself to know what's real and what's not. Then because I thought this was true, it became a belief that ran my life. I didn't trust myself for a long, long time. Looking back, I feel sad to think I spent my childhood and most of my adult life believing these things.

God: What other beliefs did you develop from the experiences you had?

Beth: The first belief I can remember came from my picking up other people's energies. I made that mean I'm not safe, people are dangerous, and I need to protect myself. It took me a long time to start trusting people again.

The belief around the toilet paper was that I am different from other people, strange, a weirdo. I must hide my weirdness or other people will get upset and not like me or hurt me. Once again, people are dangerous and I'm unsafe.

There were so many! The experience when I felt very small and thick and was told it was my imagination led me to believe that I can't trust myself or my feelings. That what I think is true may be false. Therefore, I believed that I was flawed, and other people knew better than I did. These beliefs caused me to hide who I was, look to others to see how I should act in the world, and left me feeling very tense, nervous and insecure.

Many years later I discovered that I worked hard to compensate for these beliefs by developing the qualities I thought were missing, in an effort to "fix" myself and therefore not feel the pain. So to overcome my perceived shortcomings, I became very resourceful. I created a facade of confidence; developed concrete, strong and unshakable opinions; and became very rebellious if anyone told me what to do. In this way, I became more successful in my interactions with others, but underneath the surface, the old beliefs were still running me.

God: Are they running you now?

Beth: Now, they're barely operating. Although I'd done a lot of personal exploration during my life to get conscious about them, they still ran me until the last few years. It's amazing to me that now I just can watch these beliefs pop up and then just as quickly let them go. I have found an acceptance within myself I never knew existed. I can trust to the point where I'm sitting here at the beach on a gorgeous morning, being interviewed by God, and it all seems perfect.

God: And perfectly normal?

Beth: Well, yes, normal!

CHAPTER 4

When the Student is Ready...

"The decisions you make and the actions that you take upon the earth are the means by which you evolve."

- Gary Zukav

I JUST DON'T FIT IN

God: Did you continue to have unusual experiences throughout high school?

Beth: Actually, no, my teen years and early adult life were fairly normal. I had shut myself down because of what Phoebe had taught me.

It is true that I had difficulty finishing high school because I have dyslexia, a learning problem that makes it difficult to read and spell words. In those days, at least in my school, they didn't have alternative types of learning – it was one size fits all – and I just didn't fit.

God: What was it like for you to go to school?

Beth: It was a never-ending nightmare. I would walk into the classroom day after day, sit in the back of the room and pray the teacher wouldn't call on me to read. I learned when

I was in first grade not to read out loud in class. I read very slowly and struggled to pronounce the words. The other kids laughed and called me 'stupid' and 'retard'. I felt ashamed of myself, frustrated and angry, and I wanted to scream at them to stop laughing. I didn't know why I couldn't read like the others.

Being called an 'idiot' and told, "You belong in the dummy class" was a daily given. No one stuck up for me. At recess I sat by myself in a corner of the schoolyard.

God: What about the teachers? Did they help you to understand and cope with your dyslexia?

Beth: The teachers weren't much better than the students. I guess they didn't know how to deal with a dyslexic student. I had a good vocabulary, I was obviously bright, and I was outgoing, so the teachers may have thought that if they teased me enough about my grades I would work harder. One of their favorite things to say is that I was lazy – I heard that word many times – but their strategy backfired. I was already trying so hard that being called lazy drove me into a rage, and instead of working harder I would mouth off and end up in the principal's office.

I spent most of my senior year of high school skipping school and experimenting with drugs. I had a friend, Tom, and we'd just look at each other before class and head out the back door. We used to sneak off before the bell would ring and head out to a spot in the woods. We tried almost every drug you can think of. The drugs helped me forget my pain and shame about not being able to read well. One drug I didn't try was heroin, which was as easy to get in Newburgh as anything else. I had a fear of needles and enough common sense to know that it was very addictive, thank God.

God: You're welcome.

Beth: What?

God: Just a little joke. Go on.

Beth: People don't usually think of you as having a sense of humor.

God: That's a shame, because everyone would have a lot more fun if they did. Tell me more about school.

Beth: I hated it so much that 'ditching' school and doing drugs seemed like a great alternative to the endless badgering and ridicule. This became a problem towards the end of the year because I was in danger of not graduating. One of my favorite teachers, Mr. Posner, said he would help me catch up if I came to his classroom after school each day. He was my history teacher – a short, dark-haired man with eyes like a kind German shepherd and a funny pockmarked nose. I loved his class because he made history so interesting with his storytelling, and he never asked anyone to read out loud. I always got a B+ or an A in his class, which made me feel great. He was able to draw out the best from me, when my other teachers couldn't.

God: How did he help you catch up?

Beth: He taught me many strategies for learning that I've used throughout my entire life. He showed me how to figure out what words meant by the context of the sentence. If I knew that the sentence was about George Washington and war, then I could figure out the word 'Revolutionary.'

He suggested that I sit by the window and read in the sunlight because I told him the light in the classroom made the words jitter on the page. As long as I could express what wasn't working, he found a way to help me manage it. His class and my art classes were the only reason I ever came to school. So I spent the last six weeks of my high school year in Mr. Posner's classroom catching up. Thanks to him I graduated – with a GPA of 68% – but still I graduated.

God: He sounds like Phoebe, in that he knew how to support you when others didn't.

Beth: Yes, in a way he was. He showed up when I desperately needed him. Mr. Posner and his funny nose – he was an extremely generous and creative man.

God: Did you want to go to college?

Beth: Yes, very much. Before graduation I was told by the vice principal of my high school that I should try to find a more creative outlet than going to a traditional college. I didn't like the insinuation, and I ignored him. Mr. Posner had opened a new world to me, and I wanted to try it out. So I enrolled in a few college classes. I thought I'd be OK if I continued using Mr. Posner's strategies, and I was. For the first time in my life I got decent grades, but what took other students an hour to read took me three hours, and the work that seemed easy for them was very challenging for me.

One afternoon I was walking past a construction site, and I saw how hard the guys were working. Then it occurred to me that I was working as hard as they were just to keep up. I was often working like a dog on my homework into the early hours of the morning. I was exhausted and realized that it would never be easy for me. And I thought, *there has to be something better than this.* The next day I dropped out. So the vice principal was right after all.

That's when I decided to go to acting school in Manhattan. It seemed like a natural step since I'd grown up around actors. My mom was a set designer in college and my dad always considered himself an actor first. His other jobs were just to make money until he got another acting gig. So I guess you can say it ran in the family.

SHEDDING MY OLD SKIN

It was now 1977. I was nineteen years old and working as a waitress at the Clam Casino in Fort Lee, New Jersey, to pay my way through acting school. There was a cute blonde bartender named Greg in the restaurant where I worked. He was nice and funny, with a smile that lit up his face. We had so much fun working together that we began dating. During this time I continued pursuing my acting career, taking the train to New York in for cattle call auditions, clutching my photo and resume. One time I stood four hours in line on 43rd Street, in the rain, with about 300 other actors, just to hand in my resume. On the way home I leaned against the bus window and cried. I realized going to acting school and being an actress were two very different things.

Acting school was exciting and creative, but auditions involved endless hours of standing in line, with all the other desperate out-of-work actors, just so I could smile at some nameless producer. I wasn't cut out for that. I performed in a few little plays and a student film, but the level of rejection and competition was more than I cared to endure.

God: So you gave up acting school as well as traditional college.

Beth: Yes. I was good at giving up in those days, but really both choices were right for me. In the meantime, Greg and I decided to move in together. I continued to wait tables to pay my bills, but I began to wonder what life was all about. Was this it? Living here in New Jersey, a drab, gray, concrete place? Waiting on people who seemed mostly unhappy and worried about one thing or another? This couldn't be it, could it? Greg was also dissatisfied. He was unhappy much of the time and I worried that he was becoming depressed.

One night my friend Louise and I were sitting at the restaurant, folding napkins, getting ready for the evening rush. We fantasized about moving to California. What fun it would be to live by the ocean, enjoy the sun, and be with people who were happy to be alive. California seemed like paradise. I had no idea that my fantasy would become a reality.

But within a few years, Greg and I had had enough of New Jersey. We got married, filled our Volkswagen bus with our stuff and in June, 1983, we drove across the country to California to capture the dream.

God: Was California what you expected?

Beth: No. I was a New Yorker. I'd never been around people who hugged so much, did yoga, and held full moon ceremonies and drumming circles. When we attended some of the more woo-woo events we were skeptical and couldn't help but mock them afterwards. But it grew on me, and soon I noticed that I felt more at home in California than I ever did on the East Coast; it was laid back, relaxed and suited me well.

A few years later we had our son Spenser. Greg and I had each started our own businesses. Greg had a successful mobile cell phone business. I was making and selling jewelry, caring for Spenser, and really enjoying my life.

This period of happiness lasted for five years. Then the economy took a turn for the worse and Greg's business declined dramatically. Our income decreased, which put stress on us both. Our bills were harder to pay, we were working twice as much with fewer results, and our marriage bore the brunt of it. I had unknowingly recreated a relationship like my parents. We started arguing all the time, mostly about money, and it turned ugly.

God: Did you still love him?

Beth: Yes, but it had dawned on me that we weren't well-suited for each other. I wanted more adventure and was drawn to different pursuits than Greg; I was changing, and I couldn't stop or control it. A divorce seemed inevitable, and terrifying. I had never lived alone before, never really fended for myself. And now I had Spenser to think of. Although I was frightened of divorce, this life that I was leading seemed like a lie. Even though I still cared deeply for Greg, staying with him because I was scared to be on my own didn't seem like a good reason.

But friends who were single told me, "It's rough out here on your own. There aren't really any good guys left, so just work it out with Greg and you'll be better off."

So for a while I stopped thinking about divorce and Greg and I tried to get our marriage back on track. We went to see a psychologist. We took a course called The Forum, a personal growth weekend workshop designed to help people live happier lives. Nothing helped for long, but at this time we were still living in our heads, as opposed to our hearts, and we only participated in these activities from an analytical perspective.

God: Were you aware of that?

Beth: No. I didn't even realize there was another way to be, a way to make decisions other than "thinking" about them. But ultimately, nothing helped our marriage. We were living in a kind of private hell. At night, we'd lay in bed like strangers, facing away from each other, careful not to touch. As the divorce moved closer to reality I started turning inward, really observing myself for the first time from a spiritual perspective.

I don't consider myself a spiritual seeker; I consider myself more of a spiritual finder. It's like when I need answers, they find me. When it's time for me to gain new knowledge or transform myself in some way, people, books, events or whatever is needed just seem to show up in my life.

God: When the student is ready...

Beth: The teacher appears, yes! That has been a consistent theme in my life. In this case, the teacher showed up in the form of a book called The Seat of The Soul, by Gary Zukav. I wasn't much of a reader because of my dyslexia, but I couldn't put this book down. This was a new kind of book for me, and I was drawn to the words as though they were The Truth, a truth that no one ever told me before. "We are in a time of deep change. We will move through this change more easily if we are able to see the road upon which we are traveling, our destination and what it is that is in motion." These words stayed with me as I savored the book. Somewhere deep down inside, I knew that this was the road I was to travel now. I was unsure of my destination, but it was clear that something in me was in motion.

I had Gary Zukav to help me. His book became my constant companion, and I bought the tape series so I could listen to it over and over. This was a powerful period of growth and change for me. This new spiritual perspective opened my eyes, opened my heart, and opened my mind to much more than I thought possible. As I was growing out of my marriage and the life that Greg and I had made, I was also growing out of the person I knew myself to be. I was shedding my old skin to allow for the new person I was becoming.

God: Was it sad to let go of the old Beth?

Beth: It was sad and lonely and scary and exciting and wonderful. It was all of those things. I decided to get away by myself for a few days and so I rented a cabin in a little mountain town called Julian, near Mount Laguna. Each day I wandered around in the beautiful evergreen forest as I listened to the tapes. On the third day I was sitting with my back to a very large old pine tree, gazing up to where it seemed to touch the sky, when something strange happened. It was as though the world had stopped around me and there was only this moment. I could see dust particles shimmering in the shafts of sunlight that poured through the branches. The sharp evergreen smell prickled my nose. I could feel the rough bark of the tree through my shirt, and I became part of the tree, part of everything. This experience was very physical; it enveloped me and filled me with an odd tingling. But I was scared by the sensations, and so I tensed up and it stopped. I had no idea what was happening to me.

God: Do you know now?

Beth: Yes. I believe this was the first true glimpse into my expanding awareness. I was beginning to remember who and what I truly am – one with you, and one with every living thing. In that moment I knew that I must begin this new life that was calling to me. I returned from the trip with a deep sense of calm. I was ready to move forward with the divorce.

CHAPTER 5

A Strong Foundation

"As we learn to speak from the heart we are changing the habits of a lifetime."

- Marshall Rosenberg

ALL SCREWED UP

God: What was your life like after you went out on your own?

Beth: I was on a crazy roller coaster ride, never sure when the next downward plunge would happen or if it would send me off the rails altogether. I'd never lived on my own before, and I was trying to figure out who I was outside of a 13-year marriage. Additionally, I had Spenser to think about; he was only six years old and I was finding out that he had serious learning disabilities.

Greg and I filed for bankruptcy and our house went into foreclosure. I lived there alone for a time until we lost it for good, but at least I could breathe again without all the tension and fighting with Greg. Still, I felt lonelier than I ever had before. My money was limited to what I could earn from my jewelry making, and I didn't know where I was going to live or how I would pay for it.

Then it got worse. The Waldorf School told me that Spenser could no longer attend there because they weren't equipped for his type of challenges. That's when I discovered that he needed even more testing. I didn't know how much longer I could continue to dodge this landslide.

God: How did you and Greg get along?

Beth: We had to talk to each other because of Spenser, but Greg was very angry, and I let him have his way in the divorce settlement to make it as easy as possible and limit the drama. So I only asked for my jewelry-making tools and my computer – I told him he could keep everything else. Although Greg was our main source of income, I did not ask for alimony because he was so upset I knew there would be a struggle. I don't know if I was being courageous or just an idiot, but I didn't want to fight for money every month.

When the house went into final foreclosure I had to find somewhere else to live. If I'd been realistic I probably would have found some cramped apartment or a roommate situation, but beauty and space were important to me. Although at that time I didn't know how or why it happened, I always seemed able to manifest things in my life. So I decided to commit to what I really wanted – a beautiful and spacious house with a backyard and a separate bedroom for Spenser. My friends and family thought I was crazy. "How can you possibly afford that?" I heard over and over again. But sometimes, instead of being practical, you just have to follow your heart.

However, there were times I doubted myself, and I searched for cheaper alternatives, but looking at crappy apartments and rooms for rent was depressing. One place had cockroaches and mouse droppings; at another the creepy old man next door kept staring at Spenser. What was I going to do? I knew in my heart that something better was on its way, so I just waited.

Shortly before I had to leave our home, a neighbor told me that they had a house that was coming up for rent and asked, "Can you afford $800 a month?" She told me it was a cute three-bedroom house, on a canyon, with a big grassy backyard. It sounded perfect for us!

With what little I earned by selling jewelry, I knew that $800 a month was too much money. But I told her, "Yes! Yes I can," not knowing how I would pull it off. The very next day a friend of mine told me about her foreign exchange student and the proverbial light bulb lit up in my head. I contacted the foreign exchange service and learned that I could make $500 a month hosting a student from Japan. Three weeks later Spenser and I moved into our new little house.

God: When you line up your desires with the natural flow, anything can happen.

Beth: Yes, and somehow I knew we would find the right place. Now we were settled, but I still felt so insecure and alone. For much of the next year I questioned myself: Why am I so scared? Why do I feel so lonely? Sometimes I spent hours in the bathtub crying, letting the warm water soothe me. Old memories came up and this practice seemed to help release the pain. Of course, having to take care of Spenser kept me functioning in the real world.

God: What was your first adult experience of awakening?

Beth: By now I was comfortable with the New Age practices so common in California, and part of my exploration involved learning some self-help modalities. These led to my first adult realization that there was more to life than I was consciously aware of.

I was trying to figure out who I was – to find my new place in the world, and I'd heard about a modality called Rapid Eye Technology (RET). It's a process of moving a wand back and forth over your eyes to move energy and release trapped trauma. I was interested and immediately set up an appointment. I don't jump on everything I hear about, but this just felt right.

The originators of this technique, Joseph & Ranae Johnson, came to my house to work with me. We quickly got started. I lay down on my massage table and they waved a wand back and forth over my eyes. After about ten minutes I began to feel a very low frequency vibration inside my body. I tried to stay calm and talk about the things that were coming up for me, but the vibration became stronger until my whole body started shaking from top to the bottom. Then suddenly, it seemed as if intense rays of light were exploding out from inside of me, out of my mouth, head, hands and feet. This was the same sensation I had as a child when I was stuffing the toilet paper down my pants.

God: Did you try to stop it this time?

Beth: No. I was trembling from head to toe, and very scared, but I reminded myself to relax. As I calmed myself the sensation grew stronger and stronger until it seemed as though I was leaving my body, shooting out along with the rays of light. A feeling of euphoria or bliss came over me. I was gone, but at the same time I was there, more fully awake and alive than I had ever been in my life. I wanted this experience to last forever.

But as soon as I had that thought, it abruptly stopped. The shaking subsided and I was back in the room, back in my very limited body. And then I felt my hands – they were literally screwed up. My fingers and wrists were tight and twisted, and they hurt.

I tried to relax my hands but they wouldn't release. This frightened me and I looked into the practitioner's eyes and said, "Help me, please. What's going on?"

Ranae believed that I'd had what was called a kundalini awakening, and she suggested that I just rest for a while. I asked her what was wrong with my hands and she told me that I'd be fine if I could relax as best I could and let my body integrate what had happened. I was somewhat reassured because she sounded confident that I'd be OK. So I said goodbye, and after she and her husband left I went to lie on the couch. Here I was, with my body tied up in this very strange knot. I decided to just stay on the couch until something else occurred to me. Scary "what if" thoughts ran through my head. *What if I remained twisted up and hurt?* I worried until finally I was just too tired to be scared anymore.

At that point my breathing became deeper and less erratic. I calmed down and started to get curious about what had happened. I felt a combination of excitement, intense longing and some concern about how my body was feeling. My hands were still screwed up tight against my side. Eventually, with some breathing and meditation, they loosened.

Over the next few days I became obsessed to return to that state of bliss again. I started fanatically trying to figure out what had happened to me so I could re-create it. I thought about having another RET session, but the practitioners didn't seem to know much about the kundalini experience – they seemed almost as surprised by the whole thing as I was.

I began reading about kundalini on the Internet. One reference said that it is an energy that exists in everyone's body, but most people never even know it is there. But in a very few people, perhaps less than one in one thousand, this energy becomes aroused and activated. This can be a happy event or it can be scary and disruptive, depending on whether your kundalini is aroused on purpose or by accident. I also read that it is considered a metaphor for the creative potential within each of us.

God: And was it a metaphor?

Beth: Absolutely not. For me it was very real, so I kept investigating. I found there were people who repeatedly had experiences just like mine, so I felt encouraged that I could recreate it. I tried meditating, I tried praying, I tried willing it to happen, I tried jumping up and down and yelling. I was just desperate to feel it again. I knew about depression, but I never understood what that was like until now. Now I understood it all too well! I felt a deep sadness and lonelier than I thought possible. Would I ever again feel as good as I did during the RET session? It became the most important thing in my life.

After about two weeks of this I realized that I fallen into a serious depression and that it had taken over my life. So I decided to stop chasing this elusive experience and to get back to my day-to-day routine.

God: Before enlightenment, washing dishes. After enlightenment, washing dishes.

Beth: Now you're teasing.

God: Just a little.

Beth: It was very hard to let go of the kundalini awakening. But the depression scared me and kicked me back into my life. Slowly I returned to normal, but in the back of my mind there was always a glimmer of hope that the bliss would return and stay with me forever. The hope faded as the years went by. It wasn't until 2010 I got a glimpse of it again.

BUILDING THE BRIDGE

God: What did you do in those thirteen years?

Beth: I didn't know it at the time, but those thirteen years would prove to be the necessary foundation for my journey back to the source, to you. After the kundalini experience, I decided caring for Spenser, finalizing my divorce and maybe even dating would be my primary focuses.

Even though Greg and I were living separately we still had to work together to raise Spenser and settle on the details of our divorce. Spenser needed health insurance, he needed to be tested for learning disabilities, and I had to figure out where he could attend school now that Waldorf said he had to leave. All of this would cost money that I didn't have. Greg and I were not in agreement about who would pay for what and what to do about Spencer's needs, but we had to figure out a way to make this work. I wasn't sure how that was going to happen.

During this, time I went to an event called Rumi's Field Weekend. The name referred to the poet Rumi's line, "Out beyond ideas of wrong-doing and right-doing there is a field. I'll meet you there." This sounded like just what I needed.

The weekend showcased Nonviolent Communication (NVC), the work of Marshall Rosenberg. A beautiful man named Neill led the introductory session. He was tall and dark-haired, with a full beard, and had a centered and peaceful presence. I was so intrigued about what I had heard that I asked many questions, which Neill patiently answered. NVC is a communication model that encourages a clear and compassionate way of interacting with others, rather than the typical "violent" verbal and physical ways that most of us learn and use to get our needs met. For example, instead of yelling "Shut up!" we could say, "I want to concentrate on my work. Would you be willing to carry on your conversation somewhere else?"

God: Is such a polite request always possible in the heat of the moment?

Beth: I learned that it's not so much about being polite; it's more about being conscious and knowing that you have a choice. Once I learned to shift my perception, I could choose how I would respond. From the minute I was introduced to NVC I knew it contained an important missing piece in how people relate to one another. And when I applied these concepts in my own life, I experienced the world differently. It was life-changing for me.

God: When did you first notice a major difference?

Beth: The first improvement came in my relationship to Greg. When we separated, he was quite angry that I had asked for a divorce. Sometimes when we talked on the phone, he'd raise his voice or hang up on me. I had just begun learning NVC and wasn't very skilled at it, but I figured that things between us couldn't get any worse. I still cared about him, we had our son Spenser to think about, and my deepest desire was to maintain the best quality of relationship possible. When we spoke and he was angry about something, I tried out the tools I was learning. Our conversations noticeably improved.

For example, once when we were discussing child support, he told me he wanted Spenser half the time, and that meant he wouldn't have to pay child support. He also told me he didn't intend to give me any more money because he was the one that supported our family all those years and if I was leaving him, the well was going dry. At first I thought, what nerve! I had already agreed to no alimony, so how dare he act this way? And then I remembered the NVC I was learning. Normally I would have gotten angry and righteously reminded him that I had worked as hard as he did to start his business and contribute to its success, while simultaneously raising our son and running my own business.

But this time I didn't do any of that. Instead, I used what I knew of the NVC model. I said to him, "You must be feeling pretty frustrated being asked for money when you didn't even want a divorce. Is that right?"

There was silence for a moment, and then he said, "You're damn right I am." In that moment the whole conversation seemed to shift and we both relaxed. As I continued to learn and practice our communication got better and better. The NVC tools made what could have been an ugly divorce bearable. Greg and I raised Spenser separately but cooperatively, and we're still friends today.

I spent the next few years learning as much as I could about Nonviolent Communication, applying it to my life and discovering that the underlying consciousness of this model was the key to changing the ineffective and destructive ways people interacted with one another.

CHAPTER 6
The Opening

"Get very clear about the kind of world you would like and then start living that way."

- Marshall Rosenberg

Calibrating My Internal Compass

THINGS SETTLED DOWN between Greg and me. We worked out a divorce settlement, agreed on what to do about Spencer's needs and slowly moved into relatively peaceful co-parenting relationship. Now that things were a little more stable in my life I turned my attention to using NVC to work on myself and benefit others as well.

God: Tell me more about how this work you did on yourself led you back to me.

Beth: Neill, the man I'd met at the first workshop, was by now a good friend and helped me to expand my understanding of NVC. We were both excited about examining relationships – how they work and how they don't work. Over the next year and a half, as we became closer, I learned what a complex and wonderful mind he had.

As we connected more deeply with one other, Neill and I

fell in love and moved into an intimate relationship, and he's still my life partner to this day. He and I have similar passions about contributing to people and helping to support the world in a positive way. So much so that we decided to do this work together.

After some trial and error, we created a series of successful personal growth seminars and workshops. You know the saying, "If you really want to learn something, teach it." It was when I began teaching the underlying principles of NVC that I understood them deeply and incorporated them into every aspect of my life. This experience shaped me and helped to establish a profound new perspective in which to see myself and the world. This allowed me to loosen my grip on my opinions and judgments enough to open myself to the possibility of connecting with you, the true source of who I am and who we all are.

I learned to be less afraid and worried about the world outside of me. I now understand how the normal 'us-against-them' perspective, which runs rampant in this and many other societies, reinforces the belief that we need to protect ourselves. I remember thinking people were "wrong" to be late or change their plans with me; I was always on time and I kept MY commitments, and that was the "right" thing to do.

Each time I practiced un-learning my judgments – my cultural training about appropriate and inappropriate behavior – I was able to understand that we are all doing the best that we can, that being late or not keeping commitments wasn't a personal affront to me, and actually it wasn't about me at all. I learned that each of us is only always trying to experience happiness the best way we know how.

God: So you no longer felt the need to protect yourself?

Beth: I did let down my guard, but much caution remained. I know now that each distinction Neill and I uncovered, each level of understanding I integrated into my life, was an opening to a new world. This practice allowed me to open my mind enough to see you, feel you, and be with you again. But the old beliefs were like roots that dug themselves deep into the core of my being. The key was to relax enough to crack a hole in the surface so I could see what was really going on underneath. All my judgments, all my opinions that I believed were "the truth" were keeping me defensive and on guard all the time.

You can see this very clearly by observing how nearly all societies function. The majority operate with an us-against-them, right/wrong mindset. Beginning when we're very young, we're taught to identify who's right and who's wrong. It's so ingrained in our culture that we hardly notice it. It's practically in the air we breathe. This is why most of us are rarely able to relax.

God: When did you first start noticing this mindset and its effects?

Beth: When planning our seminars, we knew we'd have to be able to clearly explain these principles to our students. This led us to examine and challenge many assumptions we used to take for granted. Once I did that, I saw examples of this everywhere. For instance, movies usually contain clearly recognizable heroes and villains – us against them. Only recently are some art forms starting to show that the 'villain' could use some understanding and empathy as well. As a case in point, in the play Wicked, based on The Wizard of Oz, Elphaba, the Wicked Witch of the West, is actually cast as the heroine of the story. We see events through her point of view. When we look more deeply at the motives and actions of those very different from us, we may find that we can understand and relate to them. Once I saw that I could relate to people's motives, it was easier to relax and stop protecting myself from them.

THE ABILITY TO CHOOSE

God: Please talk more about how the seminars you and Neill developed supported your spiritual expansion.

Beth: A few years after Neill and I got together, we were both working as NVC coordinators here in San Diego. Whenever Marshall Rosenberg would come to town we would organize, advertise and staff his workshops. Neill had always been very curious about the unique distinctions underlying the consciousness of this work, and we began to explore these. This became the basis of the work we teach today. Through years of experimentation and refinement, we put together a set of distinctions that we believe made the biggest difference in our lives.

For instance, understanding the difference between integrity and morality helped me connect to my inner integrity and to let my old judgments of what's right and what's wrong fall away. When I integrated just this one distinction into my life, it changed the way I saw the world forever.

We define integrity as "being whole and complete." And you can't be whole and complete without being true to your word, your chosen values and yourself. We define morality as "judging what is right or wrong based on culturally accepted standards." In other words, instead of blindly following the dictates of society, I learned to examine my core values to determine what to do in difficult situations. In the end, we discovered a set of thirty-seven distinctions, and as I understood them better and practiced integrating them into my life, they shifted the entire way I related to my world, not only on a mental level, but also on a physical and spiritual level.

God: Only thirty-seven?

Beth: Very funny! I'm not saying that it was easy. It took time, but the more I integrated these understandings into my life, the more my perceptions changed. Like most everyone else, I grew up projecting my thoughts and feelings onto others. If somebody didn't wave to me as they drove by, I would think they were upset with me. If the man in the grocery store line argued with the clerk, I might think, "What a jerk." This is a terribly small box we put ourselves, and others, into without even knowing we're doing it.

I came to understand that my thinking, opinions, and perceptions were mine alone, and that others could be in the exact same situation and perceive it completely differently. When I really integrated that understanding, I was able to do more than just believe that people were doing the best they could; I could actually guess what they were trying to accomplish by their words and actions. This helped me to have great compassion for myself and others.

God: How was it for you to recognize this?

Beth: I had a lot of regret about how much of my own life was spent focusing on "who's right and who's wrong." I used to say to myself, *How stupid,* or *I should've known better; I'm such an idiot.* But when I realized how much human suffering is caused by this habitual conditioning, I was filled with grief.

As part of developing our work Neill and I learned that

being raised in this judgmental culture limits how we are able to respond to situations in our lives. In effect, our choices are limited only to submission, agreement, or rebellion. Submission might sound like, "I'll do what I'm told, but I'm not going to like it," and rebellion like, "Don't tell me what to do!" In agreement, we agree with the judgments and opinions of others. For example, we might concede that "I am stupid, or I should've known better."

God: How did you respond to situations in your own life?

Beth: When I was very young, I mostly "agreed." I remember being in elementary school and the teacher asked me to write an answer on the board. I didn't hear her because I was daydreaming, and when she looked at me she knew that I hadn't a clue. She tightened her lips, narrowed her eyes and shook her head. She said, "Oh Beth, at this rate you'll never make it out of fifth grade." The whole class laughed and I was devastated. I thought about what an idiot I was, and why I couldn't do anything right. I had been told often enough that daydreaming in school was bad and wrong, so I agreed with her judgment of me.

God: When did the rebel come out?

Beth: As I got older I grew tired of these judgments. I became very rebellious at around age fourteen, and if anyone tried to tell me what to do, I refused. In junior high a teacher caught me passing notes to a friend. She grabbed the note out of my hand and told me to get in front of the class and read it. I said no, and told her that if she made her classes more interesting, people wouldn't be passing notes around.

Then I got up and stormed out of the room. It's that right/ wrong split again. If I did what she asked, I would be admitting I was wrong. But instead, I made her look like the one who was wrong. This rebelliousness continued for much of my life, though in adulthood it became subtler. I would just ignore people or not call them back; in other words, I acted in ways people might call "passive aggressive."

God: Did rebelling feel good?

Beth: In the moment it did, but afterwards I would still feel irritated, and that left me confused. I didn't realize I was so limited in my choices. My confusion was trying to tell me that there must be a better way to deal with the situation.

In the past, I wasn't able to make conscious choices because I was running around trying to be right or not to appear "wrong." If we have learned to only recognize behaviors as either "right" or "wrong," then our options for responding are limited to those patterns of thinking. All you need to do is look at our movies, novels, and TV shows to see a reflection of our cultural choices. Hurt feelings, anger, repressed communication, and lack of honesty are abundant everywhere you look. Our options and choices are always limited by what we are able to discern or distinguish in any situation.

So many people believe that their cultural values are the truth – the only truth. They take these values as their own. They rarely stop to ask themselves, *What is important to me? How do I feel about this particular situation?* or *What do I value, and how can I live in harmony with those values?*

If I had learned these new distinctions when I was younger, I might not have believed my teachers' negative opinions of me. When someone told me what to do, I could have stopped and decided whether it was important to me as well, or expressed my feelings about it or tried to understand what was going on with the other person. But all I knew was that it was better to be "right" than "wrong." And my only options at the time were to submit, agree, or rebel.

THE CONSEQUENCES OF JUDGING
AND LABELING

God: Do you have an example of how this right/wrong thinking negatively impacted your life?

Beth: Yes. My father worked a lot, and when he came home he just sat in front of the TV watching one sports program after another. I used to label him a workaholic, and I thought that he was distant and selfish. These ideas caused me pain – who wants to have a distant, selfish workaholic for a father? This also affected how I treated him; I held myself back from feeling and showing my love, and how much I wanted us to be closer. He obviously didn't care about me, so why should I care about him? It wasn't until I learned how to get beneath these labels that I was free to love my father for who he was – a deeply caring man who was scared and didn't know how to show his love. There's a lot more to getting underneath the labels then I can explain here, but the judgments kept me from reaching out to him for many years.

God: What was it like when you were able to love him?

Beth: So sweet. It was a great gift for both of us. I was able to tell him how much I loved him, and see his eyes light up. We were able to have real conversations and we opened up to each other as never before.

Don't get me wrong. Our work wasn't a magic pill that I took, and presto, my life was perfect. It continues to take commitment and practice to change lifelong beliefs and patterns. Even now my life is not completely void of conflict, and there are times when I think I'd rather have different outcomes, but I'm much more accepting of what occurs. Now, when there appears to be a struggle with another person, instead of reacting I slow down and do my best to empathize with myself or the other person. I then consider my options and choose the actions I think will serve everyone best. Life is much easier this way.

MY GUIDING LIGHT

God: What about more spiritually minded people? Do you find that they have the same kinds of judgments?

Beth: We worked with a wide range of people, not just "spiritual" ones. But I was amazed that even highly conscious people still have this right/wrong, us-against-them mindset. It can be subtle and mostly subconscious, but it's still there if you look closely. Even those of us who have learned to express ourselves in a spiritual and politically correct manner demonstrate this attitude in our language and our actions. This indicates that at some core level, we still believe that we are separate and in competition with one another.

As more humans are becoming more conscious and accepting the concepts of oneness, love, and compassion, many of us feel frustrated when we don't embody those ideals. At these times we tend to deny our psychological and emotional tendencies. Our work also helps me to avoid this so-called "spiritual bypassing." This is when we consider ourselves so "spiritual" that anything less than perfection is a failure. We think we must deny the fact that we have a body and a personality. We especially want to reject those unwanted parts of ourselves known as the "shadow." We push them away and cover them up by going to our "peaceful place" and do our best to ignore the ups and downs that life brings. To believe that we can instantly transcend our habitual humanness through spiritual understandings alone is an attempt to bypass these things and avoid dealing with them.

God: So sometimes spiritual people deny their less acceptable feelings? For instance, "If I'm spiritual, I can never get mad or feel depressed?"

Beth: Yes. As feelings are pushed underground, conflicts arise. The consequences of ignoring feelings and parts of ourselves can result in codependency, denial, fear, shame, confusion, frustration, and all-or-nothing thinking. We futilely attempt to control ourselves or others. Some of us go to the extremes of compulsive behavior and addiction. This kind of spiritual bypassing can cause unnecessary pain and suffering. However, there is an alternative, and that's where our work comes in.

God: Tell me how your work has helped you in this regard.

Beth: At times, my deeply ingrained beliefs about myself – that old programming learned in childhood – led to thoughts such as "I'm not good enough, smart enough, or attractive enough," or to feelings of fear, and loss of hope. For some people, those beliefs can lead to serious depression or to even questioning the value of life itself. These parts of ourselves can seem dark and scary, but as I internalized the truth that there isn't a fixed "right way" and a "wrong way" to behave I was able to accept myself and became much more accepting and transparent with others. As I embraced my humanness I could allow the less than satisfying thoughts and behaviors come to the surface so that I could transform them; in other words, see them as the sweet messages that they really are.

I discovered that spiritual bypassing can be avoided when I understand the reasons for wanting to bypass my shadow side – the side of me that has just not yet been seen in the light of consciousness. As I deeply integrated these distinctions into my life, I began to see myself and my habitual nature for what it really is. Not good or bad, right or wrong, appropriate or inappropriate, but simply as thoughts and behaviors that I might want to either explore or change. There is nothing to hide.

The years of developing and delivering our work that followed my glimpse of oneness during the RET session allowed me to transform the way I saw the world and showed me the trail that led me back to you. During this time I unearthed and examined the cultural values that I'd unconsciously taken on, I rediscovered my internal landmarks, I gained clarity about what's most deeply important to me and how to make choices that are in harmony with my innermost truth. I am so grateful because I once again participate in my life with joy, creativity, and enthusiasm.

The more I let go and allow my true nature to reestablish itself as my guiding light, the closer I grow to you. There's really nothing for me to do other than sense and feel how I am in each moment and to follow my internal wisdom with a childlike curiosity. Even with how far I'd come on this path, one day early in 2007 my whole world was turned upside down. I received a phone call that my 77-year-old mother was seriously ill with pneumonia and in the hospital. I was scared; mom had always been so strong. It was clear she needed help, so I started flying back and forth from California to

Florida every four or five weeks. I made sure she was getting the proper care in the hospital and took care of her bills, her house, and other affairs. The doctors told me that because part of her lung needed to be removed, she would be in the hospital and rehab for a very long time. I wasn't sure how I was going to handle this; how would I take care of my mom and continue living my life?

In the years leading up to this, I had developed a strong sense of my purpose in life and I was constantly looking for ways to fulfill on my mission through our company, Focused Attention. I was a serious worker; there were many things to be done and I did them. For years, Neill and I gave live seminars until we reached the point where we realized that our expansive vision of serving millions of people would never be accomplished by continuing to give small, local seminars.

We decided to go online with our work so we could reach the world. I spent my days learning online marketing, writing articles and blog posts, figuring out Facebook and Twitter, and all the other strategies recommended by the experts. For four years we tried to hit the ever-moving target of online marketing, but as we took three steps forward, the target took two steps back.

God: Had you been close to your mother during this time?

Beth: We had stayed in touch by phone, but my life was so all-consuming that I hadn't seen her for three years prior to her illness. Fitting long-distance travel into my schedule so that I could care for her drove me to reassess my priorities. It was clear that my mother came first, but these events tore a gaping hole in my perfectly laid plans for my life and my business. Still, in the end, I was grateful.

Even before mom got sick I was busy running our business

full–time. Spenser, now nineteen, still needed much time and care because of his learning disabilities. We had hired a tutor because he was reading at only the second grade level. We were making sure he was learning life skills both in school and at home. For example, we used his allowance and chores to teach him budgeting and fairness in the context of our family relationships. There was still so much to do to prepare him for adulthood! Now I crammed caring for my mother into my already crowded life.

God: Why were you grateful?

Beth: I realized I'd been living my life on auto-pilot, like a greyhound chasing the rabbit around the track, always with my eye on a goal. I was forced again to examine my life, as I had after my divorce. I would soon become closer to my mother than we'd ever been. And as one thing led to another, I began walking down the path of awakening once again.

But at first, I was determined to do it all. I brought my computer with me everywhere and struggled to write articles on the plane and between my mother's appointments. My life had once flowed easily, but now I couldn't keep up. I was in conflict between a desire to work towards my vision and my determination to support my mom. I was exhausted, and something had to go. But our work, mission, and plans had been everything to me. It was as though I needed to die and be reborn.

God: Were you scared to let go?

Beth: At first, yes. But slowly I surrendered the idea that I had to keep the same pace, that I had to fulfill my mission, and I shifted my attention towards my mother's pressing needs. And then came something unexpected: a relaxing of sorts, a softening, a smoothing out of my jagged edges, a subtle but weirdly profound change that I felt inside. I began to question if all my plans, my vision and the extraordinary amount of work I was doing to "get" somewhere – to arrive at some destination – was it what I was really meant to do? Was this plan bringing me happiness? I began to wonder what was the true meaning or purpose of my life.

God: You questioned the mission and the vision you had?

Beth: More than that, I questioned everything. I put everything on the table. All my beliefs and all my dreams.

SIX MONTHS TO LIVE

God: What happened next with your mother?

Beth: After a completely debilitating surgery, it became necessary for my mother to move in with us here in California. She couldn't take care of herself. She needed help going to the bathroom, changing her clothes, and getting in and out of bed. I now had to assist her with these most intimate tasks.

And then there was my mother's personality. She was no shrinking violet; she was a strong opinionated woman, and even as she deteriorated and became as helpless as a baby, she never had a problem with expressing her opinions. When she first moved in with us, we sure had our ups and downs. During this time I also faced my own inevitable mortality. I know we all die someday, but when hospice gave her six months to live, her imminent death was staring me in the face.

God: Did you think your mother was getting in the way of your mission?

Beth: Not exactly, but I began feeling an intense agitation.

It wasn't quite dissatisfaction, because I love my mother and I wanted at a very deep level to support her. But I did worry that our business was coming to a standstill after all the years of hard work and all the forward momentum we'd created.

I mean, we had a BIG mission. Neill and I knew that our work had a lot to offer people around the world through seminars, products, and online classes – information that would support them in powerful ways – but I couldn't keep going at the pace I had been. I had to back off from the intense effort the business required, yet still try to keep it afloat so it didn't disappear altogether.

God: How did all this affect the changes that were occurring inside you?

Beth: Surprisingly, even with the increased agitation, the softening and relaxing of my internal state continued. At the same time, other shifts were taking place.

Being with my mother was fertile ground for examining myself. Mom liked to tell me what to do and how to do it. In fact, she enjoyed giving orders to everybody, but now all her attention was focused on me. This has always pushed my buttons. Once, when I was about five years old she asked me to sweep the floor, but instead of letting me sweep she would grab the broom out of my hands gave me blow-by-blow directions for every push and pull. Even at five I didn't want her telling me what to do. I clearly remember how irritated I felt. I looked her straight in the eye and said, "If you don't like the way I do it, do it yourself."

And now she was living in my house and telling me how to do… everything! My buttons were constantly being pushed, and I turned into that five-year-old over and over again.

God: What gifts did you discover in the conflicts with your mother?

Beth: As I softened, it became easier to let my mother just be herself, that perfect expression of my mother that she always was. The major turning point came when I was preparing one of her family recipe called pizza chicken. She pronounced from her throne – I mean wheelchair – at the kitchen table, "Really dear, after all the years of watching me make that you should know that you brown the chicken first," she said.

I looked at this old, dying woman and for the first time, I saw her for who she truly was. My mother gave advice in order to feel good about herself! She was trying to contribute, and sharing her knowledge helped her to feel confident and competent. And rather than react with irritation or frustration, my heart melted with love for her.

Now Neill and I often say in our seminars that what people say and do really isn't about you, it's about them. Everyone is simply trying to meet their needs in the best way they know how – always and without exception. I had learned to easily see this in people who weren't close to me, and now I finally saw it in my mother. So instead of becoming frustrated or angry at her comment, I began to engage her, asking her for more advice, more of her experience. I saw her face relax and a little smile came to her lips as she softened along with me. It became the most enjoyable cooking experience we'd ever had together.

God: How was this part of your awakening?

Beth: After the pizza chicken experience, I began searching for ways to let my mother tell me what to do. She was so weak by now that it was difficult for her to physically do anything, but she could experience life through me by giving me directions. My mother was quite artistic, and one day Neill and I had a gate-painting project. True to form, my mother had many opinions about it. Instead of telling her to leave me alone, I asked for her advice.

"Mom," I said, "How would you do this?"

It was as though a shot of life force energy started rushing through her; her face lit up and a big smile appeared. And before I could say another word she started giving me explicit directions about how to paint the gate. "Well," she said, "I would definitely have more drop cloths because paint can get all over. And make sure you put enough paint on that brush so you don't get streaks. And honey, you're going to mess up your clothes; I would change if I were you. She went on about colors and how to hold the brush. While listening to this, all I felt was joy. What a relief for both of us!

I was letting go. I let go of what I thought I knew and just welcomed what showed up. And what showed up was my mother and me. Without effort, almost organically, I now saw my mother just as she was – the truth of who she was – this beautiful soul just wanting to live life, express herself, contribute, and be seen. At the same time I was able to relax into the truth of who I was.

And guess what? We were the same! I always just wanted to live my life, express myself, contribute to others, and be seen. As I realized these truths I was able to just be myself, and to love more openly and completely. This shift in how I responded to her "contributions" was a gift for my mother, yes, but also a huge gift for me. I unwrapped this gift inside of myself: finding me, knowing me, loving me, and relaxing into me. Waking up to the truth is letting go of what we "know," and allowing pure reality to shine through.

CHAPTER 7
Cracked Wide Open

"Your task is not to seek for love, but merely to seek and find all the barriers within yourself that you have built against it."

~ Rumi

THE MASKS

THANKFULLY, MOM HAD NOW OUTLIVED her prognosis of six months, perhaps because of her renewed interest in life as we became closer and more loving with each other. After she had been living with us for over a year I was worn out by the twenty-four-hour a day responsibility. It all started mildly enough. I felt a curious agitation, and realized that I needed support in order to shift how I was relating to the situation. So as I normally do, I asked the universe to send me someone who could help me.

A day or two later my ex-husband Greg told me about a technique he was trying that involved a pendulum and affirmations. Affirmations hadn't been too effective for me in the past. But even so, I called Daniel, the practitioner, and I sensed that he could help me so I scheduled a session.

Daniel lived in Colorado so we "met" over the phone. During the first session, he explained he'd be using a pendulum to guide our sessions. Each time we spoke, using his pendulum, he suggested remarkably fitting affirmations for me. Then he would ask me to repeat that affirmation over and over again with my eyes closed and my hands wrapped one way and my legs wrapped another.

God: What kinds of affirmations?

Beth: He started with, "I am ready, willing and able to feel love unconditionally in every present moment," and then would move to another, like, "I have the courage to follow my passion, faith in my ability to choose my path wisely, and I am at peace with the unknown this creates in my life." Each time I repeated one I felt a shift inside. Each time, I relaxed a bit more, as though something unwanted was falling away. We would talk about what came up for me, and then he would ask me to repeat a different statement, sometimes totally different and sometimes only subtly different than the one before. I was intrigued enough to schedule another session.

It was during our second session that things got wild. Over and over, I was repeating, "It's safe and okay for me to live in plain view for the entire world to see." My eyes were closed, hands crossed one way and feet crossed another. "It's safe and okay for me to live in plain view for the entire world to see. It's safe and okay for me to live in plain view for the entire world to see. It's safe and okay for me to live in plain view for the entire world to see."

After about a minute, an intense vibration rushed through my body. The affirmation cracked me wide open! A very strong visual image entered my mind's eye. It was a face with no eyes and no mouth. Then appeared another face with a big broad smile and gigantic teeth, and then many other faces filled my mind. One looked like a wolf, another was covered in material like a shroud, and an angry old man face with red and black stripes on its cheeks.

I saw that they had no backs to them – they were masks. Then I felt them moving up through my body from very deep down inside of me. One at a time they would rise up, with a jolt, and hover around my face for a moment. Then with an intense pressure I felt them erupt out through my skin, one at a time. Each mask was a different shape, had a different feeling, and each expressed something different than the one before. With each came a release of a kind of emotion and tension, like lava erupting from a volcano and oozing out of me. I knew that each one of these masks was an expression of some crusty old façade I wore to protect myself. I recognized some as they passed by: the happy girl, the cunning one, false modesty and overconfidence. As they moved up and out, I felt the anger, guilt, fear and sadness that were hidden behind these masks release with them.

As soon as the last mask – an unrecognizable muddle of eyeballs, lips, noses, and ears – moved through me, my whole body started vibrating as if there was an enormous force pushing on every inch of my being, as if the whole volcano was about to explode. Then up from the pit of my stomach came a deeper vibration, which moved into every part of me. This energy was different than the thick oozing type of movement I had felt as the masks were moving through me. This energy was fast and bright and moved around so quickly I could hardly follow it. Then it seemed to explode out of me, and out of every pore in my body. Suddenly I felt my body still sitting in the chair, but somehow I wasn't in my body; I was somewhere else. Yet I wasn't hovering over myself like in the movies. The "I" that I knew myself to be was simply not in that body.

I was breathing faster and faster until I started to hyper-ventilate. I managed to tell Daniel, "I can't catch my breath; I can't catch my breath." He told me to lower my head down between my legs. This relieved some of the intensity and pressure that was building up in my head.

I sat there with my head down for what seemed like a very long time. I was unable to move, unable to speak. I just sat there, feeling the residue of the energy, my mind whirling with thoughts. *What just happened? Am I really going crazy this time? Should I move?* Then I faintly heard Daniel's voice from the phone, "Beth, how are you feeling? Can you tell me what just happened?"

I was able to say, "I'm okay. I'm not sure what just happened to me." As I told him about the energy trying to explode out of me, I realized something. This energy wasn't trying to explode out of me; I just wasn't a big enough container to hold it. I wasn't even sure what this meant, but in time it would become clear to me.

God: You were not a big enough container to hold the energy. Some people spend their lives searching for that realization.

Beth: In a sense, I had been searching as well. I just didn't know it. Eventually I stopped working with Daniel, but I discovered that the process he was using was called Psych-K, which helps you identify and change subconscious beliefs that mask your recognition of yourself as a divine being. Psych-K has become part of my essential toolkit for restoring my connection to you. I continue to use it even today.

God: This event brought you closer to recognizing who you really are.

Beth: Am I far from a full recognition?

God: Not very. No one ever is very far away. Tell me more about that explosive energy.

Beth: I realized that as I grew up, I drew my energy in closer and closer to my physical form to protect myself. As my belief in myself as a separate person grew, I became a much more encapsulated being than I was meant to be. I believe this is true of most of us. The experience that I first interpreted as the energy trying to explode out of me could be more accurately interpreted as my being attempting to re-shape itself. I've come to realize that we human beings are inherently much larger than our physical form would have us believe. We are energetic beings that are only limited to our physical bodies if we believe we are.

THE SHAMAN

God: What happened after you worked with Daniel?

Beth: Despite all the self-help work I'd done, all my work with Neill, and all the new modalities I'd learned to support myself during this expansion process, I still sometimes felt troubled. The December before my mother passed away I felt worse than usual. Most of the time I could let the feeling pass, but at that point days of discomfort had turned into weeks. I wondered if, after all the opening experiences I'd had, this heavenly feeling of peace and relaxation was leaving me again. I was angry and disappointed. How could this be happening?

One night I was sitting on the back patio crying, looking up in the sky – as if you were literally up there – and I expressed my dissatisfaction. Excuse my French, as my mother would say, but I yelled, "What the @#%@# is going on? Why would my peace and my happiness disappear this way? What the #@@$% am I supposed to do now?"

I had been caring for my mother now for over two years. The sheer amount of effort this took drained me, and the agitation depleted any stores of energy I had left. But I didn't get any answers that night. When my cursing didn't work I decided I'd have to find help elsewhere. Maybe I should talk to a spiritual counselor, or maybe I needed to go to the doctor, or maybe I should start meditating again, or doing more yoga or... or... or? The uncertainty was driving me crazy. Then a friend told me of a man who had studied with shamans in Peru. As usual when the next step along my path appears, I knew intuitively this was for me, and I registered for the next healing journey.

God: Please tell us about this journey and how it contributed to your expansion process.

Beth: I took the train up to Los Angeles where the ceremony was to take place. Although the house was in the middle of the city, the property was perched on the side of a secluded hill and far from the nearest street. That and the thick screen of trees gave it a country feel. I walked into the rustic old home to find the shaman, a tall man with wavy gray hair and a warm smiling face. He looked at me as if he knew me. I felt a deep sense of knowing him too. As the others arrived, we all settled in and the shaman gave us instructions on how to get the most benefit from our journey.

The ceremony started with an invocational prayer, and then each of us was given what the shaman called "the medicine." The shaman paced around the room, chanting prayers, and handed each person a tiny cup of thick dark syrupy liquid. Within about a half an hour people all around me were having their own unique experiences. One woman was crying; one man was sitting stoically, hardly moving an inch, with his eyes closed as if in deep meditation. Another person's eyes darted back and forth, and up and down and around, like they were seeing something that was not visible to me. Our experiences seemed so different we might as well have been in different rooms.

The shaman continued walking around the room and performed a healing ritual on each person, with sacred tobacco smoke, bells and rattles. I couldn't see much in the dim light, but I sensed their energy change as he stopped and performed a similar yet unique ceremony with each person. Then he'd move onto the next.

God: What were you experiencing?

Beth: Nothing physically, emotionally or mentally changed in me for close to an hour. Then he moved towards me and even before he touched me I felt a slight vibration in my body. As he came closer the vibration grew stronger, and then he put his hands on my shoulders. My body exploded as a rush of energy, from deep down in my core, moved intensely up through my stomach into my chest, then expanded in my head with a powerful shaking motion.

The Shaman blew smoke in my crown chakra at the top of my head. He chanted as he moved around me, holding his hands over me, touching my head and my shoulders. The internal movement persisted, moving up and down through my body as he continued. Back and forth he went, chanting strange and unrecognizable words. At this point I was shaking from head to toe. I was just about to ask him what was happening when he said, "You are experiencing a kundalini rising. Allow it to continue until it's complete. Relax into it as much as you can; you will know when it's done."

The intense powerful movement in my body and the mixture of excitement and fear were similar to the experience I had those many years before with the Rapid Eye Technology. But this time I was in a room with many other people, and along with the movement, strange noises started emerging from me. "Ya ya ya oh ah ya ya Ahhhhhhh, oh ya ya ahh!" These sounds seemed almost tribal in nature, rhythmic like a drumbeat and curiously familiar.

God: Were you self-conscious?

Beth: Yes, I felt embarrassed that I was the loudest person in the room, but this self-consciousness came in small waves and quickly left. With each thought, my body moved, as though the movement was dissolving the energy of that thought-form. The energy flowed up and down my body in huge waves. Each movement seemed to stop, and then explode out of parts of me, as though it was opening each of my chakras and clearing them. The rhythmic noises turned into slow deep howls as if I were about to give birth.

Unexpectedly, I was compelled to stand up. The movement became stronger and more purposeful. Energy ran up and down through my body, stopping at points that seemed stuck, as if there were blocks in its way. It lingered at these points with a deep, intensified vibration – stopping but not stopping – moving but not moving. My whole body shook, making way for the energy to flow. And when it was ready to move again, there was a weird sensation like a cork popping on a champagne bottle. Then the energy expanded past the bounds of my body, and areas that were blocked seemed to clear.

God: What else did you feel?

Beth: It was beyond words. While I was shaking, I felt a sense of connection to everything, an open free feeling – a profound experience of joy, of love, and yes, even bliss. And yet none of these words can describe the depth of what I felt. At this point I was sobbing with joy. It was a relief and release of all that ever held me back, caged my spirit, or kept me small. It was as though there were no bounds to my spirit or my body or my sense of being.

This intense shaking and blissful feeling went on for what felt like hours, until I wondered if it would ever end. But how could I be tired of bliss? Looking back, I suspect I was becoming physically tired, like all the movement was hard on my body and my nervous system as well.

God: Many people prepare their bodies for years to experience what was happening to you.

Beth: I know that now, and I realized even then that I wasn't prepared. So I called over the shaman and asked, "Is this normal?" He assured me that it was perfectly okay, and to allow it to run its course. I would know when it was over. So I just relaxed into the movement, allowing this energy to have its way with me.

At one point I felt compelled – almost assisted – to bring my hands into a prayer position in front of my face. I stood there and cried tears of joy, feeling connected to everything and safer than I'd ever felt. I knew that everything was as it should be. I opened my eyes in the dimly lit room with my hands still in a prayer position, my fingertips at my forehead and the rest of my hands flowing down in front of my nose and mouth. An awareness or sense of recognition came into my mind. Between me and what I see in the room there is a space, a place of stillness and quiet, where nothing can bother me. This is my place of peace, this place between my hands that looked different than what I saw on either side of them. I understood then that my stillness, my peace, is in my hands.

I spread my hands open and knew, at a very deep level, that inner peace is always within my reach. Having peace in my mind, body and soul was one hundred percent my responsibility. We always have the ability to choose how we respond in a situation, and in that moment my hands became a tangible, visual symbol of that truth.

As I'm writing this, I realize I would like to offer this process I experienced to the reader.

Peace Is In Your Hands (Exercise)

As you're reading this, you can try it for yourself. Close your eyes and place your hands in a prayer position. Now put your thumbs on your forehead and open your eyes. Around the outside of your hands you will see your environment – the place where you are. However, your hands will now appear as a clear space without any visual clues from your environment. This space is always there in every situation; it is the stillness. It can be your place of peace if you choose it.

As you continue to stand with your thumbs at your forehead, imagine a situation in your life that is not going the way you would like. Just for a moment, see this clear space created by your hands as the true peace and stillness within you. Now, while lowering your hands in front of you, open them, palms upward, as if you are accepting a gift. Now imagine that in your hands are the peace and the stillness that is always available to you, in any situation. Press your hands, your gift, into your heart. Your peace is always there, always attainable, never very far away. It's in your hands – always in your hands.

God: Not everyone is ready to feel this, you know.
Beth: I know, but it is such an incredible feeling that if

even one person senses what I'm talking about it will be worth telling about it. It seemed strange at the time because I had done so much personal growth work, and I long ago understood that I was responsible for my own happiness. Being responsible for ourselves is even one of the major distinctions we teach in our work. But for the first time, I got it in a physical way, not just as a concept or mental practice. I was so inspired by this awareness that I wanted to scream it into the room, but I was so enthralled with this sense of peace and calm that I couldn't even open my mouth.

At that point I saw that excitement and peace are not mutually exclusive; I could have both of them at the same time!

God: Many people think they are mutually exclusive. It keeps a lot of people away from seeking peace because they're afraid it will be boring.

Beth: At that moment I truly got it. We can have both. It's not either/or. And with that recognition, the movement in my body began to slow down and a low hum, a vibration, took its place. I would know when it was done, he said. And then it was.

The energy left me, my hands fell from my face, and I sank slowly back in my chair to a deep place of stillness that I had never felt before. It was as though my entire existence had been confined in a small hard protective shell and these last two experiences helped crack that shell wide open. My sense of intense joy and connection changed, but it didn't disappear. I wondered if I would again lose this blissful bond, as I did after that Rapid Eye Session years before. But that thought quickly disappeared as I rested in the beauty and peace of that moment. It was a homecoming of sorts – coming home to you.

CHAPTER 8
Lifting the Veil

"The eye through which I see God is the same eye through which God sees me; my eye and God's eye are one eye, one seeing, one knowing, one love."

~ Meister Eckhart

WHAT A GIFT

God: What happened afterwards? Were you able to maintain this sense of peace?

Beth: It was a mixed bag. I was able to maintain it most of the time with much attention and practice, but it didn't feel like a strain and struggle. This time, there was no sense of depression or longing or loss, only a sense of expansion, and growth, and fullness, love and hope.

What fascinated me was that I could experience all my emotions and a deep sense of peace at the same time. I started feeling everything, all at once. It was as if a veil had lifted, or become thinner. I was much closer to the heart of what felt like the truth.

God: Did you behave differently after this experience?

Beth: Yes, I noticed that my emotions – all of them – continued to surface more readily. I cried more easily, I slipped into anger more quickly, I laughed more easily at ridiculous things, and I became more honest and straightforward than I had been. When I returned home after this journey I noticed that I felt frustrated and even angry whenever I needed to do something for my mother. This was very disturbing to me, but at the same time, deep down in my being, I knew everything was absolutely perfect. I wondered what was going on.

God: How did you handle the anger towards your mother?

Beth: I had an energy clearing ritual. I remember one morning in particular; I walked into her room to get her out of bed, dressed, and washed up. Before I went in I did my usual clearing ritual so she wouldn't be disturbed by the impatience I sometimes felt about caring for her. One morning, after seeing the shaman, I felt particularly annoyed. There was a struggle within me between the life I thought I wanted – being free to do as I wished, including the work I love, and the life I was living – cooking for my mother, doing extra laundry, cleaning out her potty, and even wiping her butt. It was like having to care for a 110 pound, gray-haired, wrinkly-skinned baby. Sometimes I conjured that image to make me laugh, and trust me, laughing any time I could was a very good thing.

I began doing this clearing process because I was torn about the life I was leading. I knew I consciously chose this life, and I truly wanted to care for my mother. It was a gift in so many ways, but at the same time I was afraid my frustration would impact her in a negative way.

The ritual went like this: I would stand outside her door

before walking in and release any upset, dissatisfaction, or irritation that I didn't want her to pick up. I did this by first sensing where in my body I felt the agitation. Then I would shake it off by jumping up and down, or shaking my arm or a leg, or whatever part felt most uncomfortable. Then I would quiet down and remember a sweet and loving time my mother and I had spent together. This whole process only took a minute or so, and made a huge difference.

So on this day, I did the clearing ritual as usual and then walked into her room. And though she hardly looked at me I snapped at her: "I'm doing the best I can! Give me a break, for God's sakes" My extreme anger surprised me and I was left almost speechless. But I quickly apologized and told her I needed a few minutes by myself and that I would be back to help her soon.

I left the room and sat with my head in my hands, wondering what the hell had happened. Why did I react that way? The intensity behind my words shocked me. This woman wasn't the "me" I knew myself to be. This contrast was especially strong because only a week before I was in that place of unconditional love, joy, and peace.

My confusion prompted me to call the shaman and ask him if he could give me some insight. He said that these raw emotions were common after a kundalini experience, especially for people like me.

I asked, "People like me, what does that mean?"

He said, "It means people who have done a lot of personal growth work, who have a lot of compassion and caring for others – people who want to take responsibility for their lives."

I asked him to explain further. He told me that very often

when people learn to take responsibility for themselves – to stop being a victim of circumstance – they stop blaming other people for their situation. This is a wonderful thing, but it doesn't allow for certain feelings that arise to be expressed. The energy of these feelings has to go somewhere, and where they end up going is deep down inside – they get pushed down to an unconscious place within us.

I said, "But I don't really think I'm upset at all. I made a conscious choice, I understand the consequences of the choice, and I'm willing to accept them in a loving way."

But the shaman told me these feelings build up on an energetic level, and not at a conscious thinking level. A kundalini experience such as I had begins to break down the veil between what we think is real – our plans, decisions, our ability to control our environment – and everything else. And within this "everything else" are all our emotions, all our sensations, and all our expressions of them. So from now on it would be harder and harder for me to keep the deeper level under wraps.

God: Did you expect that everything would be easier after you experienced this awakening?

Beth: Yes, I guess so. But instead of everything being easier, there was more for me to pay attention to. The shaman suggested that I pay more attention to my feelings, flow with the energy, and allow it to move. He said by doing so the energy would soon dissipate. After we talked I sat for a long time and explored the emotions and sensations I was feeling and what might be triggering them. I realized I was doing a lot of things for my mom that deep down, I really didn't want to do, and I was angry. I also saw that I wasn't caring for myself in a way that replenished me.

A day or two later I talked to my friend Dale, a vibrant woman in her early sixties with platinum blonde curly hair. She's a great friend and part of my support system. Dale is an accomplished healer, using Reiki and many other modalities. I told her about my experience with the shaman and what had happened afterwards. "What would you do if you knew your mother had another fifteen years to live?" she asked.

It was the perfect question. When my mother moved in, the prognosis was that she had approximately six months to live, and now it was nearly two and a half years later. Don't get me wrong; I was very grateful that my mother was still with us, especially since she seemed so happy, but I had no idea I would be caring for her this long. So the question Dale asked really hit home – fifteen years! – what would I have done differently if I knew the commitment was for fifteen years? The answer was simple; I would hire someone to be with her part of the time. I realized that I could delegate some of the care of my mom. This gave me some peace for the moment.

WAITING TO DIE

The conversation with my mom about hiring a caregiver didn't go as simply as I had imagined. She had become very attached to me being her caregiver. At the same time, she worried about being a burden, and that she needed too much from me. I reassured her that she was an exceptionally easy "patient" to care for and hadn't done anything wrong. It was just that I wanted to get back to my work, spend more time with Neill, and have more of a life outside this caregiver position. She worried about how we would afford it, and I told her that we would figure it out; there were lots of options. For over an hour we thoroughly talked through all the concerns she had. By the end of our conversation she seemed calmer.

Within a week I heard about a possible caregiver – another reminder of how often the right things turn up when you focus your attention in new directions. I felt excited after hearing this good news and ran to tell my mother. But when I went into the room I saw her quietly slumped over in her wheelchair.

"Mom, what's going on?" I asked her. She didn't answer so I asked her again.

She looked at me and said, "I am waiting to die. We're all just waiting for me to die."

Even as I write this tears come to my eyes. She looked so incredibly lost, as though she was at the end of a road and didn't see anywhere to turn, nowhere to go. Worried thoughts flooded my mind. *Did I cause her to feel this way? Am I pushing her towards death? Am I just waiting for her to die?*

But no, I just needed help. I stood quietly for moment and then reminded myself that what she was feeling wasn't about me, it was about her. It's funny; in the past I would have started reassuring her, letting her know that I loved her. I would have talked about the reality of the situation and how well things were going. But all I did was put my arms around her and hold her.

My mother wasn't very demonstrative, so she sat there rather stiffly as I embraced her. A moment or two later she looked at me, and I told her that I loved her and asked her why she believed we were all just waiting for her to die. She said again that she was being a burden and that it was too much for me – she saw how this care-giving was wearing me out. Otherwise I wouldn't be hiring somebody. I let her know that my deepest desire was to joyfully and lovingly care for her, and that with help I could continue to do this. It was just that I wasn't Superwoman. I was okay asking for help and hoped that she would be as well. She said that she was, but I wasn't quite convinced.

But as it turns out, we never brought anyone in to help. My mother's health declined quickly and she died within a few weeks of that conversation. Now, in hindsight, I realized that for my mother, the answer to this idea of "being a burden" meant dying.

God: Why do you think that?

Beth: Looking back on my mother's life, I believe that her mind, thoughts, and beliefs were a tremendous affliction. She had a very difficult childhood. When she was very young she was sickly and spent most of her time in bed. She also grew up during the depression in a poor family, and then was sexually abused by her stepfather when she was an adolescent. How could she not be carrying the painful weight of her past? She knew what it felt like to carry a burden and she didn't want to inflict that on anyone, especially not me. Her generation did not have the emotional resources that are available to us now. And as she told me many times – each time I tried to help her cope with the pain of her past using some of the "tools" of our work – she was an old dog and not about to learn any new tricks. So she believed nothing was going to change for her in this lifetime, and death was really the only option for relief.

God: Did you blame yourself?

Beth: Of course I deeply questioned whether it had been best to express my need for help and the desire to get back to other parts of my life that had been put aside for so long. But at the end of this soul-searching, I came to the conclusion that my mother would have known my feelings, one way or another – energetically or in words. At least it was overt and nothing was left to the imagination.

This way, I got to express how much I loved her and how my genuine desire was to care for her joyfully. So in the end I'm glad I followed my guidance and was honest with her.

After that, my mother's emotional states became more extreme. One day, for example, she was taking an afternoon nap. Neill and I decided to go out and get some of her favorite split pea soup for dinner. I went into her room and found her sleeping so soundly that for a moment I was afraid that she was dead. I looked at her chest to make sure she was still breathing and she was.

I leaned over her and whispered, "Mom, Mom, we're running out to get some soup. Do you want some?" She didn't move, not at all. So I nudged her on the shoulder and whispered to her again, but she remained still and quiet. I became concerned because normally she is a very light sleeper. I shook her shoulder a little harder. "Mom, wake up!" I said, "Mom!" Still nothing.

I called Neill into the room for support. I tried again to wake her up, but still nothing. Oh my God, I wondered to myself, is she in a coma? So I raised my voice and almost screamed, "MOM, MOM, WAKE UP!!!"

Finally she moved her head and slowly opened her eyes. "Bethie,'" she said to me, with a big smile. "Sweetheart, so good to see you, what are you doing?" I told her we were going to get soup and she squealed with joy saying, "I looove soup, how wonderful, oooh thank you!"

Although my mother often expressed appreciation, this level of sweetness was extreme. She seemed like a different person – light, almost childlike in her expression of joy. I asked her if she was okay, and she replied with this over-the-top kind of happiness. "Yes, I'm wonderful," she said. "I feel so good and you're so beautiful and soup sounds wonderful!" It wasn't like her at all, but I loved seeing my mother so happy.

"Okay," I said, "Do you need anything before we go?"

"No, nothing," she said. "I'm wonderful." A little worried, we reluctantly left to go get soup. When we returned with the soup she was still in this state and she ate her soup like it was the best thing she had ever tasted. And she went to bed that evening happier than I've ever seen her.

THE EYES OF GOD

God: What happened next?

Beth: By the next morning everything had changed. She was very sad, even depressed, and her energy was so weak that she could hardly get out of bed. It was as if she was fading right before my eyes. She moved so slowly that morning as we went about her normal routine, brushing her teeth and hair and changing the diaper that she wore at night so her bedding wouldn't get soaked. I was hoping she would perk up, but she seemed more impaired than I had ever seen her.

As we finished her routine she looked at me, thanked me and told me how much she appreciated me caring for her. I made her usual breakfast – two eggs over medium, toast and yogurt – placed it in front of her, and watched as she tried to eat it. But this morning she only finished a small portion instead of cleaning her plate as she usually did. Well, she had her good days and bad days. The only reason it seemed significant was that it was such a huge contrast to the night before.

That day, as usual, she watched TV, ate lunch, took naps, and was visited by a hospice worker. It was Tuesday and that night I had a Toastmasters meeting. Neill would meet with a friend of his for coffee and pick me up when I was done. We did all the usual things to get mom ready to spend an evening alone. After dinner, I got her into bed with her TV remote control in hand. Just before we left we put Petra, our little six-pound poodle, with her in bed. She loved having Petra sleep with her. When everything was just the way she liked it, she told me to have a good time. She seemed perfectly fine and even happy again, so off we went.

After the meeting, we drove home and pulled the car into the garage. It was still fairly early, so I opened the door to the house and yelled, "Mom, we're home." When I didn't hear anything, I walked into her room and was shocked to see that she had gotten out of bed and was sitting in her wheelchair, slumped over.

I quietly said, "Mom, are you all right? What are you doing in your wheelchair?" I hoped she was asleep. But no answer.

I touched her shoulder and moved her a little and realized something was wrong. *Oh my God*, I thought to myself, *I think she's dead.* A chill ran through my body. I felt terrified, confused, and overwhelmed with emotion.

I screamed, "Neill, Neill, I think Mom's dead." He ran into the room and looked at her, then touched her hand.

"Yes baby, she's dead," he said. I just stood there. I didn't know what to do.

But Neill knew what to do. He thought I might be going into shock so he put his arms around me and walked me to the living room. He sat me down, threw a blanket around my shoulders and sat down next to me. I sat quietly for a time and then said, "What do we do now?"

He replied, "We don't have to do anything right now. How are you?"

"I'm just so shocked. She was fine when we left. I'm not sure what happened." We sat there for another few minutes without speaking and then I realized that we had to call hospice. They would take care of things.

I made the phone call and of course they knew what to do. What a gift this organization had been to all of us during these past two and a half years! They let me know that they would be there within the hour and for me just to relax until they got there.

I went back to my mother's room and looked at her. There she was – my mother – there but not there. It wasn't the first time I've experienced someone's death; I had been with my father when he died. I was able to say goodbye to him, and to experience the lifting and leaving of his essence from his body. But this time I was not here to say goodbye. I wished I had been able to let her know one more time how much I loved her and what a gift it had been for me to care for her, to tell her how wonderful it was for me that we had two and a half years to heal old wounds and to restore our relationship.

She had told me more than once that she didn't want to cause me any pain. I'm guessing this was the way she wanted it; it was easier for her to die in peace, with no one around. Maybe she thought it would be a gift for me not to have to be there – she didn't want me to suffer, she didn't want to see me cry. Maybe she even struggled out of bed and into her wheel-chair so her death would cause us the least amount of trouble, so we could just wheel her out. She was ready to go: no fuss, no muss. That would be something my mother would do.

I thought back to the day before when she was so bliss-fully happy. Maybe while she was sleeping that afternoon – so difficult to wake up – she was experiencing what was on the other side of death. She had a glow about her, and as she woke up and looked into my eyes, an angelic radiance beamed from her. As I remembered her face, I realized I had been looking into the eyes of God.

Now, as I looked at her lifeless form, I understood what she had experienced the day before – the joy, peace and hap-piness – she was one with All That Is – one with God.

Here in this room, only the shell of the mother I knew remained. I sat there for very long time just gazing at this limp, lifeless form, empty and quiet. This experience brought me to a profound understanding. We are not our bodies – in the body, or not, we are part of everything. My mother was truly no longer present in this form, and yet I knew in that moment she was and always will be alive, eternally part of All That Is – whole, complete and joyful.

Then the doorbell rang – it was the hospice nurse.

CHAPTER 9
Perfect Timing

"Body and mind, and spirit, all combine, to make the Creature, human and divine."

~ *Ella Wheeler Wilcox*

LETTING GO

STRANGELY, MY MOTHER'S DEATH paved the way for one of the most wonderful times of my life. I was again about to experience the sense of oneness with everything that I had come to know. However, there was much to do immediately following my mother's death; it was as though I were leading two separate lives. One part of me was mourning and reevaluating, opening and expanding, exploring and discovering. Then there was another part of me that just took care of the details: the death certificates, banks to notify, legal papers to get in order, the cremation and memorial service to organize. I mechanically completed each task until they were all done.

My son Spenser had moved out to share a place with a roommate a few months prior to this and was doing well, and now Neill and I realized that it was just the two of us.

For more than twenty years we had always been responsible for others – his children, Spenser, my mother – and now we were alone. This created a void, an emptiness, with nothing obvious to fill it. It felt strange, but at the same time filled with possibility.

Of course I was mourning my mother's death. She was a character, and I would miss her. But in the last years we had worked through all our old issues. After she was gone I realized I had nothing to regret. What remained was just love, and missing her. Now I felt totally unencumbered, with my whole life ahead of me. I could choose to do anything I wanted!

God: How did you respond to so much freedom?

Beth: There was so much room for whatever I wanted, so many choices, that for a time I didn't know what to do. So I booked an appointment with Allison – an intuitive massage therapist that we knew. I was hoping that a massage would help clear the restless energy and confusion.

On the morning of my appointment I was running a little late. I hit every red light, got behind every slow driver, and even took a few wrong turns. My fingers were gripping the wheel and my heart started beating faster. All the way I kept saying to myself, you have plenty of time, the timing is perfect – but this didn't reassure me.

On some level I knew this was true. I usually seem to arrive where I need to be just at the perfect time, but when I arrived on her block I felt frustrated and tense. Finally I squeezed into a parking space, stopped the car, and started to cry. As I stepped out of the car I saw Allison's previous client, my friend Dale, just coming out. So, if I'd arrived on time I would've been sitting in the office for twenty minutes, waiting. But for some reason I continued to cry. I thought to myself, *Boy, I need a massage; I just need to relax.* Dale gave me a quick hug as we passed.

I walked up the stairs and saw Allison just changing the sheets on the massage table in her office. I tried to pull myself together by focusing on what was around me. I smelled the orange scent of the massage oil in the air. I watched as Allison's delicate form moved around the table as if she was barely touching the ground, and I felt the hard seat of the chair as I sat and tried not to fall apart.

"What perfect timing," she said as she glanced up and saw me.

Those three simple words tore down the last of my defenses and I crumbled. Why had I been torturing myself by rushing and worrying? She saw my tears and said, "Let's get you on the table." She left the room and I undressed. I lay on the table facedown, still crying; it was as though a faucet had been turned on and I couldn't turn it off.

When she came back in the room she said, "Well, let's just start where you are," and she began doing some energy work.

This was not the relaxing massage I had come for. The buckets of tears that had built up over my mom's passing poured out. Allison slowly and gently moved her hands to different places on my body. First down my back, then down my legs to my feet and back again. The touch of her hands on my skin felt like wind flowing through silk, and I could feel the energy in my body moving and changing its intensity. When my tears began to subside, she told me she sensed that I'd done well clearing myself energetically and that now we could clear the rest.

God: How did Allison clear the energy in your body?

Beth: She "swept" it away. She told me to imagine myself sweeping together all the stressful energies in my body. Then, using her hands, she gathered up what needed to move and guided it out.

With each sweep, waves of feelings and emotions coursed through me – sadness, fear, regret, and strands of anger. I tried not to think too much and just let them flow. After these came another wave – now, a sense of longing, ribbons of loneliness, and more tears.

This was about much more than mourning for my mom. As the emotions were swept away, a sense of calm and peace came over me and my body began to tremble.

I recognized the kundalini rising once again. Waves of energy rippled through my body and I had uncontrollable urges to stretch my legs, move my arms and shake my hands out rapidly.

My body seemed to have its own intelligence and it knew what to do. I got up on all fours, moving different parts of my body as I did. Each movement brought more energy to that part, and as it did it began shaking rapidly. First my arms, then my chest, my stomach, my legs, my feet – they all shook in turn, Allison moved her hands up to my head to steady me as I now turned onto my back and continued to shake, experiencing the same sensations as during my last kundalini experience.

It was another clearing – a housekeeping, or cleaning up of what I now know as my chakras. When the energy moved in, the shaking increased, and when the energy moved out it felt as though it was bursting out and then back into me. Feelings of lightness and connection to All That Is moved into my body and my thinking mind. It's as though I was connected to everything: the energy in the room, Allison, the soft music playing in the background, the off-white walls, the soft brown chair in the corner of the room, and the very air itself. I was one with it all – one with everything. Waves of joy, bliss, and otherworldly emotions rippled through me. Here I'd landed once again in this place of such knowing, such peace, such grace, though none of these words truly do it justice.

Then a thought came to my mind: *How do I stay connected to this full, real connection to All That Is? How do I keep this connection in my day-to-day life?* And the answer came: through your skin – your skin is your connection to All That Is. I didn't really know what that meant, but I knew that it was the truth.

A deep love filled me. I felt Allison's warm gentle hands still at my head and I embraced her arms with both my hands, looked up at her and told her how much I loved her. Her smile was deep and warm. Allison smiles with her eyes, dark almond-shaped eyes that looked at me with such love. I explained to the best of my ability what was going on inside me.

As I talked I began to feel my words through my skin – this might sound strange but with each word I spoke, instead of hearing them I was feeling them on my skin. As she replied to me the same thing happened – I felt her words through my skin.

God: Can you describe how this felt?

Beth: It was as if the skin around my entire body was humming with each word, with each sound, like an exquisite field of movement. It felt like a delicate dance on my skin being choreographed by angels.

Something profound had just happened. I had asked a question about how to stay connected, how to stay present to everything in my day-to-day life, and the answer was through my skin. I didn't know what to do with this information or how it would affect my life. All I could do at that moment was relax and enjoy the experience. Allison left me, and I lay there for what felt like an hour and watched the sun cast shadows across the walls in Allison's office, cocooned in my miraculous skin. A deep sense of gratitude washed through me and I had a multilayered knowing that there is much more to our day-to-day lives than we are able to perceive.

I got off the table and I felt like I was floating, as if I were in a gentler world, one that was easier to navigate. The connection – the joy and gratitude, the lightness and ease – stayed with me as I got dressed and left the office. But when I got in the car and started driving it faded, and slowly I slipped back into the more dense reality that I knew as my normal life.

God: What about this insight you got on the table – the one about connecting to All That Is through your skin? Did you ever understand it better?

Beth: Not at first. After resuming my normal life, when I recalled the answer to my question, I had to laugh. It seemed so profound at the time, but later it seemed so strange. Connecting through my skin, what the hell did that mean?

A couple of weeks later a friend of mine brought over a DVD called *As Above – So Below*, by biologist Bruce Lipton. He makes biology understandable to the average person, like me, and he talks about how we're affected by more than our genes. We watched his video and in it, much to my surprise, the idea of connecting through my skin became clearer to me.

He says that we are created in the likeness of a cell and that each cell has a brain. In his book, Biology of Beliefs, he explains that the brain of our cells is not the genome, as was first thought – it is actually the cell membrane – the equivalent of the cell's skin.

God: The brain of each cell is in its skin.

Beth: Right. But – you know all this.

God: Yes, but your readers might not be so up-to-date on their biology.

Beth: Okay. So here is what Bruce actually says in his DVD:

"Built into the membrane are protein switches that respond to the environmental signals by relaying their information to internal protein pathways."

That means that the surfaces of the skin around our cells are like little relay stations. They pick up all kinds of information in the form of signals from the environment, and they carry it back to the switching stations on the inside of the skin, which then decide what actions to take. The signals represent environmental forces that switch on the various motors within a cell and cause protein gears to move.

God: So these signals, or environmental forces, can be anything that has an effect on a cell?

Beth: Yes. Signals represent both physical and energetic information that comprise the world in which we live. The air we breathe, the food we eat, the people we touch, even the news we hear – all represent environmental signals that activate protein movement and generate behavior within our cells. And the way our cells behave causes how we behave.

Simply put: people, air, food – or even the news – can all activate the cells in different ways and cause our behavior. Bruce says that when he uses the term "environment" in his discussion, he includes everything from the edge of our own skin to the edge of the Universe.

And now it made sense to me. In the same way the cell has skin that relays information to the switching stations and creates behaviors, our bodies do something similar. Our skin is the first connection to all the information there is – it is pure and unfiltered. Our other senses are different – our eyes see and our ears hear, but this information is filtered through our thoughts and our past experiences.

I saw the effect of the filters all the time in the seminars we taught. A group of people would come into the room and hear the exact same words, but experience them completely differently, depending on their history and where they were in their personal growth process. You can see the same thing in a family where the children were brought up with the same parents but have different childhood memories of the same event.

It's as though our skin is a huge open field that takes in every bit of information around it and then decides what to do depending on what it's taken in, without any filtering from our conscious mind. This was completely new information to me, but it made so much sense. Now I better understood the insight that I should connect with my skin, but I still didn't know what to do with that information.

CHAPTER 10

A Hard Nut to Crack

"The lives of animals are woven into our very being – closer than our own breathing..."

- Gary Kowalski

STRANGE THINGS BEGIN TO HAPPEN

AFTER MY LATEST KUNDALINI EXPERIENCE with Allison, I was truly open to maintaining the connection to All That Is, but not in the compulsive way I had before. This time it was more peaceful, this time it was a quiet knowing that there was something greater than myself. So I put my intention out to the universe that I was ready to embody this connection. Then I just went about my business.

After that some very strange things began to happen. Animals started finding their way to me. I had heard of totem animals, so it's not like the idea was strange – but these beautiful creatures physically put themselves in my path over and over again until I finally paid attention.

First came the turtle. Since this was my first totem animal experience, the poor sweet turtle had to come to me three different times for me to take notice. The first time was in a food court at a local strip mall with a beautiful garden. It had a koi pond with a little bridge where you could stand and feed the fish. Neill and I often came here when we wanted a break, to sit, have a cup of coffee, feed the fish and relax – it was quite lovely and peaceful.

Now the pond also had quite a few water turtles, who would sit up on the rocks and sun themselves. They loved competing with the fish for the food we tossed into the pond. But this day as I walked up the path towards the koi pond a turtle had somehow gotten out of the enclosure and was walking towards me. I thought she was lost so I just picked her up, climbed down some large rocks, and placed her back in the water.

That was the end of that, or so I thought. But much to my surprise, the very next day I walked out into my backyard – and guess what I saw? A turtle. This was a different kind of turtle but a turtle nonetheless. I couldn't imagine where this turtle came from, in the middle of our housing tract, or how it got into our fenced back yard, but there it was, looking at me.

Anyone who knew much about animal totems may have been suspicious by this time, but not me. I started checking with my neighbors, and found out that one of my neighbor's turtles had gotten out of its cage and somehow crawled through the fence into my backyard. I couldn't see a way for that turtle to actually get through the six-foot, solid wood fence surrounding our yard, but even so, there he was. So I gave the turtle back to the neighbor and I thought that was that.

But no, that turtle energy wasn't done with me yet. A few

days later we went back down to the koi pond and as we got out of the car, a turtle came walking towards me, right in the parking lot. I picked up the little turtle and brought her back to the pond and gently guided her into the water. Now they finally had my attention!

God: So by then you were "turtley" convinced?

Beth: Oh no, not puns too?

God: All forms of humor are part of my nature.

Beth: All right! Anyway, all these turtle encounters got me wondering if they were trying to give me a message. I decided to look up "turtle" as a totem animal and see what medicine they offer. So as soon as I got home, I checked on my computer to find out what these turtles were up to.

I found a website called Lin's Domain, with information about many animal totems. Here's a synopsis of what I discovered:

> Turtle Medicine carries us between dimensions, like a bridge between our waking state and our dream state. It helps us to slow down our thinking mind and the energies that keep us playing our earthly games. It is as if Mother Earth is calling us to release the tight hold we have upon any nightmares in our waking state. If a Turtle totem shows up in your life, you should slow down and pace your life more. Bigger, stronger, faster are not always the best ways to reach your goals. Turtle also teaches the art of grounding to Mother Earth's power and strength. By focusing your thoughts and actions in a collaborative way with the Earth's limitless energies, you're no longer all on your own.

I found all this interesting, but I wasn't sure what to do

with this information so I just let it be for now.

But then I started seeing crows everywhere. There had always been a lot of crows around the house, but I began noticing them more than ever: one sitting nearby as I got out of my car, or when I stepped out on the back patio. This had been going on for a week, when one day as Neill and I were taking a walk in our neighborhood, I noticed down on the ground right in front of us was a very large, perfectly formed black feather. Neill picked it up and handed it to me as if he knew it was for me. You would think because of my experience with the turtle I would pay more attention, but finding the feather didn't faze me. I guess sometimes I'm a hard nut to crack.

So once again the universe pushed me a little harder to wake up. Crow took the matter into his own hands and began talking to me – well not in English or anything – but he did start squawking at me. One morning soon after finding the feather, I woke up and went downstairs to find the crow sitting on my back fence staring into my kitchen. I looked at him, not too surprised, and turned to get a cup of coffee. And he began to squawk. "Caw – caw – caw," the crow cried with his ragged, raspy voice. It was very loud and impossible to ignore. I glanced at him, and he looked almost directly into my eyes and continued to squawk. " Caw – caw – caw, caw – caw – caw, caw – caw – caw."

"Okay, I get it," I told him, "You want to tell me something. What is it you want me to know?" As soon as I acknowledged this he flew away, so back to the Lin's Domain I went. And here is what I found:

Crows are the keepers of the Sacred Law and to have

a crow totem is very powerful. Personal Integrity is your watchword and your guide in Life. If you have a crow totem, your prime path is to be mindful of your opinions and actions. You must be willing to walk your talk, to speak your truth and to know your life's mission. Crow is an omen of change. Crow lives in the void and has no sense of time; therefore, it sees past, present and future simultaneously. Crow merges both light and dark, both inner and outer. It is the totem of the Great Spirit and must be respected as such. They are symbols of creation and spiritual strength. Look for opportunities to create and manifest the magic of life. Crows are messengers calling to us about the creation and magic that is alive in the world today and available to us.

These beautiful creatures had really gotten my attention, so when the red-tailed hawk came to speak with me, I was clear that she was there for me. About a week after the crow had made himself known, a red-tailed hawk came and positioned herself in almost the exact place on my fence that crow had. I woke up, came downstairs for coffee, looked out the window, and there was this majestic bird. She was quite large as far as birds go, with a dark brown head, white and russet chest feathers and intense dark eyes.

She sat there quietly but purposefully looking at me. Now that I understood she was there to give me a message I asked her straight out, "What is it you'd like me to know – please tell me what message you have for me."

I sat quietly and closed my eyes and waited for an answer. But none came. I opened my eyes and she was gone. I walked outside and around the side of the house but she was nowhere to be found. As I continued to look for her I noticed a feather on the ground. A small rusty red and black tipped feather lay right in front of me. I picked it up and I knew that hawk had left it for me. I went online to discover that the red-tail hawk had a unique message:

> Hawk is the messenger, the protector and the vision-ary of the Air. It holds the key to higher levels of con-sciousness. This totem awakens vision and inspires a creative life purpose. A hawk totem is filled with respon-sibility because hawk people seek the overall view. They are aware of omens and spirit messages. A Red-Tailed hawk totem is special. It has direct ties to the Kundalini, the seat of primal life force. It is associated with the base chakra. If you have this totem, you will be aware of and work towards fulfilling your soul's purpose. It reflects a greater intensity of energy within your life: physical, emotional, mental and spiritual forces will all be strong within you. The Red-Tailed hawk is a permanent totem – it will always be with you.

The link with kundalini energy was perfectly fitting, and I was past the point of surprise about any of this. But I had a question – were these animals now all my totem animals for life, or were some just messengers for a moment? I found out that they could teach me about myself as well as connecting me to divine energy.

We can tap into the energies of these animal totems for strength, guidance, personal answers for questions that we may have, as well as for healing ourselves and others. They ultimately help us to learn exactly who we are emotionally and spiritually. Ted Andrews defines animal totems in his book "Animal Speak," as "any natural object, animal, or be-ing whose phenomena and energy you feel closely associated with during your life." A totem is considered to be a power, also called 'medicine,' and is capable of walking down our path with us on our spiritual and personal journey in this lifetime.

So it seemed that they were to be my lifetime compan-ions. I felt honored, and delighted, and confused. After all of the visits from the animals and the information I'd received I still wasn't clear what this all meant. I knew there was still something – an opening – wanting to emerge. And more was to come; I hadn't seen the last of these animals.

CHAPTER 11
Emerging Realities

"Magic ... is a sudden opening of the mind to the wonder of existence. It is a sense that there is much more to life than what we usually recognize; that we do not have to be confined by the limited views that our family, our society, or our own habitual thoughts impose on us; that life contains many dimensions, depths, textures, and meanings extending far beyond our familiar beliefs and concepts."

- John Welwood

THE RITUAL

BY NOW I REALIZED THAT EACH TIME I was about to experience a new opening, expansion, or an important insight I would feel a physical pressure, as if I were a balloon being filled to the bursting point. This uncomfortable sensation was a stark contrast to the peace I felt most of the time.

The latest kundalini episode had relieved the tension for a while, but soon the pressure returned. This time I again sought help from my friend Dale, who invited me over for a weekend. The plan was that one day I would help her to set up her website, and the next day she would reciprocate and use her skills to help me. I hoped Dale could facilitate whatever wanted to emerge in me.

The very next weekend I went to her beach house. I know a lot about online marketing after the years spent developing our business, and Dale wanted to bring in more clients. On Saturday we put my expertise to work and reinvented her website. We added an eye-catching design and then gave it the ability to capture the names of possible clients. By the end of the day it was clear, simple and inviting, and we were happy with our work. I slept well that night, with the rhythmic sound of the waves rolling in near my window.

Sunday morning it was my turn. Dale started with a Reiki and an energy balancing session. I could feel the warmth radiating from her hands as she worked on me, and my whole body softened. I felt more relaxed than I had in days. Then she wanted to do some Gestalt therapy – not my favorite. Usually with Gestalt, rather than helping me get to the heart of the matter, I tend to get tangled up in my conscious mind. But I trusted Dale so I agreed.

Gestalt is a process that uses dialogue to communicate with different parts of yourself. We started out by talking to my agitation. I would move back and forth between two chairs, speaking first as me and then as my agitation. I asked questions, and it would answer. Dale moved with me and she added a few little twists to the process, like spraying aromatherapy scents.

Back and forth we went for a while. My "agitation" let me know that there was much stress in my body – my physical form – caused by grief for my mother and also from the strange, opening and expansion experiences. My body, apparently, was exhausted.

"What can I do about this?" I asked.

"You can care for this beautiful creation better than you have," the agitation said.

"In what ways might I care for myself better?" I asked, "How can I relax?"

I was surprised to hear myself say, "Start taking baths!"

I never much enjoyed taking baths. The last time this even occurred to me was after my divorce, over fourteen years earlier. Now I was being directed to design a ritual around bathing that would soothe and nurture me, and to use bath salts and essential oils. In other words, to care for this physical form with love and reverence. I wondered – was this how I was to connect to the universe – through my skin?

I asked the agitation what my skin had to do with this, and all I heard back was that I should also stroke my skin, love my skin, and honor my skin as the great gift that it is.

As this "dialogue" went on, I felt my body and my mind ease. I now had a sense of direction, and felt grateful to Dale for her highly developed intuition, her skill as a healer, and her loving support. That night she cooked me a wonderful dinner of crispy Brussels sprouts and salmon. We took our plates down to the beach and were serenaded by the ocean and the neighborhood seagulls as we savored every bite.

Afterwards she taught me about different aroma therapies. I particularly loved the oil called Humility; it had a stirring scent, like an exotic flower from a far-off island. I also chose lavender, for reducing stress, and two blends called Joy and Inner Child to take with me for my first baths. I went home the next day feeling hopeful and excited to see where this would lead.

I spent some time just thinking about what I'd discovered, to integrate what I learned. The first thing I did was to stroke

my skin, as directed – my hands, my arms, my neck – noticing how it felt, allowing what came up. This immediately
helped me realize how out of touch I was with my body! I
closed my eyes and allowed myself to just feel these unfamiliar sensations. With each caress I could feel where every hair
connected with my skin, and the stroking stimulated a sense
of warmth within me. The exercise brought me to a rare place
of stillness; it was like a form of meditation. My mind was
quiet but alert. I practiced giving this attention to my skin a
few more times before I actually took a bath.

Several days later, I created the bath ritual that was suggested. I had a very nice bathtub, a large oval with a shelf
all the way around it. First I set out candles and crystals and
things that were meaningful to me, such as Reiki symbols
and a picture of a lotus flower. I would use essential oils and
salts from the Dead Sea and the Himalayas. I would burn
sage, cedar and incense. And I put out the feathers I got both
from the crow and the hawk. I found a small brass turtle that
was able to hold some crystals, happy that all my new-found
totem animals could be with me for support.

I found it was easy to create the physical expression of
the new ritual – it was like any other art form that I had ever
created – make it beautiful, make it feel good, include color,
shape, smell and texture. Finally it was all ready to go, but
what came next? What exactly was the purpose of this bath?
Would I know what to do? Should I just relax and see what
happened? I decided to stop asking questions and just get in
the bath already.

As I turned on the water and plugged the drain, I realized
that the ritual had started. Each part of this was connected to
everything. I slowed down and became more present to each

step I took. I gathered the salts carefully in a cup and mindfully poured them into the running water, watching the large pink grains settle to the bottom of the tub. Using my lighter, I lit the sage and watched the leaves begin to burn. As the dark orange-red edges of the leaves burned down, the black gray ash fell away. Smoke rose up in the air creating movements, like a slow dance, peaceful and serene.

I watched the water rise higher in the bathtub. The swirling turquoise liquid had a very appealing quality that invited me in. When the tub was almost full, I turned off the faucet, disrobed, and stepped one foot, then the other, into the hot water. Like liquefied velvet, the water closed over my skin. I lowered myself into the bath, finding it easy to be present to the heat of the water against my body. Then I slowly sank down until I was sitting cross-legged on the bottom. Okay, now what?

So I sat there, and sat there, for what seemed an hour, when finally something began to happen. My mind quieted and I noticed my breathing become deeper and smoother. I remembered back to the time after my divorce when the warm water of a bath would soothe me. I just sat there enjoying this peace. After some unknown amount of time it occurred to me that I was done; my fingers and toes looked like skinny white prunes. So I got out and dried myself off. I was disappointed because I had expected some kind of special healing experience.

God: Maybe the ritual needed to know you were serious. A few wrong turns in the beginning are often part of any journey.

Beth: You mean they're like a test?

God: Not exactly, more like the twists and turns on an unknown path.

PARTS OF THE SAME WHOLE

Beth: A few days later the idea of a bath popped into my head again. But really, I couldn't take a bath every time I felt tense; the whole process took over an hour. I had work to do! I needed to revive my business and start earning money again.

Just then Neill came in the room and asked me what was going on. When I told him what I was thinking, he looked at me and said, "Beth, your mom just died. Relax, there's nothing critical that needs doing. It's time for you to take care of you. Please go take a bath; everything is fine."

I began to cry with relief. "Thank you," I said. I felt such a deep sense of love in that moment that I could only say "thank you," and embrace him with gratitude. Then I got up and went to take a bath.

Again I ran the water, put in the salts, added the oils, lit the sage and the candles and made my way into the tub. The candles threw deep shadows on the wall. I felt as if I was floating in a hidden lagoon. I leaned back and relaxed in the water, wondering if anything else would happen. The hot water felt so comforting. Was just resting here in this moment, without needing to accomplish or understand anything, the whole point of these baths?

I wasn't much of a meditator, though I'd tried meditation on and off for many years. Even so, I realized that quieting my mind and just "feeling" would be the best thing I could practice at this point. I focused on my breathing, feeling the air move gently in and out of my nose, feeling the hot water on my skin.

Then I remembered being on the massage table when I had asked the question, "How do I stay connected?" Through my skin – that's right, through my skin – so I placed my attention there. With this, my skin began to tingle. The skin around my nose where the air flowed in and out became more sensitive. The skin on my body where the water touched me felt more sensual, more delicate.

Paying attention to these sensations allowed me to deeply relax. *This is wonderful*, I thought, but as soon as the words came into my mind the sensations lessened and I felt my muscles tense. I knew the idea of meditation was for thoughts to come and go, like clouds. The warm water seemed to help me let them flow. So for the rest of this bath, thoughts floated in, and I allowed them to float out by returning my attention to my skin. I practiced this bath meditation many times over the next few weeks. Then one day an image of a crow came to my mind.

My eyes were closed, and I "saw" the view of fence through my kitchen window to the patio. On the fence sat a large black crow, the image identical to when the real-life crow came to me. As he looked at me, his eyes glowed with a golden sparkle. As I looked back at him, instead of just seeing him, I began to feel him. The connection grew, and I felt I was becoming part of the crow. My body in the bathtub was less noticeable and his body became fuller within my consciousness. I could feel his strong little heartbeat. I felt the breeze running down to the tip of his feathers, and the fence tucked firmly within his claws. I sensed how he balanced between his head and his tail. The sensation of being a crow intensified. It was all crazy and amazing!

God: Some people call this shape-shifting. What happened next?

Beth: With an intensity that shocked me, he lifted both his wings and began to flap them, and I was so startled I opened my eyes. Then I was back into my body, and not placed gently back, but thrown back violently. I was alone, scared and confused, sitting in the cooling water. But it had felt so real. Did that really happen, I wondered, or was I going crazy? I wasn't sure, but I needed some time for the experience to sink in, so I drained the water and got out of the tub.

I sat on my bed and thought about what had just happened. *Am I crazy?* – I didn't think so! Yes, I knew I was sane, but that whole scary, intense, wonderful experience seemed so real. It was as though I was becoming that crow. Finally I decided just to leave it for now and see what happened next.

A day or so later, I once again was drawn to take a bath. I began my ritual as before, but now I added my new invocation – an opening prayer. My experiences have shown me that there is much more to "reality" than I can normally see, hear, or feel, and I wanted to acknowledge this. I wanted to affirm my willingness to see, hear and feel everything available to me, so I asked for words that would support this at the beginning of my bath rituals and this is what came:

> I see all there is to see,
> I hear all there is to hear,
> I feel all there is to feel,
> I say all there is to say,

and I am one with All That Is.

I leaned back in the tub, rested my head on the pillow, closed my eyes, and almost immediately the image of the crow appeared in front of me. I felt my body tense up, but as soon as I noticed that I slowed my breathing, kept my eyes closed, and focused on the image. Soon enough I began sensing him again.

As the sensations of the crow grew within me, my own body seemed less and less real to me. It was as though I was seeing out of his eyes; my peripheral vision seemed to decrease.

My senses changed; I knew what was happening around me/him by the subtle movement I felt in his feathers. There were people nearby that I couldn't see, but I could feel their presence. As I sat with him quietly I sensed an unfamiliar feeling of wholeness, or fullness, or oneness, as if through the crow I was now connected to everything. Through this sensation I understood that there was no separation between things. Everything was connected. It felt as though there was one large sheet of energy that ran through everything, each part connected to the next.

I watched, I listened, I sensed as the crow. When something moved in the yard near us I could feel, hear and see the movement in my adopted body. This was a different type of sensing. I didn't just see with my eyes and hear it with my ears – I saw and heard with my entire body. I can't explain it, but as I stayed with these sensations I knew that the crow had a message for me. I relaxed my body even more so that the message could come through, and then I began to perceive the message in my mind, as though the crow were talking to me, but using no audible language.

God: And what was the message?

Beth: It wasn't what I'd ever imagine a bird would say, but I had let go of all that with my prayer. The message was this: *What human beings perceive is not the fullness of what there is to perceive, and the separation you think is between us is not real. What is real is that we are all connected; we are all parts of the same whole. There is nothing that we do or say or think that is not affecting every other aspect of reality.*

As these ideas took shape in my mind, the overwhelming nature of them propelled me back into my own body. I felt the water around me; the image of the crow was gone and I wondered again if I was losing my mind. Was that just my imagination? It felt so real! I sat up, drained the water from the tub, and went to lie down, trying to absorb the experience.

CHAPTER 12

The Unfolding

"Fear is born from our concepts regarding life, death, being, and nonbeing. If we are able to get rid of all these concepts by touching the reality within ourselves, then nonfear will be there and the greatest relief will become possible."

~ Thich Nhat Hanh

I MIGHT NOT BE CRAZY

DESPITE THESE WILD EPISODES, I clung to the certainty that I was quite sane. And if this could happen to me, then maybe I should open my mind to the possibility that reality was quite different than I'd always believed. So I paid careful attention and allowed these new experiences to unfold with as little judgment as possible. When the thought came that I was going crazy, I just allowed it and reminded myself that I couldn't possibly know everything there is to know about how reality worked. This allowed me to continue exploring what was coming through me, and gradually the confusion and worry subsided. Whenever I had doubting thoughts, I would let them float by.

God: What happened to your other totem animals?

Beth: Soon I received messages from both the hawk and the turtle. First came the turtle. One day I was lying quietly in the tub with my eyes closed when she appeared, walking towards me as she had at the mall.

As I watched her I consciously relaxed so as not to scare her away. When her little green body moved closer I saw the padded claws of her feet and the yellow streaks on the side of her head. When I tensed up with doubt, she'd slow down. When I relaxed again, she advanced. This went on for another few moments and then I began to sense her, as I had the crow. She was calling me inside, and I soon felt her cold hard shell cover me. Her back became my back. Strangely, as her shell embraced me, I felt warmer; it became secure and comforting.

The idea that I was imagining this or making it up kept popping into my mind, but I allowed those thoughts to float away.

I felt myself, not the self I know me to be – but rather my essence or soul – embodying the turtle as I had with the crow. But the turtle's experience and her message were completely different. She gave me a sense of separateness, isolation and protection that had not been evident with the crow, as if I had safely arrived home. I felt grounded, calm, and with a self-assured knowing. There are no words to explain; it came in waves of feelings, sensations and impressions.

As I melted more and more into the form of this creature I began to hear her message. *You are safe; you are protected; you are loved.* The words flowed into this body in warm waves. *You are safe. You are protected. You are loved.* They repeated over and over again as waves of feelings flowed through our joined being. Tears began to form and then I sensed myself return back to my own body. I felt the water, and I heard the words again: *You are safe you are protected you are loved.* I sobbed as if I had never heard words like this before – *I am safe, I am protected, I am loved.* The bath water became a warm soft blanket covering me, nurturing me, and taking care of me. When I was a child and told my mother I didn't feel good, she would call me up into her lap and wrap her arms around me. Now I felt the same kind of warmth and love in which she had held me and comforted me. The turtle disappeared and I was sitting all wrapped up in my mother's arms once again.

But like all the other thoughts, this memory of my mother floated out of my consciousness. As soon as that memory left, the turtle reappeared and offered one more message: *Your answers are within you. Go inside, be still, stay the course and be patient.* This message, unlike the others, came from outside of me – more of a mental picture or thought that I seemed to hear with my ears.

You might think having these experiences would be easy – all joy and bliss, beautiful messages and extraordinary experiences, but on the contrary, often there was a turbulent fight between my pragmatic reality-based mind and this expansion into the unknown. It was as though I was a little boat on the vast stormy ocean. This final message threw me overboard.

Stay the course, what course? I thought. Be patient? Patience is not one of my strong suits! Then the image of the turtle disappeared and my thoughts became louder and more pronounced. *Crap,* I thought, *what do you want me to do now?* I looked up – as though you were going to throw me a life jacket, and come down and comfort me or tell me what to do.

Just as I looked up, the hawk appeared. I slowed my breath

and focused on her image, and my anxious thoughts released their grip on me. My mind grew quiet again and I began to feel her majestic form. She felt light and bright and almost airy, as if the wind were whispering through my skin.

I began to merge into oneness with the hawk. I felt stable and firm-footed yet at the same time there was a mystery that I didn't understand. When she moved, I was moving. My arms waved up and down but they were not my arms. I felt a lifting off and, oh my God, we were flying. I had balance, coordination, grace, and a kind of freedom that I have never known in my own body. As we flew and I looked around, I realized I couldn't actually see anything with my eyes – I couldn't make out details of my surroundings, all I could do was feel the strangest sensations. I felt the air on my arms, the tingling of the wind in my face, and the lightness of my body. I was dancing on the wind. As we continued to soar above everything, the hawk's message came to me. *Live in the moment; allow yourself to be free, and just fly.*

All at once I was back in the water, but this time I was calm, relaxed and free. I was back in my own body, yet I retained the sense of freedom I felt as I was flying with the hawk. I sat there for some time just soaking in this magnificent sensation. Finally I got out of the bath, blew out the candles, and crawled under the covers -- this time, to revel in the sense of freedom.

God: How did these messages affect your life?

Beth: In the moments they occurred, these things seemed so profound, as though they would change everything. But the truth is, they do and they don't. That's the good news and the good news. Certainly I was affected deeply. I spoke my truth with less fear of losing friends or not being liked, because I knew at a deep level that I was loved, safe, and protected. I also felt a whole new level of connection to All That Is. My senses were heightened and I acted on my guidance more quickly. I felt much freer to trust myself and to know what to do, and that's good news. At the same time, outwardly not much changed; my life went on just the same, and that was good news as well.

The crow and hawk became my constant companions. I don't know what happened to the turtle; maybe it's not easy for her to get to me, but the crow is always around. There are plenty of crows where I live and on a regular basis they approach me and we chat, and I remember how connected I am to everything.

I see red-tailed hawks much more than I used to, and they seem to position themselves right in front of me so they're hard to miss. They are reminders that I'm as free as I choose to be, and that my perception of what is real may be less real than I think. This allows me to relax into the present moment.

FINALLY FREE

I continued to take baths and as I did, I developed new rituals that assisted me in clearing out my old "stuff." One major area to clear centered on my fear about not "doing" enough. After all, being busy is one of our cultural epidemics. I started a breathing practice in my baths where I breathed into the physical areas of my body, my arms, my legs, my back – I breathed in peace, and breathed out stress and fear. Each time I left the bath after performing this practice, I felt clearer and lighter.

At other times I released layers and layers of fear, jealousy, judgment, and more. Various clearing processes would come to me – different ways of clearing at different times. During this time I bathed at least four times a week, and each bath was unique and cleared a different aspect of myself, like the masks I'd shed so long ago. My hands got warm and my feet tingled. I cried, I laughed, I shook, I did Psych-K balances, and I moved energy, and as I did I got more and more connected to All That Is.

I also received much guidance during these baths. For example, I got a message to spend a whole day practicing being completely present and to do nothing unless something called to me loudly. If there was something to do, I would know it. Otherwise I was to just experience what came up about not doing anything. I was just to experience calm, peace and presence.

The rest of that day and for weeks to come I practiced as the message had instructed me: I paid attention to being calm and peaceful. I practiced doing only what called to me loudly – I played with knowing when there was something important to do or when I was to just do nothing, to just be present. This was one of the most challenging and confusing experiences of my life. I remember sitting on my back patio trying to figure out what being "called to do something" would feel like. I realized that I had a deeply ingrained habit of being constantly in motion, flitting from this thing to that thing with no presence of mind or knowing why I was doing it other than it was on my to-do list. My mind kept rambling on about all the things I could go do, but with each thought no feeling of being drawn to it was present – there was nothing that I really wanted to do.

The amount of agitation that came up during this time gave me much to clear during my baths. How can you feel so peaceful and so restless in almost the exact same moment? I was experiencing this dichotomy more and more lately. Again, in my experience, this was a sign that something was emerging within me – something was trying to have its way with me. Those few weeks were very tiring, but extraordinarily interesting ones.

God: What was trying to have its way with you?

Beth: It didn't reveal itself for a while. But one day, I had a sense that it was time for another bath, so I prepared it and lowered myself into the hot steamy water. After a few moments of relaxing I suddenly started feeling very small. It was a sensation that was familiar to me – that same sensation I had as a very young child. My hands felt thick and tingly. My body was unfamiliar to me, as if dense and tight and very, very small.

This was the same sensation that had scared me so much as a child that my parents started taking me to a psychologist. I was told it was my imagination, not real, and nothing to worry about. But now as an adult I knew that these feelings were not just my imagination. At first that old fear popped into me, and then I relaxed into the experience. I breathed slowly and deeply, and let the sensations of smallness and denseness became stronger. I sat there for a very long time like this.

Suddenly a flash of insight came. Oh my God, this was my connection to All That Is. My body was the conduit – the connection to everything out there – and I mean everything. It was all mine to experience from this place.

Now I understood that I felt this denseness because my essence is so much bigger than my body, and at the same time my body was the only tool I had to experience it with. With this thought, an expansion took place. It was as though my head gushed opened and my essence joined with everything. I recognized that my body was connected to the totality of all things – I was able to join with everything through my sensations, my skin, and through my physical being. This time there was no shaking or intense energy movement, just a quiet knowing, with every pore of my being, every cell of my body. This time instead of having the experience, I became the experience.

In that moment everything was perfect. The water became cooler and cooler and I just continued to sit. I couldn't think of a reason to get up. Everything I needed, everything I wanted, was right there with me. So I just sat there.

After some time Neill popped his head through the door. "Are you all right?" he said, "You've been in here for hours." *Hours*, I thought..., *strange, it didn't seem like hours*. By this time he was used to my bath experiences and didn't seem too concerned. Just a warm sweet caring emanated from him.

I looked at him and let him know that everything was fine. Well, better than fine – everything was wonderful and I was just where I needed to be.

God: So you understood what it's like to just "be" until it's time to "do."

Beth: Yes. Finally. And as I talked to Neill, it was time to "do". My body started to move – almost by itself – it was time to get up and out of the bathtub. The weeks of practice doing only what called to me seem to culminate in this moment. For the last few hours I was just "being" until there was something to do. It all made sense to me. As I stepped out of the bath I realized that everything – I mean everything – was different in my life: who I knew myself to be, how I felt, what I saw through my eyes, what I heard in the room. It was all different and at the same time absolutely nothing – not a single thing – had changed.

As I often did after my bath experiences, I wrote about what had just happened. There weren't many words in me, but what came out was, "Today I know things that I cannot explain – not with my mind but with every cell in my body. Today I reconnected with the source of who I am – on a physical level – fully and completely. I am no longer afraid."

God: What had you been afraid of?

Beth: I realized that my whole life to this point had been spent in some level of fear. I'm not talking about being afraid physically. I seemed to be like anyone else – relatively competent, relatively happy and content. What I mean is being afraid to connect with, see, feel and know the truth of who I really am. There was always an underlying anxiety, a ripple of tension that came anytime I thought about, wanted to do, or did anything that was bigger than I thought myself to be.

I played small. All my life. The fear was debilitating, and it had kept me from doing so much, being so much, feeling so much. And now as I stepped out of the bathtub, all of fear and the anxiety seemed to be gone, and I was free.

CHAPTER 13

This Wild and Beautiful Ride

"If you are not willing to risk the unusual, you will have to settle for the ordinary."

~ *Jim Rohn*

RIGHT HERE, RIGHT NOW

SOON AFTER THAT LAST profound bath experience, Neill and I decided to take a day off and go to Balboa Park in San Diego to enjoy the gorgeous May weather. At first it seemed like a typical trip to the park. The day was bright, the sky was blue and the park was filled with green and gold leaves and brilliant flowers. We wandered in the direction of our favorite little outdoor cafe for lunch. As we walked I was acutely aware of the warm soft breeze – how it smelled of the ocean, and how it caressed my skin.

Ever since I learned that my skin was a large part of how I connected to Source – to All That Is – I've been paying more attention to it as a means of sensing the energy around me. Rather than thinking about, seeing or hearing things, I was experiencing them through my feeling sense. So as we

120

strolled towards the restaurant I experienced the walk in a deeply connected way.

Suddenly everything I saw seemed to glow with a special brilliance. As I walked by each individual flower, the pink, red and gold seemed to pop off the intense green background. The park looked like a brightly decorated watercolor painting. At the same time I began to feel a number of different vibrations. It was like tuning forks of different tones were being held to my ear, but I could feel them quavering throughout my body. Everything I saw and heard seemed more vivid and alive.

This might have felt good if it wasn't such a shock. I didn't understand what was happening, and it was so intense that I began to feel physically overwhelmed, nauseous and exhausted. As usual, I cannot find the exact words that get to the essence of how it felt; these experiences cannot be described accurately in words. I had to stop and sit down until the feelings subsided a bit. As I rested there on a bench, looking around, I watched the colors dim. The intense feelings dissipated until everything was back to normal.

God: How did you explain this extraordinary feeling to yourself?

Beth: I believe that when I'm connected to everything – God, spirit, the universe, All That Is, – the quality of that connection is different than in my day-to-day reality. The extraordinary feelings that come are a physical experience of my connection to the universe. The more fully connected I am, the brighter and more uniquely intense everything is.

When I reflected on it, I realized that my previous experiences of being one with All That Is came when I was in a meditative state. But now they began to occur randomly as I went about my normal activities.

The next one happened when I was sitting at the kitchen table talking to Neill. Out of nowhere a flash of energy rushed up and down my spine, surprising me. It was the first time I experienced the kundalini energy move when I was just sitting and talking.

The energy began simultaneously at the crown of my head and at the base of my spine, and then it moved together towards the middle of my back. It was so intense that I wondered if something was physically wrong with me. The forces continued to move together and then part, flowing in the opposite direction. I couldn't even explain to Neill what was happening; I just sat there with an odd look on my face. As my concern about my physical well-being rose, the sensation faded. Then, I tried to get the feeling back, but it didn't come!

God: You were concerned about your body and yet you wanted the experience to continue.

Beth: Yes, I wanted it both ways. The kundalini experience can be wonderful when I relax and allow it, but this time it caught me off guard. And it was different; usually it's one energy moving in almost a circular motion, but this time it started in two places. Just when I think I know how a kundalini experience will affect me, or when I think I know what color flowers are, or how I relate to animals, then I'm shown something extraordinarily different. I keep learning that I know very little about how "reality" works – especially metaphysical reality.

It's as if I'm being educated in a new type of truth, one governed by different laws. Or more accurately, I am able to perceive the world as it really is, without filters. I now believe my senses are what tell the truth; only our thoughts and beliefs distort what is accurate and real.

Yet another experience happened in our backyard. It was a day just like any other day. We woke up early. I meditated, grabbed some coffee, and went outside to sit in the sweet fresh air of the morning, and Neill joined me. There were big fluffy clouds drifting across the sky, hummingbirds were making their regular morning visit to drink from the fountain. We sat there chatting about our work as we often do in the morning: discussing things like what motivates people or causes them to act and react as they do.

We weren't that far into discussing the question when, as I sat there with the sun just rising over the rooftops, I declared, "This is what people want. This is what they want – right here, right now." At that point I began experiencing the moment... the air touching my skin, the energy of All That Is. "Right here, right now, this is what they're looking for," I repeated. And as I said that, everything lit up as if a gigantic light was switched on. Colors became brighter and my whole body started to tingle, just as it had that day in the park. Again, that sense of being connected with everything came over me and heightened my awareness. My connection to All That Is became manifest and filled me with pure joy.

This time I didn't feel shocked at all; instead it was as if I were being poured into the experience. There was wholeness and lightness and a beauty that no words can describe. Tears ran down my face, but there were no emotions attached to the tears. No thoughts caused the crying; my sensations were at the heart of the tears. Now, I could call it joy or bliss, but in that moment no words were present. All I knew was that I had reached a new level of connection. I know I keep saying this, but it's true. With each experience, each expansion, my connection and feelings of peace and joy deepen. Each experience feels fresh and new, and more profound than the last.

After a while, when Neill looked over and noticed the tears, he asked me what was going on. By this time I was able to speak. I told him that I was having an extraordinary experience of light and color, connection and joy. I wondered how long it would last, and for once it didn't dissipate as I played with the thinking around it. I continued to feel and sense this wild and beautiful ride even as Neill started asking me questions. Our conversation became a wonderfully supportive avenue in which to understand my experience.

First he asked, "What are you feeling?"

I replied, "I feel like my body has expanded into everything around me and that everything around me has become a part of me. I feel more than I've ever felt, like there's a door just outside our normal perception. If you can open it, you can walk through and enter a different world, with the ability to sense and know the real truth. It's as if I'm in one big cosmic jumble connected with everything else."

Then he asked, "Why tears, why are you crying?" I told him I wasn't sure. Thinking didn't cause the tears; there was just a feeling of peace, relaxation, joy, and a knowing that everything was perfect just the way it was. With this combination of sensations came tears.

Then I had this desire to stand up and see if the sensations continued as I walked around. To my surprise they did; it was as if I was on some kind of drug. I was definitely in an altered state. Now, I had done my share of drugs when I was young, but none of them caused me to feel like this. I laughed to myself, thinking that if the drugs had felt like this, I probably would've become a drug addict.

I wondered how long this would last and decided to just go about my day. So I went upstairs, brushed my teeth and washed my face. Washing became a new and wonderful experience. The water bathed me, the warmth washed over me, and the movement of my hands felt like a dance that slid and twirled on my face. As I dried off and looked around, the colors in the room were still bright, but they were starting to fade. The experience was coming to an end. The whole thing lasted about twenty minutes.

MUCH TO MY SURPRISE

Then there was the other side: after the joy, the crash. Each time I had one of these intense experiences, afterwards would come the doubt and concern about whether I was going crazy. To reassure myself, I began looking for confirmation I wasn't alone, that these things also happen to other people. I started investigating online, and to my surprise, I found that these events were common in some circles.

There is a whole online TV channel of sorts, Conscious TV, dedicated to offering interviews with people who say they're "connected to all" in the same way I seem to be. I also found books by yogis and gurus filled with accounts of kundalini experiences. I read Gopi Krishna's book called Living with Kundalini, in which he expressed his concern that he was going crazy.

I also read parts of Swami Muktananda's book, Play of Consciousness, which talk about his deep, unexplained sexual feelings. This was very comforting to me, because I sometimes encountered sexual responses while I was meditating or bathing. I would just be sitting there, when my groin would begin to throb as though I was being sexually stimulated. At other times, thoughts and feelings of past sexual encounters slid into my head unexpectedly: soft lips on mine, the urgency of a man's body pressing into me. I would become extremely aroused.

During one point in Muktananda's awakening he had also experienced these feelings in many of his meditations. He said, "Now everything was directed outward toward sex, sex, sex. I could think of nothing but sex! My body boiled with lust, and I can't describe the agony of my sexual organ. I try to explain to myself in some way, but I couldn't. The only thing was that I was able to keep firmly in the lotus position; that was as steady as ever."

It's not comfortable for me writing about these things, so I can't imagine how it was for him, a holy man who was had chosen to be celibate. But I was reassured to know that my feelings had been experienced by others.

And yet, even as I read these accounts, I had a sense that I needed to experience all these things for myself and not be influenced by the stories of others. So I became very selective about what I read, what I watched, and who I talked to about all this. I decided that from now on, I would be guided to find my own truth rather than adopt the truths of others.

CHAPTER 14

The Bridge Between Two Worlds

"It is good to have an end to journey towards; but it is the journey that matters in the end."

- Ursula Le Guin

EBB AND FLOW

ALTHOUGH THE BRIGHT COLORS, the tingling sensation and intense feeling of connection of my last experience had faded, something truly had awakened within me. There remained a constant flow of energy – a low-grade vibration that was new to me. It was like an underlying movement in my body, like a tide ebbing and flowing. It wasn't agitation or nervousness, because there wasn't an emotional component to it – just movement of energy, and at times very intense.

Of course during this period, the normal responsibilities of life still needed my attention. My son Spenser required my help, I was taking some steps to revive our business, and there were the simple day-to-day chores to do, like paying bills and buying food. I noticed that when I focused on what I needed to "do," the spiritual sensations within me became more subtle. Then when I quieted down, such as during meditation or bath time, they came back strongly. I realized that my beautiful connection to All That Is was not a given – at least not at this point.

God: You mean that you could lose it if you did not return to it frequently?

Beth: Yes. If I did not focus on keeping it in my life, it diminished. It was my choice – how I chose to focus my attention would give me either a highly aware life or a more mundane life. But I was confused about how to maintain the balance between that real and beautiful spiritual awareness and all the day-to-day tasks.

I began to ask for guidance because I wanted some direction and some understanding about what was going on inside me, and I also wanted to know how to maintain the inner connection in the face of my daily activities. Until now my only experiences had come spontaneously. I could either accept them or not accept them, but I didn't ask for them. Now I found myself asking for support about how to maintain awareness, and not from a human advisor. I wasn't sure who I was asking!

God: No comment.

Beth: Well, I didn't immediately think of you because I wasn't sure if I believed in you. You see, I didn't have a very religious childhood. I was brought up Jewish, but with little understanding of the religion itself. My mother came from an English Jewish background and mixed various holiday traditions, so she first celebrated Christmas by putting presents under the bed instead of a tree. However, my brother became so overexcited about all the presents that we changed to a more traditional Hanukkah. But aside from that holiday, religion wasn't part of our daily lives. My father came from an Eastern European Jewish family who kept kosher, but he was a rebel of sorts, so I didn't get any clear religious understanding from him either.

What I did get from my mother was that there was something more to this world, something bigger than we could understand with our mind alone. She always had an unspoken sense of spirituality about her.

My mom was a mixed bag – caring and loving on one hand, and practical and brutally honest on the other. When I was young I asked her what religion we were, and she said, with much conviction, "The only real religion, is to be a decent human being."

Another time I asked her if we were Jewish, and she told me, "You know you're Jewish for sure because if the Nazis came they would take you away – and they would take you away because you have a Jewish mother – that means you're Jewish."

Yes, I know this sounds awful for a mother to tell her ten-year-old child something like this. As a kid, it scared me, but I grew to understand that she was trying to take care of me in her own way. She grew up during World War II and witnessed the horrible things that one group of human beings could do to another. She had lived through it, and so she really believed that being Jewish was dangerous. She wanted me to be careful and vigilant.

So you can understand why I was just not convinced about the existence of God. This is why I had always counted on my intellect and things I could see and accept as true to take care of myself. Now I was faced with phenomena that I could not comprehend with my rational mind – things outside of normal reality – and this changed how I asked for help. I couldn't use the same tools that I'd always counted on. So I asked for answers silently, as if the answers might lay dormant deep within me. I asked out loud, as if God or some external being had the answers. And I asked before going to sleep, hoping that my dreams would give me some insight. I kept asking, and the answers started to come in very interesting ways.

THE PERFECT CIRCLE OF ENERGY

From my earlier experiments with metaphysics, I understood that it was worth it to pay attention to coincidences. Consequently, when in one week I started hearing friends talk about yoga, seeing yoga magazines, finding yoga coupons in the paper, and noticing, for the first time, a yoga studio near my house, I knew it was probably a synchronicity that I should check out.

I had tried yoga over the years, knowing that it was highly recommended for my physical well-being, but I found it physically uncomfortable and preferred other forms of exercise. But here it was, popping up everywhere. Yoga might be the answer to my prayers.

In my first class I experienced yoga in a whole new way. The focus was more on our spiritual nature than our physical being. As I moved in the ways the teacher instructed, I felt that intense kundalini energy move and stop, move and stop. I learned that I could control the intensity and rhythm of the energy so that there was less resistance and more flow. The movement became a dance: cat, cow, downward facing dog, plank, sphinx, upward facing dog – the dance released energy!

My connection to All That Is could be found here, found in this movement, in this flow. Once again I realized that my access to All That Is came through my body, this form that I inhabit. This practice would become an important part of my life. For the next two months I tried all the different teachers until I found the ones with whom I could move the most energy.

I practiced yoga six or seven times a week, sometimes twice a day, so I could keep the energy moving. My system became very sensitive to the forces moving within my body, and to light, sound, and smell. As long as I kept the energy flowing I could handle the change in my senses.

During the time following that intense experience in my back yard, light seemed brighter, sounds were louder, and smells were stronger. These sensations were often uncomfortable, because the intensity of lights hurt my eyes and the sounds irritated my nerve endings. The smell of garlic that I used to love became overwhelming, and I could no longer tolerate spicy food. Doing yoga lessened the discomfort.

God: What do you think was the cause of this increased sensitivity?

Beth: I believe it was because I was bridging two worlds – my physical reality and this new, broader spiritual world. This bridge heightened my experience in the physical world. As I focused more on connecting with the new, unfamiliar part of my reality, I was led right back to my physical world. The broader spiritual connection brought me right back to my body; it felt like the perfect circle of energy.

God: Can you give me an example?

Beth: Because I was spending so much of my time

developing my spiritual awareness, I was becoming less and less social. I spent my time meditating, bathing, and experiencing myself as a spiritual being.

The clearest example of being led back into my physical world was during a bath experience. After I completed the initial bath rituals – the candles, incense, aromatherapy, prayer and gratitude – I would relax for a few moments, empty my mind, and allow a thought to emerge. This first thought showed me what needed to be examined or cleared in that specific bath.

So this particular time, I relaxed and lay back, letting my arms float, letting my muscles release their tight grip on my bones. As usual, a thought rose in my mind as I sank down into the water. I remembered an exercise from a Psych-K course that I had enjoyed very much. The idea was to imagine the worst possible scenario for my death.

It might sound morbid, but for me, it had been profound. When I first did this exercise in the workshop, my worst scenario was to be sitting in a wheelchair all by myself in a nursing home, not having done anything of real value, and never having helped the world. It was just to have led a normal, boring life.

As the memory entered my mind, I heard, Do the exercise again. So I did as this internal voice asked and again tried to imagine my death scene. I was astonished when, instead of sitting alone in a wheelchair, I was lying in a bed surrounded by family and friends. *This couldn't be right*, I thought. There are dozens of people in the room, loving me, and me loving them. What was so terrible about this?

As I continued imagining, I saw that the people in the room were grieving my impending death. My heart ached for their pain, and also with the love I felt for them. How could I leave them? I loved them so; I would miss them so. The thought of leaving everyone and everything in my life deeply saddened me. And yet the next step of the exercise was to imagine myself dying and then experience what was on the other side of death. During the Psych-K seminar, I was deeply moved by this. I realized that it made no difference how my life turned out because I was one with the universe and one with all things. A sense of bliss had filled my body, and I felt that death – when the time came – would be a welcome and wonderful transition.

But this time the bliss was mixed with sadness. I questioned what was going on. How could my simple life and the people in it mean more than the extraordinary feeling of being connected to All That Is? How could this sadness coexist with my joy and bliss?

Well, at this point in my life, I would've been content living in a cave and spending my days meditating with all the joy and wonder that my new reality had to offer. Being connected in this way seemed a wonderful alternative to any normal life, even a life full of loving people.

As I sat with this contradiction, my body began to move and I had a strong urge to start shaking my head back and forth, up and down very quickly, and my arms shook rapidly as if someone was shaking them for me. Then my legs began shaking the same way. The water splashed in rhythm with my body, which trembled as if releasing something unwanted.

Then I settled down. Peace flowed within me and these words formed in my consciousness: You are not meant to die now nor are you meant to live as a monk; you are meant to integrate All That Is with your physical existence. You are meant to be an example – an embodiment of heaven on earth. Now is the time to begin, now is the time to move back out into the world.

Upon perceiving these words, tears streamed down my face. My heart was so open; I was once again connected to everything, and I knew that this message was the truth for me. In that moment I knew how I was meant to spend the rest of my days – to bridge this expanded reality with my everyday life.

I sat in the bathtub for a long time, just taking it all in. The candles had burned down to stubs and the incense had long since gone out. After a while I stepped out into the chilly air, and soon the profound sense of connection began to fade.

I was left with the idea that I'm supposed to fully live in both worlds. I think this is what creates the perfect circle of life, flowing from spirit into physicality and back again. I was to bring this newfound bliss into my everyday life, to love and be loved as deeply as possible and to continuously replenish myself spiritually.

So now I had the mission, but not the map. How was I supposed to implement all this? How was I to embody the connection between my soul and my physical world? How was I to integrate this physical reality with my newly realized spiritual world?

CHAPTER 15

You Ask and I Will Answer

"I am open to the guidance of synchronicity, and do not let expectations hinder my path."

~ Dalai Lama

TRUSTED SOURCE

SINCE MY MOTHER'S DEATH I had been quite reclusive. I worked only sporadically and socialized only with a few close friends. Then two separate events took place that brought me back into the world of ego and personality. They also gave me some direction and sent me down a new and unexpected path.

The first event came while I was meditating. One day I heard the words, *Move north; it is time for you to move north.* Move north? We lived in a beautiful house and I was happier than I'd ever been in my life. Why in the world would we move? Then I heard it again: *It is time for you to move north.*

I thought about this "suggestion" and the possibility of moving. The real estate market was terrible, so selling the house could cost us a lot of money. Renting it would bring its

135

own set of problems. So I just continued my meditation and let it go. But later that day the same message pressed itself into my consciousness again, and this time I felt something different – a rush of energy and excitement bubbled up in me.

I decided to talk to Neill about moving north and see what he thought.

After his initial shock – because Neill really doesn't like moving – we discussed how this crazy idea might happen. If we rented out both the main house and the granny flat, we could actually cover the full monthly mortgage, insurance and taxes with the rent money. But if the main house went empty for even a month, it would be impossible to pay our mortgage and also a large rent payment for where we would be living. We'd have to go into credit card debt, which we try not to do.

But Neill and I had learned that my intuition does not lead us astray, so we resolved to at least start looking for places to rent. I began checking the northern San Diego County Craigslist offerings. We couldn't move too far because I needed to be close to Spenser, who was now 22 years old and living in San Diego. Every week I took him shopping and checked to make sure he was taking care of himself. Where in North County would be close enough, and still somewhere we wanted to live? We decided to take the next few weekends to investigate different areas, look at some houses for rent, and see what felt good to us.

The second event came during the same period of time we were house-hunting. I got a call from Dale inviting me to an event called "Big Mission, Big Sales, Big Life." by a sales and marketing expert named Lisa Sasevich. In my "old life" I had listened to some of her teleseminars and was impressed with what she taught and how she taught it. Immediately I had an urge to say yes, despite the fact that learning new sales techniques seemed in opposition to my present inner journey.

Old feelings began to well up in me, as though my brain somehow switched back on again. I had a renewed sense of excitement and possibility about my business, which I hadn't experienced in a long time. As I'd been getting more and more connected to All That Is, I'd become quieter, my mind more peaceful, my body more relaxed; I was just more present inside and out. It wasn't a bad feeling, but it was quite a contrast. I wondered if being more engaged in my business life would affect my ability to maintain my peaceful, joyful state.

I was drawn to this event, but also hesitant. There would be hundreds of people there, and I hadn't been around crowds of people since this whole expansion/awakening process started. I worried about being overwhelmed with all the noise, the energy and the smells. But the event was pulling me like a magnet and I had to go and find out why. Maybe there would be something that would help me bridge the two worlds, as unlikely as this seemed. In any case, I registered, and planned to keep my eyes open for anything that could help me.

But on the day of the event, as I drove up to Hyatt Regency in San Diego, I had second thoughts about coming. There were people everywhere. Just walking into the energy of the hotel lobby with its ringing cell phones and mountains of luggage overwhelmed me. Excited entrepreneurs from all over the world were checking in, and chattering non-stop to each other. I immediately walked outside, found a bench hidden behind a thick stand of bamboo, and sat down to collect myself. How was I going to bridge this gap between this physical everyday world, with all its distractions and intensity, and my connection to All That Is? I would have to learn a lot in order to pull this off, especially when faced with these high-energy entrepreneurs.

As I sat there I felt very alone. My connection suddenly seemed all too fragile. When I was home meditating, relaxing in my backyard feeling the air on my skin, or enjoying nature, the connection was strong. But now I felt distracted and disturbed. I had to keep bringing myself back, back to my peace, back to my joy. It took concentration, and I realized that I would need frequent breaks.

I went back inside, registered, and stepped into the huge event room, filled with hundreds of talking, laughing people. There was a big stage with two tall screens. Rock music blared from giant speakers. I found a seat in the last row, and as the day went on, whenever I felt overwhelmed by my senses I just got up, left the room and went outside, where the air and the sun on my skin brought me back to my peaceful center.

During one such break I had a feeling that it was time to go back, and I walked in just as Lisa was introducing her next guest, Tim Kelley, the author of *True Purpose: 12 Strategies for Discovering the Difference You Are Meant to Make.* When she brought him on stage my body simultaneously tensed with excitement and relaxed. I knew I was about to hear something important.

Tim Kelley first asked everybody in the room whether they believed in some higher power – some source of knowledge that had the answers to their questions. About 75% of the audience raised their hands. Then he asked who believed that somewhere inside of us, we have the answers to the questions we asked, in our subconscious mind. Most of the rest of the audience raised their hands. He labeled this higher power your "trusted source." Tim worked with us to clear the fears that typically block people from communicating directly with their trusted source. He called this "getting permission from the ego."

Then he asked everyone to pick a name for this part and have a conversation with it in writing. It went like this: You'd first write your name, then you would write a question for your trusted source, and you would then write the answer that came from this source next to its name. Tim explained that this exercise was based on Carl Jung's "active imagination" process.

He suggested that we ask questions such as:

> What is my essence?
> What is my mission?
> What is my message?
> Who are the people I am meant to serve?
> How do I transform their lives?

I named my knowledge source "God." I'm not sure why I chose that word. Usually, when talking about the universe, or Source, I call it "All That Is." Perhaps I just wanted to make it easy. I've always been a skeptic, and faith in something unseen comes to me only after I've experienced it for myself. I was intrigued by this exercise and at the same time committed to asking hard questions and getting specific answers. This was the first of my conversations with God. Many more would follow.

COSMIC ARTISTRY

My first conversation with God at the seminar went like this:

Beth: Hello, God.

God: Hello, Beth.

Beth: How do I transform people?

God: You are the transformer; you are meant to be the light.

Beth: The light of what?

God: The light of the world.

Beth: I don't know what that means.

God: Yes you do.

Beth: Is it what I do now?

God: Yes and no.

Beth: What is the difference?

God: You.

Beth: What do you mean by that?

God: You will be seen now.

Beth: In what way will I transform people's lives?

God: You will help them know themselves – their true selves.

Beth: I thought that I would help people through relationships. Did that change?

God: That is the only way we can truly know ourselves.

Beth: Who is really talking to me?

God: We are talking.

Beth: But how do I know that this conversation is different than one I would have in my own head?

God: You know because it is different; you know because you feel me and know that I am part of you and that when we are truly together we speak truth.

Beth: I'm not sure I understand, but I will talk to you again and find out more.

God: This is good, dear one. I hope you come back often and speak to me in great detail about everything there is that you want to know. You are very much loved.

As I finished up the exercise I realized that this is what I had prayed for, some tangible way for me to ask and get my questions answered, to have a conversation with and develop an intimate connection to this source of All That Is. Now I understood why I was so drawn to this event.

I could have gone home happy right then, but I decided to stay and so I received two more powerful pieces of inspiration that day. I spent the rest of my time talking to people that I was drawn to. I wanted to know if there were others who were having awakening experiences, and if they had been attracted to this event in the same way I was.

To my amazement, I discovered I wasn't alone – I met others who were also becoming aware that there was more to life. And like me, they didn't understand what was happening, didn't know what to do, and didn't know who to talk to about it. I met one woman who, when I told her what I was experiencing, broke down in tears and said, "Thank God! I thought I was going crazy." I was still uncomfortable talking about my own experiences, but found that when I shared with others who were also having expansions and connections with All That Is, we all felt supported and more comfortable.

I also realized that I now felt different about my mission in life. There was a lot of talk about mission and purpose at this event, and it didn't resonate with me as it used to. From a very young age – after the riot at my high school – I had been driven by my mission to help people get along better and to create a world that works for everyone. Now, though I still wanted these things, I was not driven by them.

Now my life is less rigid and more flowing, as though I create my life spontaneously, picking the design and brush-strokes as I go along, instead of working on a paint-by-number life. Now I can create my life as a piece of cosmic artistry.

I left that day knowing that something astonishing was going on with me and in the world at large. Many of us were waking up to a new reality. I wasn't alone. My life was moving in a new direction. I also came away with a new way to communicate to my higher consciousness. I was inspired and excited to begin playing with the active imagination process, so I began the very next day.

CHAPTER 16

Life Begins Here

"Anything you want to ask a teacher, ask yourself, and wait for the answer in silence."

- Byron Katie

DO I EXIST?

Beth: I know you're there. What would you like me to call you?

God: Anything you want to call me.

Beth: The word God just popped into my head again; I will call you that.

God: Good.

Beth: But that seems so separate from me, and I know there is no separation between us. And it is also not a word that I've ever been comfortable using.

God: Both those things are true and they matter not, and there is much in that name for you and others to explore. This name came to you for a reason; use it and see what there is in it for you.

Beth: Okay, but I'll want to talk more about this another time.

God: You are always welcome to ask whatever is there for you in any moment.

Beth: Where do we go from here?

God: That is the joy – wherever you want to.

Beth: You aren't much help, are you? Sorry, I know I'm a wise guy.

God: So am I, as you will see, and I will be as much help as you ask for. You are never alone!

Beth: Are you with everyone like this – closely connected and always around?

God: Yes -- but they must be with me as well in order for there to be an optimal connection.

Beth: What does that mean exactly?

God: If you do not acknowledge, trust, and believe that I am here, do I exist? If you do not talk, ask, and be with me, can I truly be with you? We are only one when we are together.

Beth: Sometimes I stop myself from writing what you are saying and I'm not sure why – do you know why?

God: Because you are afraid: afraid of your power, afraid of your weakness, afraid of your light, afraid to be who you are – one with me – one with All That Is.

Beth: It sounds like I'm afraid of an awful lot.

God: Being, living, and enjoying are all there is to do, and all else are details that have no meaning.

Beth: Even my fears have no meaning?

God: Only the meaning you give them.

Beth: How will I know what to choose or what direction to go in?

God: You will be drawn to what is next for you. It does not have to make sense. You do not have to understand. You and many others do all your choosing with the mind and the mind has taken on roles that it was not designed for. Choosing is one of them.

Beth: What if I'm not drawn to anything?

God: You are drawn to things all the time, more things than you could possibly do if you wanted to. And you know this. What there is for you to do is feel into things more often and allow your mind to take a back seat. The mind has a very important role but it is not in the choosing or discerning. That role is meant to be done by your senses, your heart, and your soul.

Beth: What if I'm not sure if I'm really being drawn to something?

God: That is the discerning part. First it is your ability to notice the attraction, then it is the ability to discern attraction from distraction. These things will come with practice. For right now you are with me and that's all that matters. You are loved, you are safe, you are protected, you are part of All That Is. Life begins here.

I was so moved by this expression of love that came from God, but also came from myself, that at this point I began to cry. It was confusing but amazingly, touching and wonderful. In the days, weeks and, months to come we had many conversations. This process opened me up to a new way of being with God – All That Is. I felt connected to everything and was able to ask questions and receive answers from something bigger than myself. It felt similar to some of my other experiences, but now the form of connection was quite different. I didn't have to do anything by myself again. I had a companion that I could talk to, and I was held and supported and loved. From this point forward I was never alone.

WE ARE THE SAME

Beth: Good morning – are you there?

God: Always – I'm always with you – in you – around you – near you.

Beth: What is the difference between you and me?

God: Difference there is not – same is all there is.

Beth: Now you sound like Yoda from Star Wars.

God: I told you I had a sense of humor.

Beth: Ok, that's funny. But if everything's the same, why don't you have a physical body?

God: But I do.

Beth: You mean me?

God: See. You know already.

Beth: Yes I have heard it said that I – and I guess then my body – is an expression of you.

God: Yes.

Beth: But that doesn't make us the same. It makes you the "one" that is expressing and me the one that is expressed. That does not seem the same to me. How are we the same in relation to what I just said?

God: The sameness comes out of form. The sameness comes as the expression. I am not you – you are not me – but we are the same.

Beth: I don't get this; could it be expressed more clearly?

God: One at a time is not the truth – you are the I and I am the you.

Beth: I believe that "we" would be able to evolve more quickly if we were clearer about these things.

God: Clarity of thought is not as important as feeling the truth of the words I say.

Beth: I do understand that – I have felt what you are saying. When I relax my body and mind, and allow your words to touch me, there is no separation between us. There is just us, but there isn't even really us, because the vibrational feeling of that connection becomes EVERYTHING. It's like hitting a big gong, and the sound is not separate from the gong. If you could see the vibration that the sound makes you would see it move out into the room, emanating from the gong, but also as part of the gong itself. So in this way the gong would be able to expand and fill the room. And you would also see the vibration becoming one with everything else. The same is true for us. It's as if we expand into something bigger, something inexpressible in words.

God: Yes, yes, be with that for now.

Beth: I think that if I could get clear simple answers to these questions it would help me and others move forward faster.

God: Keep asking then. And think about it this way. Your questions are about understanding things on a mind level, and that will only take you so far. Your sensing self, on the other hand, is a deep state within you where your true guidance and knowing lives. This guidance will lead you to all things. So questions only take you part of the way to where you want to go.

Beth: So talking to you this way may not take me where I want to go?

God: Questions from the heart lead to a beautiful connection. But questions from the mind lead only to a shallow sense of knowing.

Beth: Are you saying that the answers I get to my questions – if understood in my mind only – are not going to get me anywhere faster?

God: That is accurate. You have a beautiful mind, and it wants to understand. That is its job. But you have come to live from the mind alone and it has taken control in areas that it was not meant to control. For today, relax and allow for understanding. It will come.

CHAPTER 17
For the Good of All

"I slept and I dreamed that life is all joy. I woke and I saw that life is all service. I served and I saw that service is joy."

- Kahlil Gibran

ON THE VERGE OF CREATION

NEILL AND I CONTINUED LOOKING for a place to rent in northern San Diego County. I searched on Craigslist, and then we would drive around on the weekends seeing the houses I found. We looked everywhere from La Jolla to Oceanside. After many weeks of this we became discouraged, frustrated and tired of looking.

Now that I'd learned the active imagination process, I kept in daily contact with God. I talked to God about everything from my concern about killing the snails in our planters to the meaning of life. So asking about our house search was no different. Impatient as a kid on a car trip, I wanted to know where and when I would arrive at that perfect house that was meant for me. Would I live near the beach? Would the house be in Encinitas, Carlsbad, or somewhere else entirely?

I asked these kinds of questions and the answers came during the daily dialogues. "Why haven't we found a place to rent yet?" I'd ask.

"Stop trying so hard, have patience, and let things unfold as they will," I heard back.

"But this is not fun," I replied.

"Then only do what brings you joy," God would answer.

Before my spiritual expansion began, when I got an idea in my head I was like a bulldog with a bone until I figured it out and got what I was after. Only then could I relax and let go. So even though I know through experience that things work out perfectly when I just relax and let them, some old habits were still in place, and this advice to let things unfold was easier said than done.

I watched as my identity – the me that I used to believe was really me – wrapped around me like an old familiar coat. Much of the time now this coat just hung in the closet of my mind, but on occasion it popped out screaming to be worn. So I kept asking when I would find our new home and how I would absolutely know when I found it.

God told me, "Time, place, and matter are funny things. It's all about feeling and sensing, but not definiteness. When time, place, matter and sensations collide, then you will know you have found it."

I did my best to only do what was joyful for me, and we continued to look at rentals when we felt like it. We looked at big places and small places. Places near the beach and places inland. One place looked wonderful in the ad, but there was a gigantic Doberman residing in the shared backyard that the owner had neglected to mention. As we opened the gate to walk in, he charged at us, barking and growling, and looking like he wanted to eat Petra, our tiny poodle. It wasn't hard to figure out this place was a NO.

A few days later we were driving down the street and saw a sign on the curb. We called about it and the owner said that she could come right away and show it to us. We felt hopeful because it had two extra bedrooms for our offices and space to hold workshops. It was walking distance from downtown Encinitas and the beach, and there was even a partial ocean view. The price was over our budget, but it was a good deal for Encinitas. Should we rent it or shouldn't we? A stream of 'What ifs' flooded my mind. But I now had a source of information I could trust...

Beth: God, I know you have never let me down. I know that with all my heart, but I am worried that I'll make a bad decision about moving. We have found a place, so I need to decide right now. I have to choose.

God: And what do you choose?

Beth: I don't know! I want to live on the coast. I think I'm being called there. Or is it just my imagination?

God: It's one and the same.

Beth: My imagination is the truth?

God: Mostly yes. Your imagination is the beginning of all creation. As you feel called to someplace new, it is your imagination that is on the verge of creating.

Beth: But I'm worried I might be making a bad decision.

God: No decisions are bad – they just are.

Beth: But some decisions lead to the good of all concerned and others don't.

God: That is unlikely with you, because what you want doesn't conflict with others and you are mostly conscious of this. I believe what you are really trying to say is that you want to be comfortable all the time and always know that the choices you make will never have any bad or dissatisfying consequences. Yes?

Beth: Yes, and I know that is ridiculous and impossible!

God: You could switch the question to, "How can I make choices that are in line with my innermost being?"

Beth: I love that! Okay, how?

God: By staying in touch with it. You already know how, and have been practicing well.

Beth: But in those moments of fear, then what?

God: More practice – more quieting – more stillness – more talking to me. We can always move forward when we are together.

Beth: Can I ask for signs and then get them?

God: Yes.

Beth: Okay then – I want a clear undisputable sign that the most wonderful thing for all concerned is that we move up to North County and live in the house on 3rd Street in Encinitas, and that this sign is easily recognizable to me.

God: Okay. But be patient, dear one. You will know when it comes.

TO TITHE OR NOT TO TITHE

So I waited for a sign.

At the Big Mission event, I had been given a wonderful little book called *The Four Spiritual Laws of Prosperity*, by Edwene Gaines. While reading it, I became intrigued with the idea of tithing. I had heard about tithing for many years, but it wasn't something that I understood or found much use for. Tithing is normally a religious practice, one in which you give 10% or some agreed-upon amount of your income to your church or religious organization. As I understood it, you were proclaiming that God was your source and that if you consistently gave this 10% that you would receive it back tenfold. Even in the metaphysical community, there was talk about tithing, but they also focused on it primarily as a way of giving in order to receive back, and that didn't resonate with me.

Giving only to get something seemed odd to me. But the information in this book excited me. The idea was to practice spontaneous tithing – giving in the moment of inspiration. The author told a story about giving some money to a waitress who had inspired her, and another story about giving money to her daughter who said something that touched her. With this method, you give to anyone or anything, at any time. It sounded like fun and I wanted to try it!

For once, this wasn't about giving just to get. I know the underlying principle of tithing was about declaring God as your source, but what I had heard mostly focused on the 'getting back' part. Don't get me wrong; I'm open to receiving. But this was bigger and more meaningful than that. This was about giving from a place of being touched and inspired. I believe that money is just energy, and these days, the circulation of money is often being propelled with fear and anxiety. But *The Four Spiritual Laws of Prosperity* introduced me to a different way of looking at tithing and the use of money.

Can you imagine how the world would change if people focused on being touched, moved and inspired, instead of on what's wrong and what's not working? What might change if the movement of money was imbued with love and appreciation? If people gave money to others from a place of inspiration, not fear? I was excited, but along with my enthusiasm I worried about giving 10% of our income, because we were living right at the edge financially. I decided to talk to God about it.

Beth: What do you think about tithing?

God: It is a wonderful way to focus one's energy on gratitude.

Beth: Is that why tithing was established – to stay focused on gratitude?

God: Tithing came into being on this plane of existence because people needed to stay present and focused on the NOW, and in the moment of now, gratitude is always abundant. The 10% came from the human mind; it did not come from me.

Beth: What part came from you?

God: The part that said:

1. Share what you have with others.
2. Treat yourself as beauty and grace.
3. Live as though all is well.
4. Have joy in what you do.
5. Only ever be with others in peace and oneness.

Beth: What form of tithing would support my life and the lives of others?

God: Different forms for different people. And the way you are considering is wonderful for you.

Beth: I am at a choice point about whether to tithe or not. The car just broke down and it will cost a lot of money to repair, close to the amount that we have allotted for tithing. What do you say about this?

God: I say that money is energy – energy only. What you

do with it will create movement one way or another. Which way do you want the energy to flow?

Beth: I want to pay for the car and I also want to start tithing. If I do both things I will run out of back-up money sooner.

God: So if you don't start tithing now, it would be because of fear and only fear.

Beth: True, but how do I do both?

God: You just do it, and trust in me. There is all the money you need and more in this moment. Is that not true?

Beth: Yes – we have $5,000 in the bank.

God: And all your other bills are paid for now?

Beth: Yes.

God: And you want to do the tithing experiment?

Beth: Yes.

God: Then what is stopping you?

Beth: I guess fear of ending up with nowhere to live.

God: Do you believe that?

Beth: No, not really, but I'm worried about not having enough to pay for what I want in the near future, like living in Encinitas. I might not have enough money for the move if I do both tithing and fix the car.

God: Only if you say so.

Beth: Is there anything I can do to feel more comfortable as I am doing both?

God: Trust.

Beth: That seems like just a mental construct. How do I just trust?

God: When you are feeling uncomfortable, stop and connect to your body sensations. Get out in the air – feel the air on your skin – feel the truth of your existence.

Beth: Okay, I'll do that.

Neill and I talked about it, and we decided to begin tithing. We would take 10% of our income, split it in half and each do what we wanted with it. At first I wasn't sure how to work it. How will I know who to tithe to, and what on earth will I say as I'm handing them the money? The first time I tithed was to my favorite yoga teacher; she was calm, sweet, and sincerely cared about her students.

She always started our class with an inspiring quote. That day it was:

"You can search throughout the entire universe for someone who is more deserving of your love and affection than you are yourself, and that person is not to be found anywhere. You yourself, as much as anybody in the entire universe, deserve your love and affection."

Then she asked everyone to create an intention for their practice, and she led a short meditation. My intention was to feel the love in the room. Later, as I went through the asanas, I noticed the way she gently touched the students and moved them into position, her voice lovingly focusing our attention inward. She came to me and softly touched my arm, and it was as though I could feel her love, caring and devotion through her hand. Tears ran down my cheeks and my heart opened.

In that moment I knew she would be my first tithing recipient. After class as I was writing her a check, I watched her interact with people as they were leaving, and even that moved me. I walked over to her, looked her in the eyes and said, "Your kindness touched me. The beautiful way you interact with people makes it obvious that you care very deeply about them."

Then I let her know that I have started a practice of spontaneous tithing – any time I'm inspired I would show my appreciation by offering a gift, and it would be a blessing to me if she would accept it.

She looked shocked as tears welled up in her eyes. "It's my job," she said to me, "There's no need to give me extra; I already get paid for this."

I said, "The yoga isn't why I'm offering this. It's for your spirit, your heart, and your expressions of kindness that touched me." I watched as it sank in that I was grateful for her essence and her sheer inner beauty that I recognized. This moment of connection and mutual appreciation was extraordinary, and I wanted more of these. Since then, this form of tithing has become one of the most important practices in my life.

CHAPTER 18

Abundance is Your Birthright

"More bliss can be got from serving others than from merely serving oneself."

~ Sri Sathya Sai Baba

WHERE ENERGY FLOWS

SOON AFTER WE STARTED TITHING, some unexpected expenses cropped up. Did this have something to do with our new tithing practice? I wanted to understand what was happening, so back to God I went.

Beth: After we started tithing, money started flowing out faster than it was coming in – our car cost $900 to repair, our taxes were filed with incorrect dates and so we're being charged penalties. And we now have a big dental bill. This all seems to coincide with our tithing. What's going on?

God: Things aren't always the way you want them – they're going to go the way they go. What's more important is how you are when they go that way.

Beth: Is there any correlation between the tithing and the expenses I just talked about?

God: Yes and no. When something happens – and you make a choice – energy moves – and then something else happens. When you tithe, energy moves and also when you worry about expenses, energy moves. Until things settle out, there will be more erratic movement.

Beth: Can you give me an example?

God: When you started tithing, energy was already flowing – with fear entwined. Energies do not discriminate. All that is there will flow.

Beth: Are you saying that tithing unplugged the flow of bad things?

God: No. It is not an exact science and difficult to explain in terms that you will understand. But I will try.

You and many others move their lives forward with a great deal of fear entrenched in the energy. This comes from the collective mind and is integrated into your own personal creation. Creating from this place of fear will create fear-based realities, which in turn will create more fear. Fear energy is very dense – imagine it like a thick sludgy tar substance. The tithing that you have started, infused with inspiration, creates a different quality of movement in your field. This energy vibrates at a much higher frequency, causing the consistency of the fear-based energy to speed up. This is what you have been experiencing – fear-based energy that was already in motion.

The amount of trust and faith and courage it takes to practice tithing moves more energy, more quickly. This natural flow is a gift to be celebrated. As you continue this practice and move forward, things will even out and become more enjoyable.

Beth: So if I just continue tithing and pay the bills, everything will be okay?

God: More than okay. You are opening yourself to the wholeness that is available to you, to the great abundance of all things that are waiting for you. Abundance is the nature of your being. Abundance in all areas of life is your birthright. You have come here to experience an abundant life.

Beth: What do you mean by abundance?

God: Abundance is the feeling of fulfillment deep within your being. Sometimes that fulfillment is stimulated by some kind of material thing and other times it is stimulated by sensation or smell or memory. Abundance is the full and complete expression of all things being appreciated.

A POSITIVE COURSE

I thought deeply about this – what did it all mean? I believe that money is energy, and tithing is the energy of money in motion. The energy certainly was moving. I asked Neill what he thought, and he had some questions as well. I have never asked God questions for anyone else before, and I wanted to find out if that was something I could do.

Beth: May I ask some questions for Neill?

God: He would get answers that worked for him better if he asked for himself, but I will answer those you have now. And please know that any answers are coming through you and are not directed at him. He must hear this information and discern for himself what there is for him to pay attention to.

Beth: He wants to know if we can expect to have all our resources wiped out in order to move the fear.

God: Have all your resources been wiped out?

Beth: No.

God: How long have you both been holding on tightly to your fear? How long has your financial reserve been important to your comfort level? The flow of energy cannot be enjoyed when there is fear in the way. That fear then needs to be moved. For the flow of positive energy to come fully forward you must stay on a positive course.

Beth: How do we do that?

God: First you must understand that money is just energy. It has a positive and negative flow, as all energy does. You will always have both. If you want more positive flow, you must send more positive out. So one thing must continue – your positive flow out.

The next thing is to be present in the moment – moment by moment. Thoughts create positive and negative flow – so Neill must be quiet in the mind in order to keep that positive flow going.

Beth: Is there anything else we can do that will help to keep the flow going in a positive direction?

God: Yes, you can watch it closely and also leave it alone – be conscious and be present – be aware and trust. The flow is always there and you are part of it: guiding it, creating it, and moving it.

Beth: Why did Neill seem so tense when we started this conversation?

God: He so wants to trust, but he cannot yet let go of the past and leave it in the past. This conversation brings up for him all the past disappointments he is trying to protect himself from.

Beth: Can I help?

God: He is the one to help himself and he is doing that. He is on the verge of jumping into trust. The course you are on has an energy resonance that is irresistible to him, because he also wants what you have – trust and faith in something more than his intellectual mind. The challenge for both of you is not to be attached to the outcome. When you have an idea of what you want, and only that particular outcome will satisfy you, then you are imprisoned by the mind. Know that things change, know that as they change you are protected, loved, and cared for. Know that as long as you are following your heart and your internal guidance, whatever happens is for your highest good.

ONLY THE MOMENT

Time had passed, and I was still waiting for the irrefutable sign about whether to move north. Then signs came, but not what we expected. The house we wanted on 3rd Street in Encinitas was mysteriously rented after we were told it was available. And the same day our tenant in our little granny flat gave her 30-day notice. The signs seemed to say No, don't move north.

So I again talked with God, and I got a very clear answer that yes, we would be moving. And this time I heard that it was time to sell our house instead of renting it. This answer was contrary to the original message and I was confused.

Beth: Hi. Are you really here or is this just me talking to myself?

God: Both – we are one.

Beth: I continue to have doubts about whether this is real, that I'm not just imagining this whole thing.

God: Please always ask what comes to mind.

Beth: Knowing that I can always bring my doubts to you

is comforting, but how can I trust the answers I get from you if I doubt that you're real?

God: Let's start with a different question. When do you have doubts that I am real? Is it when you don't like the answers, or when the situation turns out different than you wanted or expected?

Beth: Well, yes. When I'm getting answers from you that make sense to me, and when things go in a way I enjoy, the doubt doesn't come up.

God: I suggest that for now, you set aside your doubt and just ask the questions that are there for you to ask.

Beth: All right. For instance, I asked if we were going to rent a house in North County, and you said yes. But that didn't work out. Then I heard it was time to sell the house now, when before we were to rent it out. Why did things change?

God: This is a wonderful question. When you ask for specifics about a small event I answer in relation to the energy that is moving at that instant. As energies flow, events and their outcomes change. With one small movement, the energies can change direction, therefore changing the outcome. That is why the answer may change, or at times I will not give information.

Beth: Does that mean that I can't get accurate information from you, or that I shouldn't ask those kinds of questions?

God: Neither. In the moment of the asking the information is accurate. But because you live in a linear reality, you can only perceive things in that reality. When you asked me if you would rent one of those houses, in that moment of the asking I told you what was likely to happen.

Yet any small change in your thinking, your actions, or the thinking and actions of others can change the movement of the energy. So if you ask me a question at 9:15, and then again at 9:20, the answer could be different. I only tell you what is in the moment, because that is all there is. You often want information that goes past the moment.

I would like you to understand that the answers you receive are about the energy in motion, not the outcome. There are no preordained scenes, there are only movements of energy for me to relay. Does this make sense?

Beth: I think so. You're saying that energy moves and changes, and there's no way to predict the future. Is that it?

God: That is simple and true.

CHAPTER 19

Longing to Be Whole

THE GUEST HOUSE
This being human is a guest house.
Every morning a new arrival.
A joy, a depression, a meanness,
some momentary awareness comes
As an unexpected visitor.
Welcome and entertain them all!
Even if they're a crowd of sorrows,
who violently sweep your house
empty of its furniture,
still treat each guest honorably.
He may be clearing you out
for some new delight.
The dark thought, the shame, the malice,
meet them at the door laughing,
and invite them in.
Be grateful for whoever comes,
because each has been sent
as a guide from beyond.
~ Rumi

OLD HABITS

WITH THE INTENSITY OF THIS new awareness and the likelihood of selling our house and moving, I began to lean towards old habits that used to comfort me. I remember years ago, during my divorce, when I was extremely stressed, I would stay up really late curled up in an old quilt on the couch, and watch old movies. The company of Bette Davis or James Cagney always left me feeling better. And when I felt confused or sad, I might eat a whole Entenmann's chocolate cake or go to McDonald's and have a Big Mac.

How could I again be drawn to these destructive behaviors as I wake up to consciousness? So I asked God…

Beth: When I feel unsettled, I choose self-defeating activities, such as eating junk food. Or I spend a lot of time watching movies or inane TV. Why do I do that?

God: These are old habits– forms of activities that distract you from your pain, confusion, and frustration. They were meant to care for you by acting as numbing agents. Now you are finding it challenging to come to terms fully with your new awareness and so you hide from it. This is part of the integration process.

Beth: When will I integrate fully – and start acting from it?

God: When the "you" that you believe IS YOU relaxes into the "you" that is already completely aware. This has, in fact, already happened on some level, but the process of full integration takes as long as it takes.

Beth: Until then, what do I do? Yesterday I had an urge to distract myself, to see a movie, eat chocolate – anything to get out of my head. What should I do in moments like those?

God: Nothing. The doing is not the issue – no doing is

needed.

Beth: Nothing? What would that look like? If a movie camera were filming me, what would it see?

God: It would see you sitting, lying, or standing wherever you were at in the moment of the feelings.

Beth: Okay, then what would be happening inside of me?

God: Now we're getting to it. You would be feeling into what was happening within you, not pushing it away. You would be sensing, feeling, being with what was moving, allowing it to move freely in you. Energy must move freely until it is ready to complete itself. Then it is done and you would be free of the agitation and upset that draws you to those unhealthy things.

Beth: That is what I do in my meditations. Thoughts come up and I allow them to be there without trying to push them away. They soon seem to be done and move out of my awareness. Is this what you're suggesting?

God: Yes! What I'm suggesting is that you take this beautiful practice into your everyday life. While your eyes are open and you are interacting with others, live this practice.

Beth: Would the agitation and the discomfort then be gone for good?

God: In that moment, the discomfort is gone from your field. As all energy does, it moves – it comes and goes. But with the desire for "all discomfort to be gone and never to return," an issue appears. In the act of wanting your agitation and discomfort to be gone forever, you are pushing it away and it does not complete itself. And so the old pattern continues.

Beth: Are you suggesting that uncomfortable sensations will return at times, and the best thing for me is to do nothing but allow them to move through me? If I do this consistently, will my habitual pattern of wanting to numb myself change?

God: Yes, that is how new patterns are made. Allow the discomfort to move through you, and you will feel peaceful again. No need to mask anything. This pattern will release and a new habit will be born.

Beth: I will try that. Thank you.

THE LOST MYSTICS

After that last conversation I started thinking about other kinds of habitual behaviors, ones that were destructive or even dangerous to a person's life. My brother, Noah, immediately came to mind. He is a genius, testing with an extremely high IQ. He also has perfect pitch and could pick up any instrument and within a few hours play it as well as people who took lessons. I remember hearing him play the flute and being carried away by the beautiful music that effortlessly poured from him. I've come to regard him as a lost mystic, because although he also has extraordinary intuitive powers, he is indifferent to this ability and seems to avoid developing that part of himself.

School wasn't much of a challenge for him either so he found other ways to amuse his extraordinary mind. He built multi-layered alarms at different points in the house to let him know when my parents were coming towards his room. He kept snakes and bred his own mice to feed them. When we were young he stole a counterculture book called Steal This Book, by Abbie Hoffman. The book described different ways to create bombs, so one day Noah made a bomb on our kitchen stove. I remember the explosion – and the excitement of putting out the fire! The house was still intact but the wall behind the stove turned to charcoal.

When he was about thirteen years old he began doing drugs. At the time he was mostly smoking pot – a lot of pot – but later he turned to pills and alcohol. He dropped out of high school, he totaled two cars, and he had a hard time creating healthy relationships. He was so brilliant, and very wise in many ways, but this didn't keep him from struggling while desperately seeking some sort of happiness.

Even with his self-destructive behaviors I always knew he loved me, because any time I was in trouble or having a hard time he knew just what to say to calm me down.

As an adult Noah found a 12- step program, which was a great blessing for him and started him down the path to a happier and more satisfying life, but I still wondered why people use drugs and alcohol, especially people who have exceptional minds and so much potential. I was curious what God would say about this.

Beth: What if I want to do things that might be dangerous to myself or others, such as taking drugs?

God: You ask this not for you; you want answers that would support others. But you must be more specific.

Beth: OK. People are drawn to drugs because they feel good, correct? How can this be a "good" thing? And, what is the difference between wanting to do these harmful things and being drawn, or called, to do something healthy – what you were talking about earlier when you said, "You are meant to always only do what you are being called to do"? I'm not sure I can tell the difference.

God: I understand the confusion. First, how can people

be drawn to drugs or things that would seem to be harmful? Those you speak of are initially drawn to drugs from the mind and the mind alone.

You see, people are not using their whole beings the way they were meant to; most use only a small part of what is available to them. The mind is quite limited, and when it is creating alone it becomes very isolated from the rest of its system – the body and soul. It becomes like a scared animal. As it experiences and creates in this isolated state it wants to feel good. But when the mind is not attached to the parts of its system that actually can discern feelings, it is drawn to drugs, alcohol or other unhealthy things, such as smoking, gambling, overeating, or even emotional outbursts, because they create the temporary illusion of wholeness.

Drugs and these other activities stimulate a low-grade experience of what is possible when the systems are integrated. These external stimuli promote a chemical reaction, which also intensifies the longing for wholeness. Once this awareness is experienced – even unknowingly – people are drawn back to the activity again and again to feel that sense of connection. The longing continues, as the mind attempts to find the connection in the best way it can from its isolated state.

So to answer your second question more directly, it is the difference between being drawn to something by a mental concept and being drawn to something by your whole integrated being. The difference lies in the wholeness. Does this make sense to you?

Beth: Let me try to summarize. The difference is that in one case, the mind alone, in its search for wholeness, is drawn to something that creates a kind of a feel-good state. But that state can't be sustained, and the mind can't really be fulfilled in this way. In the other case, when the whole being – mind/

body/soul – is called to do something from its state of wholeness, it feels good, it's fulfilling and this sense of well-being is sustainable... Is that correct?

God: Yes.

Beth: So people are drawn to drugs because they're longing to be whole? It's as though our culture has produced a whole society of lost mystics. They want to feel a connection to the rest of their "system" because their mind, body and soul are not integrated and functioning as they were meant to. Is that correct?

God: Yes. When one's system is fully integrated, one does not move towards chemical drugs or other activities that alter the body's chemicals. Your fully functioning, natural system supplies all the drug-like sensations you could ever want. Drugs are so popular because they are familiar, in the sense that your own system, when working in its divine design, creates its own comforting, altered state that some part of you remembers. You are longing to once again be fully connected to All That Is.

Beth: But since so few of us are integrated the way you're talking about, why aren't more people doing drugs or alcohol?

God: It is true that there are not many who are fully integrated at this time. But if you look around, most people are choosing some activities to either feel that connection or to mask their desire to feel it. Activities such as numbing themselves with TV, filling all their time with "doing," or sleeping more than they need to are effective to mask this desire.

Beth: So what is the solution for those who are drawn to take chemical drugs or engage in other destructive or self-defeating behaviors?

God: The same advice I gave you earlier. Do less, feel more. Be curious and allow your emotions and sensations to arise in you. Let them come to the surface and move around in you. Know that it is just energy moving, and allow it to run freely and easily through you.

Beth: Does this technique still work for people who have become physically addicted to these activities?

God: Yes, though they may need some support in the beginning to learn how to relax and do this process effectively. It can be frightening and uncomfortable to allow emotions and sensations to rise to the surface, since they have been hidden for a long time. It is important to know that it is the mind that attaches meaning to these emotions and sensations, and that meaning is what creates problems, not the sensations themselves. Support in allowing all meaning to fall away as these emotions and sensations arise is essential.

Beth: What would that support look like?

God: It could look like a friend holding your hand and softly reminding you to allow the energy to move. It could be remembering that the energy is not dangerous, and to stay present to this energy as it moves through you. It could be learning new ways to view your present reality, such as first focusing on the mind and letting it relax so that the emotions can move more freely. You have done this as part of your teachings.

Beth: Yes, I can see that, and I'd like to be even clearer about this. There have been times in my life when I felt so sad or frustrated about something that a little shopping or a big slab of dark chocolate cake with rich creamy frosting seemed to be calling my name. How do I stop myself in those moments from eating that cake or buying things I don't really need?

God: It's not about stopping yourself – it's never about stopping yourself. You can eat the cake or go shopping if you'd like. It's not the shopping or the cake that's the issue. The issue arises when you're unaware that your body/mind – your unaligned ego – is running the show. Getting conscious and making your choices consciously is the very first step in the process of integration.

It begins by slowing down and paying attention. In the beginning of this process you may not even realize that the frustration and the cake are connected. But you will learn that any self-defeating behavior is always connected to unexamined, unexpressed or stagnant emotional energy, and then you can begin to change these behaviors into ones that are more desirable.

CHAPTER 20

A Bridge with Many Obstacles

"Cease to inquire what the future has in store, and take as a gift whatever the day brings forth."

- Horace

TRUTH NEVER LIES

A FEW DAYS LATER, as I had unsettling thoughts about the prospect of selling the house in what was the worst part of a terrible real estate market, I took my conversation with God to heart and practiced allowing the emotions to come up. Instead of interpreting these emotions to mean that I was making a bad decision or that I'd never get to move north or that all this time and energy had been wasted, I just allowed them to flow into my awareness. I felt how this discomfort moved through me on the inside and sloshed around my consciousness. I played with the differences between thinking and feeling; it felt as if I were tumbling around in a cosmic washing machine as the thoughts and feelings surged through me. But I held on, and as I let all the emotions express and move where they wanted, after a time the storm subsided. But I was still left with the question: how do we choose the best course of action?

Beth: When we have a big decision to make, how do we choose what to do?

God: Always choose by how you feel.

Beth: Then I would just talk to you, do yoga, take baths, sit in the sun, and meditate.

God: Good. You are meant to always only do what you are being called to do.

Beth: But I have so much freedom. What about other people, who work for someone else or are raising their children?

God: You all have much more freedom than you believe you have. You are like caged animals pacing back and forth waiting to be fed, waiting to be freed, but you and you alone are in possession of the key. And it is not your situation that limits your freedom; it is your fear of the unknown that keeps you imprisoned. And the curious part is that you would be doing many of the same things you are doing now if you were free to choose, free to follow what you are called to do. But you are all so caught up in your mental cages that you cannot see the beautiful open landscapes in front of you.

You say if you were only doing what you are called to do that you would talk to me, sit in the sun, do yoga and meditate, but this is not true, because now you are also being called to do more than that.

Beth: Yes, it seems as though I'm now also being called to move north.

God: And this does not stop you from doing yoga and meditating and this is true for others as well. People who are raising children or working in jobs would not necessarily stop what they are doing in order to do what they are called to do. It is not an either or situation. In fact, if they were truly free to choose, they may very well be doing exactly what they are doing now, but without all the mental pain about being imprisoned they could enjoy the gifts of their situation that are hidden from them now. When you let go of fear, and allow yourself to move with the natural rhythm of your internal calling, an open road will unfold before you.

Beth: But how do I know what is the best thing to do in every moment?

God: There is no BEST – choose from the place of your feelings and what you end up doing will be the best thing for now. You know when you are drawn to something because you find yourself doing it almost before you realize it. It feels good in a sensing way. This is not a mental concept; it is a physical expression.

Beth: Can you explain more fully what you mean by choosing from this place of my feelings?

God: When you quiet yourself down and feel into your inner landscape, you will find hills, plains, and valleys. Walk along this inner path and feel the texture, the temperature, and the colors. These are your landmarks, your guideposts, and they will lead you to where you want to go.

Beth: I have a whole countryside inside of me. What a beautiful thought. But how do I interpret these guideposts accurately?

God: Accuracy is not the issue. Interpret them as feeling good or feeling bad. It is simpler than your mind will lead you to believe. All your answers are within.

Beth: Can you tell me more about what to do when I come to these big choice points, such as whether to sell or rent the house, tithe, or where to live?

God: The only one sure way to know is to slow down enough to feel your truth within – in each moment. It never lies.

Beth: When you say "truth," what do you mean?

God: Truth is what occurs to you when you are quiet – it is always there – it is who you are – but when you are "doing" it is difficult to hear – it is the knowing that only comes in the quiet space between thoughts.

Beth: How do I quiet down enough to hear it?

God: With the practice of doing without doing, seeing without seeing, hearing without hearing – it is stopping all the noise you call thinking. It is the ultimate in being present. Feel what you do, feel what you see, feel what you hear and allow yourself to be in the moment.

Beth: I get it in theory, but how in reality do I do that?

God: There are many ways to get there. The easiest of them is to be in nature. You are intimately connected to all living things – in fact, there is no separation – so when you are in nature, alive and vibrant in its natural state, the veil between you and All That Is becomes very thin. But there are other ways, ways you have been experimenting with, such as sitting and feeling your inner vibration, feeling your breath, yoga, meditation, and many others. You must choose to practice and then choose to practice again and again.

BEYOND YOUR WILDEST DREAMS

Although I was enjoying these frequent conversations with God, I noticed that it had been a while since I'd had one of those transcendent, sensory expansion experiences, when all of colors and smells and sounds were heightened, when I felt extreme bliss as a deep, palpable connection to All That

Is. I wanted to know more about this.

Beth: Why did I have those otherworldly experiences, such as the one in Balboa Park and in our back yard?

God: You had them because you were ready to experience that which you seek at a new level. It is the "how" you will be all that you are.

Beth: Why, then, when I still feel so connected, do these types of experiences fade?

God: You are in the process of opening – getting your energetic system ready to handle more and more energy.

Beth: Will I eventually just exist in that state?

God: Not as completely as you have experienced. You have said that what you want is to communicate to others. In this state you could not do that as fully as you want to.

Beth: Why not?

God: In that state you can only be there, expanded. You cannot "do" in the normal sense.

Beth: But after the experience in the backyard I was still able to get ready for my day; my senses were just heightened. So I'm not sure what you mean.

God: Your desire from even before you expressed into this life, is to experience full connection and full expression. This cannot be done in a state of expansion and elevation alone. This can only be done when fully embodied. You need much more integration in order to express as fully as you desire. In other words, you must stay more embodied.

Beth: What do you mean, before I expressed into this life? And during that experience I was still in my body, so I'm still not clear.

God: Before you were born into this lifetime – when you were enmeshed in All That Is – desire began to move energy and like energies began to coalesce. The strands of consciousness with similar desires came together and this desire created the expression that is you.

During those experiences you were in a body and you had expanded your capacity a great deal. But having a body, even with the expansion you have experienced thus far, and full embodiment are not the same thing. You have come here to experience full embodiment. That is the desire that brought your energies together and expressed into form. This full embodiment is the true gift of expressing into this material existence. It is what many want, but few up till now have achieved.

Beth: Can you explain more clearly what you mean by full embodiment?

God: Being fully embodied is when you can live in this physical reality and experience all that it has to offer and never lose your conscious connection with All That Is – with consciousness itself. When your life force energy can flow through the mind into the material world, even in the face of distraction, you will be fully embodied. It is your divine design. This is the bridge you are crossing and it is a bridge with many obstacles.

Imagine a great flowing river with its power and grace. This river must flow around many huge boulders and fallen trees, but it does so with ease because of its magnitude and ability to allow spontaneous movement. Being in a body without this complete connection is like taking a great river and making it run through a straw to get to its destination. This straw is stiff and it enormously diminishes the capacity of the water. Distraction is what constricts the flow of your mighty river.

There are many distractions present when one is embodied and they draw your attention from the great gifts that are possible for you.

Beth: What are these distractions?

God: I will mention some here, but there are many, many more. We have talked about some of them: television, foods that do not serve the flow, oversleeping, drugs and alcohol. Violence – between people, in media, and in video games. Money, in the form that it is used now. Comparisons of all kinds distract the majority of you each and every day. And then there are internal distractions which come from the collective mind: The desire for emotional safety, wanting to be included, wanting to love and be loved in a particular way. All of these turn your attention from All That Is.

Even your backyard experience can be considered a distraction if it becomes your goal. Your final destination is not to live in that world of expanded dimension. That is only part of what is available.

Beth: What is available?

God: Beauty, vision, creativity, and joy beyond your wildest dreams.

Beth: Those experiences were beautiful and joyful beyond my wildest dreams. What could be missing?

God: Without being fully embodied, you are unable to access all that is available to you. When you can tap into the bliss you experienced in the park, for example, while being fully embodied, you will be able to create anywhere you are – it is the reality of you. Then you will begin to create what you would call miracles.

Those blissful experiences were part of your wholeness but not all of it. The vehicle in which you live – your body – is the door to everything that is available to you – your access to All That Is. When you are focused and not distracted, allowing and relaxing into the wholeness of who you are, all parts of you can integrate into the whole being that you truly are.

Beth: I never considered creating miracles; I thought they just happened. What kind of miracles are you talking about?

God: What you call miracles are only miracles because of your linear perception of time. You are constantly creating them, but because of your limited embodiment, you create erratically and without focused consciousness. Each new hope, wish, and desire, births an energy creation field that is sent into the abyss of all creation. When you are fully embodied and these fields become focused you will not be distracted by all the interim reactions caused by creating a new field. By miracles I mean the things that you consider to be coincidence or luck, such as when you meet someone who directs you to just the perfect situation or person, when money comes to you just in time, when you thought there was no hope and all of a sudden circumstances change in your favor. These things and many more are your creations.

Beth: How do I do this consciously?

God: You are on your way, dear one. Do not rush; you are doing very well.

CHAPTER 21

Follow the Synchronicity

"Living at risk is jumping off the cliff and building your wings on the way down."

- Ray Bradbury

DRAWN BACK IN

I SPOKE TO GOD ALMOST EVERY DAY during this time. Each conversation was like a stepping stone, leading to another level of understanding. I continued to meditate, take baths, and go to yoga. But ever since the Big Mission event something was pulling at me, leading me somewhere. I felt the urge to start working again, but the question became, how do I balance these two worlds – the world of peace and serenity with the world of business, sales and marketing? I also wondered how I was going to integrate all this newfound spiritual awareness into my business.

Then one day I noticed a particular email message advertising a Women's Wisdom networking event, and I had a strong sense that I should attend. I still didn't go out much, nor did I know what kind of work I now wanted to do, so why this event? But I was clearly being drawn to it, so I signed up and went.

This was only a small gathering in a private home, but as soon as I walked in I felt as overwhelmed as I had at the Big Mission conference. I flashed back to my childhood, remembering how I felt each person's energy and emotions as though they were mine.

As a child I'd learned how to shield myself from this energy by turning off my ability to feel it. But in my 40s I had realized this empathic ability was a gift, something beautiful and valuable, rather than something to fear, turn off, or be embarrassed about. It was a way of connecting with people and understanding them better. Also, during this new spiritual expansion, I saw that this ability to feel my environment was also a way of connecting to everything all at once, a way of knowing at an experiential level the truth of oneness.

But now, with my empathic ability opened up, way up, as I walked into the room with this small group of people I felt as tense and nervous as I did as a child. My heart began to race, my body temperature increased and my hands began to sweat.

Over the years I've learned that when I feel this way it's best to focus on a task, so I immediately asked the woman who ran the networking group if I could help out. She put me in charge of writing nametags and greeting people. Meeting people as they came in one by one and writing down their names helped distract me from feeling so much all at once.

It's strange how easy it is to feel All That Is when I'm by myself, and how challenging it is to remain connected to that feeling when I'm in a room full of people. When I'm alone there's a sense of flow, ease and great joy to the energy around me, but when there are more than a couple of people in a room with me it's as though I'm being bombarded from all sides. The energy seems erratic and jagged and I often feel overwhelmed by it. I also knew the deeper truth of what was all around me – the pure essence of each and every person in this room – the beauty and peace of All That Is, but in that moment the beauty and peace completely eluded me.

Slowly I relaxed. Gradually I was able to move and ease myself into the combined energy of the ten or twelve women sitting in a circle in the large family room. Soft lighting came from a few lamps scattered around the room and the candles that adorned the centerpiece flickered against the walls. I sat down with a couple of women I knew and we chatted for a while. It was nice, but I still wondered why I had come. I didn't really have much to offer to the conversation and I was tired and wanted to go home.

But then the main event began, and as the leader introduced the motivational guest speaker, I heard some of the women excitedly whispering about her. They made her sound like a Tony Robbins, someone who got people standing up and clapping and yelling and all that hoopla. *I'm definitely not in the mood for that,* I thought to myself. But as she walked to the front of the room I felt her energy and relaxed. She was an attractive woman in her late thirties, with long blonde hair and a small figure. Her face was calm and her eyes were very still and present. Even before she opened her mouth my body began tingling and I felt excited. I leaned forward so I could see her better.

"The only reason any of us are alive is to become enlightened," she began. *Okay, now I'm really interested,* I thought to myself. She just came right out and said that – no hesitation.

This topic was challenging for me because despite all my conversations with God, I still didn't know for sure if my experiences were as real as they seemed, or if I was just imagining them. In that moment I got a clear internal message that it was time to feel good about my experiences and to talk about them. So this is why I had come, to hear this message.

Then she said, "Has anyone here ever had a kundalini experience?" My hand flew up in the air. As the words "Yes, I have" came out of my mouth a subtle kundalini rush moved up and down my spine. I felt lightheaded and the intensity of this energy pushed me hard into the back of my seat.

She stopped for a moment and looked at me. "Wow," she said, "this is very unusual. Everyone in this room should want to sit near her." As she spoke these words I thought, Oh no, I'm no one special, there is nothing unusual about me. I felt a dozen pairs of eyes staring at me. I was worried, and embarrassed, and the flow of spirit energy slowed down almost to a stop. Just then I remembered the message I received moments before. I was to start talking about my experiences in order to inspire others. Oh crap! I didn't think that meant NOW!

Okay fine, I thought, here I am – back in the world – and some people are going to think I'm strange, or crazy, but I can't go back to pretending nothing has changed. But what was I supposed to do? With that thought the energy started to move through me again. I took a deep breath, which allowed it to flow more naturally. There's nothing else in the world like this energy – my mind chatter slows and my senses heighten. The difference is remarkable: ordinary consciousness is like being in a room with only a small candle and then it's like someone flips a switch and all of a sudden the room is bright. Colors, sounds, and sensations that weren't available to me before are now vivid and bold. But I'd never experienced it in a room full of people before. I was so distracted by the low vibration running through my body that I couldn't focus on what the speaker was saying; I couldn't think clearly. So I got up and moved to the formal living room on the other side of the kitchen.

The room was paneled in a pale wood and there was a light blue coffee table in front of a plush sofa. I sat on that couch for a long time. This kundalini experience was different than previous ones in that I felt more physical sensations in my body, but without the heightened bliss. Still, it was moving and beautiful.

The sound of clapping brought me back to my surroundings. I realized the speaker was finished. I was excited at the chance to talk to someone who would know about the experiences I was having. I tried to get present, but there was still so much energy rushing through me it wasn't easy to get fully back into my body. I rubbed my hands together and I rubbed my feet on the floor to help ground me. As I did she walked in and sat by me on the couch. I was struck by her confidence and solid presence. She looked at me, smiled, and her eyes lit up. Then she said in a low voice, "If you ever need to talk please call me. I'd be happy to spend some time with you." With that she wrote her number on a piece of paper and handed to me. Before I could say a word she got up and started walking away, but then stopped, turned, looked at me again and said, "Don't forget to get back in your body BEFORE you get in your car." Then she smiled and walked away.

I still couldn't think straight or talk intelligibly. Then I remembered that this event was a potluck and there would be food in the kitchen. I thought maybe eating something would help. So I walked over and realized I was ravenous. I ate as though I hadn't eaten for weeks, and soon felt more grounded and present. I looked up from my plate of food and realized that the meeting was winding down, so I went to get my things from the main room.

A couple of women stopped me and wanted to know about the kundalini experience. Here was my chance to talk about it, and I answered their questions to the best of my ability. One of them seemed quite unconvinced and I realized that I had a long way to go before I'd be able to talk about this with confidence and comfort. I didn't know what to do with skeptics. I had enough trouble believing the whole thing myself. I finished the conversation and left the house that evening, unclear what to take away from the experience, except I knew it was a significant milestone. I stood by my car for a minute laughing to myself, remembering what the speaker told me, and I jumped up and down and shook my body to make sure I was back in it before I drove off.

OPEN TO RECEIVE

Beth: Good morning, God.
God: Dear one…
Beth: What happened last night?
God: You were quickened.
Beth: What do you mean, I was quickened?
God: Quickening is phenomenon that happens when you are in a place to receive more energy, more grace, more of All That Is. Last night you were open to receiving. This woman carries with her a similar frequency to the energy that is

flowing through you at this time. When you were in her presence your energies mingled and increase the flow and speed of your energy.

Also, the words that you heard from her stimulated openings that allowed more energy to flow in to you. This energy moves you and expands your ability to receive even more. As you receive more and more, you expand your ability to hold it and this quickens the process of expansion. This is what I mean by quickened. Your ability to receive and hold energy was expanded.

Beth: Is there anything I need to do in relation to this quickening/expansion?

God: Continue to be with the expanded energy and allow it to flow. That is all that's needed.

During the next few days I continued to feel an intense expansion of energy moving through me. What difference did this all make in my life, I wondered? My meditations became deeper, but my outside world looked the same as it did before. These experiences seem so profound – and they are – but if you were looking at me from "out there" all you would see was an ordinary fiftyish woman going about her day. I would soon learn the real difference these experiences made in my life. I discovered that as I continued to expand and hold more energy, and I followed my guidance more quickly, my ability to envision and manifest what I was being drawn to happened more rapidly as well.

THE MAGIC WOMAN

Neill and I were still talking about what to do with our

house and wondering about the possibilities for selling. California was in the middle of the biggest real estate slump in twenty years. There were foreclosure sales everywhere and most people were hunkering down and just hoping to keep up with their mortgage payments. Property values had dropped dramatically, and the value of our home had declined since we bought it. So we had our doubts about the guidance I'd received to sell the house. Yet once again, as we relaxed and followed the synchronicity, everything fell into place. It was all quite miraculous.

One day I told a friend about our decision to sell, and she mentioned a real estate agent, Nancy, who happened to specialize in the small community where we lived.

Nancy came to the house a day or two later with a cheerful can-do attitude. Nevertheless we let her know that there was only so much of our investment in the house we were willing to lose. If we couldn't get a certain amount of money back from selling the house we would just stay there until the market got better. Nancy told us that we were right at the edge of what was realistic, and if it became necessary she'd be willing to give up some of her commission.

At one point Neill and I had discussed just selling the house ourselves, "by owner," but knowing how bad the market was, I wanted to check in with Nancy. I asked her about the advantage of hiring her instead of selling the house ourselves. She looked surprised by the question, but recovered quickly and said, "Well I am very knowledgeable about your area, I'm very successful at selling, and I use a woman with 'magic' to help me close deals."

"A magic woman!" I said out loud, "now I'm intrigued." My instincts told me to pay attention. She went on to say that she brings in an energy worker who clears the houses of any negative or stagnant energy, though she normally doesn't tell her clients this. Well, I was sold; she certainly had something unique to offer.

When she left Neill and I talked and decided to take a chance and sell. Nancy soon brought the initial paperwork over for us to sign. We picked a date for the first open house and took pictures for the flyer. As we walked around, Nancy also pointed out areas that might be spruced up, and made some suggestions that incorporated the principles of feng shui. This is an ancient Chinese system that balances the energy of any given space to assure health and good fortune for the people inhabiting it. For example, she suggested that we put red pots with red flowers in them on either side of the front door, and get a large green plant for a particular corner of the living room. Soon we knew exactly what to do in order to get ready for the open house on November 22nd.

A few days before the open house, Nancy returned and brought the "magic woman" with her. We knew she didn't usually involve her clients in this, but we were so interested and excited about this mysterious woman that she made an exception for us. I was expecting a woman with beads, feathers, rattles, and possibly even a shaman headdress, but much to my surprise she was simply dressed and quite normal looking, just like someone you'd see at the supermarket. Her magic came from her intuitive sense. The woman – I'll call her "Magic" – walked around the house sensing and feeling the energy. By now I was no stranger to this kind of behavior – I truly knew what she was doing.

As she walked into each room she would stop and close her eyes and stand there for a moment. In some rooms she would stay for a long time and in others she would move in and out quickly. When Magic got to my mother's room, she stopped and asked whose room this was. I told her it was my mom's room and it was where she died. She told me there was some kind of a vortex still open in the room and asked if I had some unfinished business with my mom, and I replied that we were very complete in our relationship when she died. We had spent the last three years together cleaning up past hurts, misunderstandings, and childhood pain and by the time she died we were very close. Nothing was left unsaid or undone.

Magic said she would do her best to close the energy leak. About ten minutes later she came out of the room and said she'd taken care of most of it, but there was still something lingering, unwilling to dissipate. She asked me again, "Are you sure there isn't something you need to finish up with your mom?"

I thought about it but couldn't imagine what she could be talking about. "No," I said, "I can't think of a thing."

"Okay," Magic said, "I'll do some more work remotely; I'm sure it'll be fine."

As Nancy and Magic left I wondered about the energy she mentioned. I went into my mom's room to see if I could sense this energy leak, but all I could feel was a sense of peace and comfort. It was my mother's room after all, and I loved her very much. I could almost sense her there. So I didn't understand what the magic woman meant. A few days later it would become very clear.

CHAPTER 22
The Final Authority

"The intuitive mind is a sacred gift and the rational mind is a faithful servant. We have created a society that honors the servant and has forgotten the gift. We will not solve the problems of the world from the same level of thinking we were at when we created them. More than anything else, this new century demands new thinking."

- Albert Einstein

THE EXTRAORDINARY MACHINE

AS EXPANDED ENERGY FLOWED THROUGH ME, quickening my spiritual experience, so too did my life events quicken. All my excitement, anxiety and questions about the future intensified and brought me once again back to God.

Beth: I have so many questions today. First, about the house – does it still seem good to go?

God: Oh Beth, all is well, let the rest go.

Beth: What do you mean?

God: You make plans and you think you are moving things forward with your mind, but it is feeling and energy that make it all happen. The mind thinks it must take care of the feelings by creating more thoughts, and that the feelings are secondary and need to be managed. But the truth is that the feelings and energy are primary and will take care of themselves, and you, if you let them.

Beth: How did we end up talking about this?

God: You were thinking.

Beth: I'm always thinking to some extent.

God: There are different kinds of thinking. Your brain is an extraordinary machine. And your mind has the power to support you in many ways, but it has taken over areas that are none of its business. That is why the idea of ego has gotten distorted and now is thought of by many as something bad that you need to get rid of.

Beth: Are you saying that the ego and the mind are one and the same?

God: In a way. The workings of the mind and ego are designed to help you, as a physical being, to function in many ways. It was not designed to make decisions or to be the final authority. You, the essence that is you, is the final and only authority.

Beth: What is that essence?

God: It is the part of you that never changes. It is always connected, always aware, always in tune with All That Is. It is the part of you that is sure and confident, able, excited, and passionate. It is the part of you that is love, compassion and joy. It is your higher mind, the part of you that is me and the me that is you. It is the eternal and the always.

Beth: What's the difference between the mind and the brain?

God: The brain is a functioning machine. The mind is the part that allows the brain to be used by the body and the soul. There are actually two minds: the higher mind – your essence

– and the physical mind. I will now discuss your physical mind, the mind that is the doer. It links the machine and the physical body and allows information to move into formless form. It is the mind that chooses what information is released to your awareness, allowing it to be interpreted and experienced.

Beth: What exactly was this physical mind designed to do?

God: It was designed to do many things, mostly to protect and to guard. In its simplest terms this mind is meant to protect you from physical danger. In ancient times, if there was a rustling in the bush, it would alert you by stimulating your flight or fight reflex. Today it still does the same by paying close attention to the possibility of physical danger and alerting you to it, such as when you cross a street or when you hear footsteps behind you in a dark alley.

Your physical mind was also designed to protect you from an overload of information. It is a filter that allows in what is needed and necessary for your ongoing experiential evolution. In your linear reality it would be difficult to function if all information were available to you at once.

But this mind was not designed to make choices and decisions about anything other than what flows in and out of the brain's holding area from All That Is. The holding area is the way station and the storage area of all gathered information.

Beth: Then how is my essence to make decisions without the use of this mind?

God: You are meant to use this mind to function – it is part of your being. But it's meant to be used in conjunction with your feelings, which are the language of your higher mind – your essence. The physical mind has an extraordinary ability to manipulate all the selected data into stories that are assimilated and ultimately used to support the whole of you.

Beth: Sometimes all this information gets boggled in my mind!

God: That's okay. You do not have to assimilate this all at once. As you often say, it is a practice thing. Just practice.

Beth: OK then, if the physical mind is designed as a filter between the brain's storage area and physical experience, then how am I involved?

God: You – the conscious part of you is the one that experiences. The mind releases information in the form of stories, thoughts, and memories, then you sort through and experience only what rises to the top.

Beth: But often a lot of garbage rises to the top.

God: That is the issue. The physical mind was designed to allow all unimportant or nonessential data to be stored – that is its job. You do not have to analyze it all. But as time passed and generations have moved through time and space, humans have asked the mind to do a job that your feelings were meant to do.

Beth: Who asked?

God: You ask even now – your parents asked – your grandparents, and great-grandparents, going back for eons.

Beth: Why did they ask, and why would I continue to ask?

God: You ask because of fear, and because you have lost touch with the art of feeling. Feelings are the main mode of accurate guidance – they cannot be manipulated. They are always to be trusted. However, as you will see, when feelings are filtered through the mind it causes much confusion and fear.

Beth: I keep hearing that there is only love, and all else is just an illusion.

God: It is all just an illusion – even love. Love is also just energy – the energy of the universe – and there is also its opposite.

Beth: What is the opposite of love?

God: Truth is the opposite of love – truth is the other side of the same coin. They are opposed and they are also one. There could not be truth without love nor love without truth. These forces are what make up universal energy and they have formed your reality.

Beth: I have two more questions about this before we get back to the mind. How can truth be the opposite of love? And why do you say there is only illusion?

God: Let's start with the first question. Truth is just "what is," no more and no less. Truth is the sun in the sky, the ocean waves lapping on the sand, the hurricane that kills many, and it is an earthquake that destroys cities. Truth is the first smile on a baby's face and also the first tear which forms when she falls and hurts herself. Truth is all of what is, without exception. Truth is passive and cannot be experienced without love. Love is active and creative. Without truth, love cannot be expressed. Just the same way that there cannot be light without dark, there cannot be love without truth. Everyone at some point has experienced what I am talking about. When you are taken over by the beauty of a sunset, love lets you experience the truth of it. When you learn that hundreds of people have died in a massive storm, love lets you experience the truth. It is only when the physical mind gets involved where it does not belong that there is suffering. Suffering is a manifestation of the mind and the mind alone.

To answer your second question, it is all an illusion because energy is all that exists, and without the illusion there would be nothing to experience. Energy in creative action becomes form that wants to be experienced. The confusion only happens when you want to understand with your physical mind alone. If you were living as fully integrated beings, then you would be feeling into these words and you would understand completely. When the mind gets involved, it begins to interpret truth through the filters of its designated position as protector.

Beth: And what does this all have to do with the ego?

God: As the physical mind began to interpret and to guide peoples' experience, it became what you call the ego. Its primary function still continues to be protection, but now it does not just protect your physical form and the feelings from unimportant or nonessential information, but it protects you from anything and everything it determines to be a threat.

Because this physical mind no longer just filters information but is one with all information, it cannot interpret accurately any change in your system, in your environment, or in your thoughts. Change became a threat to protect you against; change has become the enemy.

As I have said, the physical mind was not meant to interpret in this way, or to choose, but it has come to take on this role over time.

Beth: How can I get back to a more natural way of being?

God: You can quiet your mind as much as possible and allow your feelings to reestablish themselves as your natural guide. Allow them to help you experience the world as you were meant to. Inhabit your physical form and feel, sense, and be with objects more than you think about them. Feel, sense and be with what you hear more than you think about it. Feel, sense, and be with the world around you more than you think about it. This is the way to reestablish yourself.

Beth: Thank you! This last piece touches me deeply and brings tears to my eyes. This is what you're talking about, isn't it? Feeling the truth of things?

God: Yes that's exactly what I'm talking about. Now feel into this even more deeply. Read what you have written again and discover all that is there for you.

THE VORTEX

During this time I did a lot of just sitting and feeling. I felt the air on my skin, the sounds of the birds singing, what I saw through my eyes as I watched my dog romping in the yard. I spent much time playing with the difference between seeing and feeling, hearing and feeling, thinking and feeling. Some days I wished that I could stay in this exploration forever, but that's not what life had in store for me.

At the same time, we put our house on the market. Balancing the day-to-day "doing" with the feeling, thinking, and expressing was challenging. Sometimes my physical mind took over and I would just fall back into the habitual doing. The good news was that now I quickly felt the contrast. I would feel my body tense up and know that my mind had taken over. I was usually aware and back in the exploration within a matter of hours.

On the 21st of November, 2010, Nancy listed the house. That evening she called and said, "You're never going to believe this, but I just got a phone call from another real estate agent who has a client that wants to make a full price, cash offer on your house." Then she added that this had never happened to her before in this economy – to get a full price offer on the first day of listing. The buyer couldn't come by until the next week, so she suggested we still hold the scheduled open house and get some backup offers in case this deal fell through. I ran and told Neill the good news. It was like a miracle; we were as excited as kids on Christmas morning.

Then I remembered what the magic woman had said about the energy leak. I didn't want anything to mess up this deal. I wondered if in fact there was something left undone with my mom that I didn't realize. I went into my mom's room and sat on the floor. Even though we had cleaned out the room I could still smell the faint fragrance of her vanilla hand cream. I closed my eyes and could imagine her thin white hands and square-cut fingernails. It was as if I could sense her in the room – as if she was there with me.

I tried talking to her, asking her if there was anything left incomplete, any reason for there to be an energy leak. But all I sensed was the same peaceful, warm loving energy that I had felt in the room before she died. So I decided to take a bath. I've experienced so many amazing things during my baths I thought maybe I could connect with my mom.

I went upstairs and prepared my bath as I normally did. I stepped into the hot water with a sense of anticipation, and as I lowered myself down I somehow knew that this would work. I closed my eyes and began my initial meditation. Within a few moments I began seeing images within my mind's eye. I saw a very large doorway. There was no actual door, just a shiny white frame, and in the center where the door would be was a grayish white mist moving gently around. As I looked at the opening I felt someone talking to me.

It was a strange sensation. No one was calling me to enter

the doorway, but someone from in the gray mist was telling me to get out. It didn't make any sense. Then I realized who was talking. It was me! I was talking to myself from inside this doorway, but I was telling myself to get out. Then I also sensed my mother on the other side of the door.

"I'm all right now," she said, "You can go."

I thought, go where?

"Go back," she said, "Go back."

But I am right here; I'm here in the bathtub.

"Not all of you. Part of you is here with me; part of you came to help me settle in because I was so scared, came to help me stay anchored until I was ready to let go. I'm ready now; you can go back."

I wasn't scared or concerned. I didn't have a clue what was going on, but the whole experience was so peaceful that I continued the conversation. It felt very good!

What do you mean, part of me is with you?

"I don't understand it myself, but part of you is with me here," my mother said. "I love you so much, but you must go now. It is not good for either of us if you stay."

But how do I go, and why haven't I left before this?

"You haven't left because you wanted to be here. But you cannot participate fully in your physical life this way. It is not the way things are supposed to be. You must now choose to retrieve this part of yourself."

I lay there in the bathtub with my eyes closed, enjoying being in this space with the essence of my mother. It was as though I was with her. I understood why this part of me hadn't left, because I had never felt this level of peacefulness or safety with her before.

I heard her say to me again, "It is time to go, sweet girl. There is much for you to do and I also must complete my journey. Pull yourself together, now is the time."

Okay but how do I get back? Then I felt this pressure around my heart, as though something from inside was sucking my chest area in. It felt intense but not painful. After few seconds the pressure released, and my whole body relaxed and let go, like I was melting into the water around me. Then my body began to tingle and the doorway in front of me seemed to vibrate. I watched it move away and disintegrate at the same time. This whole thing took less than a minute, and then it was done.

The doorway was gone, the vibration and tingling subsided, and I started to cry. The tears continued for a long time. She was gone – the peaceful, sweet feeling that I had felt with her moments before was gone. It was like she died again. The sense of being with her was so real, but as quickly as she had come to me she was gone again. Eventually the tears stopped and a sweet gratitude washed over me. I thought about how she said I helped her get past her fear so that she could get settled on the other side. I didn't remember doing anything like that, but I sensed the truth of it and I was happy I could help.

Later I went downstairs and walked into my mother's room. There were still all the memories, but I could no longer feel her in the room. I sat in the middle of the floor and closed my eyes. I was alone. I could imagine many kinds of unfinished business between my mother and I, but I have to admit that the idea of me being "on the other side" with her would not have been one of them. The words from Hamlet came into my mind: "There are more things in heaven and earth, Horatio, than are dreamt of in your philosophy."

CHAPTER 23

Learning to Trust

"Just trust yourself, then you will know how to live."
- Johann Wolfgang von Goethe

OPEN HOUSE

IT WAS A DREARY, RAINY DAY when the real estate agent showed up early to bake cookies for our open house. I loved the smell of chocolate chip cookies wafting through the house, and I knew they wanted people to get that happy home feeling. We'd been asked to leave so that prospective buyers would feel comfortable walking around inside.

So Neill and I drove up the coast to look at more houses for rent, since now we really needed to find somewhere to live. We spent the whole day looking, to no avail. We were hoping for good news from the open house, but there were no offers that day. At least we still had the original offer.

Over the next few days real estate agents and their clients came in and out. Two of them made lowball offers, below our minimum acceptable price. It was now the day before Thanksgiving and the man that made the original offer was still out of the country, so he sent his parents and a friend to look at the house for him. They all loved the house and called him right then and there to tell him so. He decided to sign the contracts over the Internet the next day.

With the signed contracts in hand – Nancy still couldn't believe it – we were all very happy, and yet at the same time things were moving very quickly. Even with all that had happened to me, there was still a part of me that poked up its head trying to get my attention. *No, don't do that,* cried my mind, *remember when, if only you knew, what if...* worry after worry, concern after concern. I knew it was the part of my mind that was designed to protect me, that sees change as an enemy, but these worries were so loud that I wondered if they'd always been like this, or did I just notice them more quickly now?

The days to come were all about learning to trust what had been developing over the last couple of years – learning to ask questions, hear the answers, and act on the information that I was receiving. It wasn't always easy, but as long as I kept relaxing into what I found to be true in my heart, I knew I would be fine.

It was now two days after we signed the contract for the house. I was excited and scared at the same time. I let some friends know how quickly the house sold and they wanted to know how that happened.

Beth: Good morning, God. It's been a little while but I know you're always with me.

God: With you I am.

Beth: I still don't understand how I am to share what I'm learning from you with others. Can you tell me more?

God: You will know when the opportunities arise, and you will take them.

Beth: That's still vague. Could you be more specific?

God: Specificity is of your world. I seem vague because as I have said many times, when energy moves, things change. Giving you specifics only holds you in place.

Beth: Okay, I understand that, but there are times when people want to know what's going on with me, and what I'm learning has been so valuable I do want to share it. But I would like to focus in the direction that would work best for everyone. What's the best way to accomplish this?

God: The best way is to stay present to how you feel in each moment. You will know if you are present. You will know if you sense your inner being guiding you. We/you, the part of you that is connected to the we, is always there guiding you if you stay present and listen.

Beth: I do feel what you are talking about more and more lately. When I'm interacting with someone or doing something, and I pay attention to my physical sensations at the same time, it keeps me present in that moment. It's as though my mind stops when I'm able to focus in this way. I will continue to pay attention.

God: That is very good, dear one. This is your mission if you choose to accept it.

Beth: Now you're doing lines from Mission Impossible?

God: It's more enjoyable to keep it light and have some fun.

Beth: I agree. By the way, we signed the contracts for the sale of our house. Do you see us in a beach house?

God: I see all kinds of things for you. And the beach is beautiful.

Beth: So as we look for new places to live, what would be beneficial to pay attention to?

God: Let's play a game. You tell me what would be beneficial and I'll fill in anything that you miss. Will you play with me?

Beth: Sure I'll play, but let me ask you a question first. Is this game to get me to stop asking you these kinds of questions?

God: You may always ask me anything that occurs to you.

This game is to show you that you have the answers. I am not the ultimate source, because you are part of me and I am part of you. As we sit here and do this questioning and answering, you are getting answers from US together. This is true whether you use my name or just ask yourself. You/ we have the answers and always have. This game is a way to have fun, build confidence, and know that you are the source, because you and I are one.

Beth: Okay, let's play. The question is, "What things would be most beneficial to pay attention to in order to create what we want in this move?"

The first thing for me to pay attention to is to stay present to how I feel. For example, yesterday I was making a list of belongings to sell in the house, I started to feel agitated so I just stopped, went outside to sit in the sun, and meditated. Then when I went back to it I felt better and was easily able to move on with the list.

It's funny; the answer felt like it came more from you than me. I think that's because I'm so connected to you right now. Is that true?

God: This is what I want you to experience. As you talk to me you are more present than when we're not talking. When you are present you are one with me.

Beth: And when I'm not present, are we not connected?

God: We are always connected dear one, but sometimes you are not aware of it. When you are not present the questions get garbled in the field of all things, and your answers are mixed with those of the collective. This incorporates your mind, your fears, and all the fears that live in the collective. These answers will not serve you well. Always settle your mind before you ask questions; get connected, be present, and feel the answers as you get them. You will know whether they come from your source or not.

LOVE WILL KEEP ME SAFE

Where would we live, now that our house was sold? As we drove up and down the coast, almost frantically, looking at one dissatisfying house after another, we kept coming back to Encinitas. We loved the community, but we couldn't find a house in our price range. Something wasn't working.

This waking up process is not the way people might think it is. I didn't wake up and suddenly become some "light being" living in an angelic realm. At least that hasn't been my experience. For me, it's been a mixed bag.

I now always have a deep, grounded sense of peace within me, so that when I'm quiet, and not "doing" much, my connection to God – All That Is – is right there, and I'm completely connected. At these times it's easy and there is no doubt; I feel, sense and know that I'm part of All That Is. It's miraculous, and I've never been happier or loved my life more.

But there's something else; I have also opened to heightened feelings and emotions. Light, sound, and touch continue to be more acute, and I sense them more quickly and intensely than ever before. Also as I've moved back into the world – talking to realtors, selling my house, interacting with people – I experience strong emotions and reactions that draw my focus of attention away from All That Is. Sometimes I feel intense anger, or fear. For example, when we're driving around looking for a place to live, a "what if" thought will come to mind – *What if we can't find a place we like?* – my throat will tighten, my heart will pound in my chest, and a rush of fear will run through me.

The difference is that the deep peace is there simultaneously, so now my emotions and reactions don't have the same kind of lingering thoughts attached to them. They don't mean much or keep my attention for long. All there is for me to do in any moment is to turn my attention to the present, let everything else fall away, and there God is once more.

I discovered that having ease in life all comes down to feeling what's going on in my body, rather than my mind. Trusting that when the time is right to act, I will know because I feel it. My mind doesn't really know what to do. It sure thinks it does, and it really wants to know, but the kind of knowing that makes things flow easily comes from the feeling part of me, not my head.

And when I say feelings I don't mean emotions, I mean my sensory self. In order to stay in that flow and gain the support that is always available, I learned to get in touch with myself in a whole new way, to reawaken parts of myself that had become dormant.

I once heard a friend say, "In the Old World our plans are what kept us safe, and in the New World, it will be the love that we have for ourselves that will keep us safe." Wanting to know what's coming and to figure everything out in advance no longer serves me. Knowing myself so deeply and fully that I can sense what there is to do next is all that will keep me safe. All I need to do is to practice this, remember this, and keep bringing myself back to what I know is true.

GO INWARD

As soon as I realized that I was making things harder than they needed to be, I stopped. I stopped looking for houses to rent and I stopped talking about houses. I just became present. I saw that I had been running around looking at every house advertised in every little beach city. When I stopped I realized I wasn't clear about what I wanted. It's important to be specific in order to get what you want. Neill and I decided to do an exercise to help us get clear and focused, one that we often taught others in our workshops.

We brainstormed everything we might want in a house, and we divided it into three categories. The first category was "essential," meaning we couldn't do without it. That meant we didn't even need to look at a house that was missing these qualities. There were about 25 items on this list. For example, since bathing had become a large part of my life, a bathtub was essential. The house needed to be light and bright, with lots of windows. Pets must be welcomed with open arms, because our cat Socrates and dog Petra were part of our family. We wanted natural beauty, such as open space, trees, or the ocean, within walking distance.

The second category was "would be nice," A quiet, beautiful and private yard was in this category. Also on this list of twenty items were an ocean view, a beautiful interior, and upgraded bathrooms and kitchen. The third category was called "perfect." This list of luxuries included being right on the ocean, and a short walk to a downtown area. As we wrote our lists we became very clear about what we wanted in our living space and what would make our life easier, more peaceful, and beautiful.

This kind of clarity brought us closer to what we wanted. Within a few days I got an e-mail newsletter from a realtor named Polly. I had never given her e-mails much attention, but this day, when I saw her picture it seemed to ignite a spark in me and I knew I should call her. She was a lovely woman in her 50s, with dark hair, bright eyes and a beautiful smile. It's strange; it was obvious from her newsletters that she didn't handle rentals, that she only sold property. But I was practicing feeling into things, and intuitively knew she could help, so I called her immediately.

When I told her that I was looking to rent a house in North County she confirmed that she doesn't handle rentals, but said she'd keep an eye out for me. So I told her everything that was on our list. I named item after item, and when I was done she took a deep breath and said, "Beth, You're never going to believe this, but my next-door neighbor called me this morning and said he was almost ready to rent his house. Your list describes it to the letter. Let me call him and see if he'll show you the property."

Two hours later Polly called back and said, "Beth, he's willing to show you the property and wants to rent it very soon." We scheduled to see the house the following weekend. But that was a week away and the closing of our house was coming soon, so my patience was wearing thin. When this kind of thinking draws my attention away from being present, talking to God brings me back almost immediately.

Beth: Help!

God: So there is a lot of thinking about everything. How do you feel when you are thinking about this?

Beth: I feel excited at first, but then I begin to feel anxious when I don't know the answers to my many questions.

God: Good. This is not the time to ask questions; this is the time to go inward, get present, and settle into the unknown. The unknown is always there. The past it gone and the future does not exist. The moments of now are all that there ever truly is.

Those moments of now are your salvation. They are the only IS that is your joy. When these times of anxiousness come to you and you want to ask questions, I suggest strongly that you do not ask. You stop, you get centered, and you feel that moment of now. Breathe deeply into that moment and feel it in every inch of your physical form. Hold your consciousness in the moment, do not stray or leave that place until you get to the point of such great gratitude that every bit of your anxiousness is transformed into the present moment of joy.

Beth: I hear what you are saying; I appreciate it. I will do this the next time I feel anxious. Is there anything else you want me to know now, anything that would support me?

God: There are many things to discuss and we will discuss them all, but there is time for that later. You are in a great transition. You are changing, evolving, exploring, and holding your light strong. You must take these steps with the entirety of your being. This is not a time for great conversations; this is a time for inward sensing, feeling and caring for you.

Make sure you rest your physical form enough so that it is strong for you when you need it. Know that I am always guiding you, holding you, loving you. We are one mind, we are one form, and we are one experience.

CHAPTER 24

Grace and Happiness

"The goal of life is to make your heartbeat match the beat of the universe, to match your nature with nature."

- Joseph Campbell

MAKING DECISIONS WITH EASE

MOST DAY-TO-DAY DECISIONS COME EASILY — like what to have for breakfast or where to get gas. Then there are those decisions you keep thinking about but the answer isn't clear. Sometimes they linger so long that the decision is just made for you. And sometimes these decisions become big problems in our lives, because they distract us and keep us from being present. How do we discern which option would bring the best outcome for all concerned? I've long wondered how to navigate this process more easily, and when a situation arose I realized I could bring this question to God.

My friend Dale had called to offer me a special deal to buy an expensive therapeutic laser. If she sold one more laser this month she would get a free one, and so she said she'd be happy to give me her commission if I bought one right away.

I was torn; I really wanted it, and yet spending $3000 on it seemed ridiculous.

Beth: I am trying to decide about whether or not to buy the laser. How do I know if doing something, buying something, or saying something is in everyone's highest good?

God: You know because you can feel whether it is or it isn't.

Beth: But many feelings come up, so how do I discriminate between them?

God: As an idea occurs in your mind, there is a corresponding feeling. That initial feeling is the one to trust.

Beth: Usually that initial feeling disappears so quickly I hardly notice it. What can I do about that?

God: The practice is being present, because when you are present, you will notice more and more what your initial feelings are. If you miss them, they are gone; you can never get back to the first one. If you have lost the initial feeling, you must discriminate between the many feelings that arise, and choose. Which feelings are positive, and where are they leading you? This is how you determine your path once the initial feelings are gone.

Beth: So let me see if I've got this. If I miss that initial feeling, then I am to determine which of the present feelings feels the best?

God: Yes. In very simple terms, that is accurate. The truth is that your internal senses are your true guides. They are the ones that lead you to where you want to go. They can lead you to the place of peace, joy, and presence – the place that people are all longing for.

Beth: Let's look at the question of buying the laser, for example. I have completely lost the initial feeling. So now if

I want to get back to it I can bring it to mind, but I notice the feelings are all mixed together. How can I distinguish between the ones that feel good and the ones that don't?

God: Try this now. Bring up a thought of the laser and sit quietly with a picture of it in your mind. Notice the feelings around it as you imagine this thing. Does the whole of the idea feel more pleasant or less pleasant? Start here, and don't think about the future of it or the past of it. Just be with the idea, the image, and the sense of the thing itself. Be with your feelings.

Beth: Okay – When I sit with the idea and a picture in my mind of the laser, I just see it and it doesn't feel particularly good or bad. It's not clear. Is there something else I can do rather than just see this thing in my mind's eye?

God: As you see it... touch it, feel it, and use it the way that you would be using it. Then sense the results.

Beth: Let me try that. When I think about Neill or a friend using the laser to ease body pain I feel peaceful. When I see myself using it to clear my allergy symptoms, for example, I feel fine, but when I imagine myself using it as a spiritual tool – clearing and energizing my chakras – I feel a quivering in my stomach.

So it seems that I'm very comfortable while using it physically, but when I imagine using it as a spiritual tool I feel the flutter. That could either be fear or excitement.

God: The flutter is energy, an energy of the unknown. It denotes excitement and possibility.

Beth: But doesn't fear feel like this?

God: No... if you pay attention closely, fear has a different element. With fear, there is an edge of pain and a mental discomfort that goes along with the flutter. Did you feel discomfort along with this flutter?

Beth: No... just an image of me using the laser as a spiritual tool and then the flutter.

God: Pay attention to the flutter. It is a very important directional tool. Look for it and see where it takes you.

THE EGO ERUPTS

So I decided to buy the laser. It seemed like the perfect time and I would be helping Dale as well, so I told her yes and purchased it. But a few days later she called me back and said that she had spoken too quickly; she didn't think it was fair to give up her whole commission. I heard tension in her voice and it resonated within me. I took a deep breath before I said anything.

I was fine about her calling to renegotiate. But at this point I had already bought the laser and wasn't able to return it, so I felt tense and confused. It had seemed like a great deal for her and a great deal for me, so where was the problem? As we talked I logically walked her through the math of it and she agreed to honor her first offer. But it didn't end there. A week later she called and wanted to meet.

As my consciousness has continued to expand, I noticed something new happening between my ego mind and my higher self. It was as though my habitual thoughts and behaviors were all rising to the surface so that I could clear them. I noticed this most during times of conflict, such as in this situation.

We met at a little Asian restaurant and sat outside. As soon as I saw her I felt a rush of intense energy, and I knew something was wrong. Dale told me she was very upset and hurt by our last phone call. She thought I had tried to manipulate her and that she was not sure how to handle it. I was stunned. After our phone call, I thought everything was clear between us, but now this. My mind was spinning as I tried to remember every detail of our conversation.

I felt myself tense up and then the conversation began to move very quickly as each of us tried to defend our positions. Habitual thoughts erupted in my ego mind as it tried to protect itself. In the past, because of the coaching work I do, I would have had this conversation logically and with little internal upset, because I knew it wasn't personal and that Dale was just trying to get her needs met. But now I felt the conversation in my body as a physical experience. As words came out of my mouth, my body felt them in a way I'd never experienced before. I started crying.

And then a funny thing happened. The tears seemed to defuse the situation, Dale and I both took a breath, and the tension dissipated. It was as if the tension stimulated my higher mind to come in and wash over the painful thoughts, like a cool summer rain. As my ego erupted, my higher mind came in and melted over "me," cooling the fire with a downpour of tears. Then I softened and the energy shifted. I asked Dale if it would help her feel better about the situation if she kept $100 of the commission. She agreed, and the situation was resolved.

I wondered about the tension between Dale and me – this wasn't the first time I'd noticed it. Was it karma – maybe something left over from a past life? For days afterwards, I thought about what had happened, and I knew there was more work for me to do around this. So I decided to ask God about it.

KARMA AND CONFLICT

Beth: Why do I continue thinking about this situation with Dale? Is there something karmic about our conflict?

God: The way the word karma is used by many of you has its basis in truth, but people's ideas about it are skewed.

Beth: Then what's the difference between what you're talking about and the typical explanation of karma?

God: The difference is that you – humans – in these bodies, think that it is you and another specific person who have unresolved and unlearned things to be worked out between you. This is not the case. There are too many strands of energy involved to take ownership of this. This tension you feel is just energy, nothing personal; there is nothing to be worked out or learned from past lives – but only energy needing to move and be experienced in this present moment of now.

Beth: Regarding Dale and me, the feelings between us during the conflict seem to be deeper than was warranted by this situation. Is that not karmic?

God: If you hold the word karma as energy movement alone – cause-and-effect – cause starts the movement and the effect either stops it or completes it – then yes, there is energy that needs to complete itself, and you and Dale can help do this. But there is no bad karma waiting to get you. There is not a good or bad nature to energy; it just is.

Beth: Then how do we help these energies to complete themselves?

God: By continuing to do what you are doing now.

Beth: I would love to understand this better. Would you be willing to show me how this whole thing works, using this situation with Dale?

God: Yes. We will start at the very beginning, in an earlier time. There were energies formed out of mistrust from the words and actions of others. Mistrust is, in other words, a missed-trust – a missed opportunity to let love express itself. These others were not the exact you and the exact Dale that exist now. This mistrust became an energetic field of its own, not attached to you or any other specific person. This is because the "you" that you know yourself to be is not the exact same "you" that expressed into form in an earlier time.

This energy, as all energies do, flowed back into the oneness, but it vibrated with a different quality from the rest of the energy strands. As it moved along with the other strands back into the denseness of life in physical form, it created an imbalance. Imbalanced energy tends to pool and stagnate because it does not vibrate at the same frequency, and so needs to be balanced.

And now about you and Dale. In this time, this space, this now, the relationship between you two contains some of these energy imbalances from past times and space.

This energy has come with you, and as it intertwines with the now – the present moment – it creates what you feel as discomfort. Unless this energy is allowed to complete itself you will continue to feel this discomfort. You can notice this by feeling what is going on in your physical form. This is your access to All That Is, and you are never without this access. You are always one with me. When you are conscious of this truth, then you are able to feel and attend to the imbalanced energies by moving them again.

Beth: How exactly do I move these energies?

God: When you become aware that your energy is out of balance and pooled within your physical form, you stop and notice that any discomfort you feel is pooled energy needing to move. Your physical mind will try to interpret it by giving it a story and making it mean more than it does. Just remember that everything is energy, and energy always wants to be moving. Then you can open the dam and let it flow.

And you already know how to let it flow. Do not live in the past; do not live in the future. Live in each moment, where your power is, where love exists, and where the energy is always balanced. You can use the tools that you know. Unearth the truth in your thinking, release the grip on your opinions and judgments, imagine, visualize, cry, jump up and down, laugh, do yoga, meditate! Any of these actions will bring you back to the essence and truth of who you truly are and let the energy move again.

You may also consciously or unconsciously be given suggestions about how to support yourself. For example, you might have an urge to become quiet, to slow down, and listen to your inner guide. This is how you can work to balance the strands of unbalanced energy that come along through time and space with all physical forms.

YOU'RE LATE!

The situation with Dale wasn't the only conflict that arose. My ego's habitual behavior of trying to protect me was deeply ingrained, and now, as my higher mind focused an intense light on these seemingly small conflicts, one after another. I was reestablishing my divine design, and learning to experience love and acceptance instead of constantly trying to protect myself.

These types of conflict might seem mild or trivial compared

to the often heart-wrenching conflicts many people suffer with their families, friends, or co-workers. In fact, soon I'd be advising a friend about her painful breakup. But for me personally, I've long been a trainer and coach on how to deal with conflicts, beginning with my own training with Marshall Rosenberg. So it's not that larger conflicts never existed in my life, it's that I've worked out the major conflicts with those closest to me, and learned to handle most situations with ease and calm, and not take things personally. What was different now was that I was getting to deeper and deeper levels of the conflict that lives within me – the conflict between my ego mind and my higher mind. This is the ultimate conflict we must all eventually face.

I had been seeing Allison, my massage therapist, for about six months, and one day I walked into her office and she was waiting for me with her arms crossed and a scowl on her normally peaceful and inviting face. Even before I entered I could feel the room weighed down with her upset.

As soon as I came in she said to me, "You're late!"

This shocked me, because for the last six months I had been coming at 10:30, and I was right on time. I said to her, "No, I'm on time; it's 10:30. What time did you think I was supposed to be here?"

Without hesitation she said, "No, your appointment's at 10. It's been at 10 for six months."

Just as with Dale, the conversation speeded up and we had a couple of quick exchanges. My body began to buzz and once again my mind reeled. I felt tense, confused and frustrated because I knew I was right.

I felt myself want to argue with her, and then the whole scene became like a movie that I was watching. I saw her standing in front of me; I felt my body sitting in the chair, but somehow I was also watching the scene as a spectator.

A minute later I was back in my body listening to my brain chatter at itself: *but I'm right, what does it matter, who cares, but she's wrong, I need to defend myself, she's angry with me, don't make it mean anything…* the thoughts went on and on. I sat with my head in my hands, my thoughts twisting me as though I were being wrung out.

Then as before, energy rushed through me, I began to cry, and my body relaxed. Once again the atmosphere in the room softened. Allison took a breath, sat silently for a moment and then asked, "You okay?"

"Yes," I said," I'm just allowing the energy to move through me."

"It's a good idea to breathe and let the energy move. Let's start over," she said as she got up and told me to get ready so we could begin the massage.

We didn't speak about the appointment time again until the end of the session. I asked her what time she would like me to be there next month and she told me 10 o'clock. I said OK, and we never spoke about it again. As I left the office many questions came into my head. *Why do I care who's right and who's wrong? I can be there at either 10 or 10:30, it made no difference to me. Why did this stimulate so much intense energy in me and why was I reacting so differently than I would have in the past? Why was it so difficult for me to maintain the peacefulness and neutrality that I have grown to count on?* All good questions to ask God, I thought, so when I got into the car I took out my paper and pen and had that conversation.

Beth: Why did I have that meltdown with Allison? It should have been easy for me to just talk to her about it.

God: You are empathic, so you felt the energy even before you went into the room. Even now, there are pockets of stagnant energy within you. When this energy gets stimulated it causes you agitation or upset. These pockets are from other times and places, and they are very sensitive to anything that feels like conflict. To protect yourself, your ego mind armored these areas so that when there was a possible conflict you would defend yourself, guarded and protected by logic, technique, and evidence for proof of righteousness. But now you have opened yourself to more than evidence, you have opened yourself to truth.

Beth: What truth did I open myself to in this situation?

God: Truth is the all and the nothing. It is both your home away from the illusion that you see before you and the illusion itself. Truth is what you can only know in your sensory self. Truth takes root in your body and resonates throughout your form. This is why when you hear truth, see truth, or feel truth, you know that it is. You do not know how you know, but you know. Truth is everything without the words. Truth is everywhere yet lacks meaning.

You opened yourself to All That Is. You opened yourself to facts without meaning. It was a fact that Allison was upset. It was a fact that she told you that you were late. It was a fact that you remembered differently.

Beth: So why did I cry?

God: Tears are for you a releasing of the tight grip your ego mind holds over your existence. So many of the beings on your planet are bottled up and waiting for your corks to be released. You could feel it, couldn't you? When you cry, you relax and can breathe again. You're then able to feel the truth that is all around you.

Beth: Why did the desire to defend myself go away?

God: Once you opened yourself, All That Is could hold you. As I have said, truth is only part of consciousness. It was love that allowed you to release the old patterns and beliefs that kept you rigid and defending yourself. You were blind, then truth and love allowed you to see. Love is the meaning of all things. Truth cannot exist without love and love cannot exist without truth. As you sat in that massage room feeling the agitation within your energy system, you opened to truth and love was able to embrace you.

CHAPTER 25
A Home Filled With Love

"Nobody can teach you love. Love you have to find yourself, within your being, by raising your consciousness to higher levels."

~ Osho

THIS IS IT!

FINALLY IT WAS TIME TO SEE THE HOUSE, the one that matched our "perfect" list. Polly was waiting outside the beautifully landscaped property as we drove up. When we entered the front door we could see all the way through to a wall of glass framing the beautiful blue sky and expansive ocean view. Right away I knew this was it. But how could we afford it? The rent was much more than we'd planned for. We had some money from the sale of our house that we could dip into each month, but that wouldn't last long.

This IS the place, I thought, but how are we going to make this work? I turned to look at the rest of the house. The kitchen was done beautifully with green swirly granite countertops, tile accents, and stainless appliances. The whole place had bamboo floors. Upstairs, the master bedroom had a spectacular ocean view, and there were two more bedrooms that were perfect for our offices.

"But I thought this was a four-bedroom house…?" I questioned. We didn't need another bedroom, but I couldn't figure out where the other bedroom was. Polly directed us to a stairway. Down we went, and as we came to the bottom we saw what amounted to a whole little apartment.

There was a small living room, bathroom, bedroom, and the laundry room. Even though it was partly below ground level, it was finished as nicely as the rest of the house. Just then I realized that we could rent this bottom floor and it would pay for the shortfall.

I dragged Neill into the downstairs bedroom and told him my idea. If we had that option, we could make this place work. Neill agreed and we went and talked to Polly about it.

"Do you think the landlord would be okay if we rented this basement part out," we asked Polly?

"I don't know, but anything's possible. I'll check with John and let you know," she said.

One thing after another had fallen into place for us, so if this was meant to be we would know soon enough. Neill and I left and waited to hear from Polly.

The next day, once again I heard Polly say, "Beth, you're never going to believe this. I didn't think he'd say yes, but he's fine with you renting the bottom floor. The house is yours if you want it. The only problem is that they can't be out of the house until the second week of January. Will that be a problem for you?" she asked.

I told her I would talk to Neill and get back to her. Our house was closing escrow on December 17, so where could we go? We really loved this house, so we decided to find a solution. I started checking vacation rentals, but our dog and cat would be a problem. No animals, I heard from the realtors. It seemed unlikely that any vacation rental would allow them, especially the cat.

I couldn't imagine boarding our cat Socrates for six weeks. He's a little crazy and doesn't like to be handled. I decided to give it one more try and called another realtor. Marjorie answered the phone and we hit it off right away. She was from New York and we both had that wry East Coast sense of humor. We chatted and teased each other for about five minutes before I even told her why I called. She wanted to know about the pets, and she told me they'd be a real problem. I let her know that they were both well behaved and that I'd be willing to sign a contract saying I'd pay for any damage.

"My partner's going to kill me," she said, "but I like you and I've got the perfect place." She sent me the address. The next morning I drove up to the condo, which was right on the ocean. Marjorie was waiting for me, and said, "I think you're going to like this place. It's all furnished, and really quite fabulous." We walked in and everything she said was true. It had a big kitchen, beautiful furniture, a room to set up our temporary office and a large and elegant bathroom. And to get to the ocean, you only had to walk out the front of the building. It was lovely. And they were willing to take pets! We decided to rent it for six weeks so that we could move into the other place more slowly.

The house closed escrow on schedule. We rented a portable storage unit and filled it with the contents of our house. It was a relief to think about taking a month off before we had to unpack everything, so this interim time at the beach turned out to be a fabulous gift.

On December 17 we packed the last of our belongings into our cars, put Socrates into a kitty crate, grabbed Petra the poodle, and off we went on our new adventure. As I drove into Encinitas I saw the glow from the Self Realization Fellowship's temple gates. The Golden Lotus was decorated with purple and pink Christmas lights that lit up the sky. As we drove down the hill toward the ocean tears came to my eyes. In that moment, I knew that trusting and following our guidance is what we are all meant to do. It is our vehicle for creating grace and happiness in our lives.

FLOURISHING IN RESISTANCE

On New Year's Day, the air was crisp and the rising sun tinted the clouds pink and blue over the ocean. I walked to the overlook to see the waves forming Christmas-tree shapes. A pod of dolphins appeared, frolicking in the whitecaps. They jumped and spun and took turns riding the waves

As I watched, my recent worries about my son Spenser fell away. Following my intuition and trusting that everything would work out had been challenging, but as I sat there I felt so grateful. I was reminded that any concern about some unknown future was only my mind taking me away from the joy that is available in each moment.

Spenser was spending a few weeks with us because the heater in his apartment was broken and the roof was leaking. This caused the ceiling and the walls to perspire and mold, which aggravated his allergies. I had talked to his landlord and the handyman to resolve these issues, since he wasn't able to take care of these things himself because of his disabilities. I worried that we'd have to find him a new place to live once again.

There was always something going on with Spenser – something for me to deal with and to worry about. It started in preschool, when I'd hear from the teachers about how he wouldn't listen, couldn't follow directions, and how he'd pick fights with the other children. He's 23 now and I'm still the one who helps him shop, deals with his bosses and landlords, and makes sure he stays healthy. Of course none of this is his fault and I love him so much, but sometimes I get tired and feel hopeless that I can make a difference in his life. Standing there watching the dolphins, I was able to soften the tight grip on my concerns. I decided to talk to God about it.

Beth: I want very much to trust that you are taking care of Spenser so I can relax and know that he is cared for. But when I see his apartment with no heat, a leaky roof and the damp bedroom, I worry. Then my mind starts obsessing that I need to fix everything in his life. Is he being cared for? And if the answer is yes, then what do I do when I see broken heaters and leaky ceilings?

God: Yes, Spenser is being cared for. You find it hard to trust because you have been so diligent in your own care for him. You have helped him for many years with great love and compassion. This is a beautiful thing. But you have cast a net of care over his existence and now you are getting in the way of his fullness. This is neither good nor bad; it just is. If you allow it, now is the time to let him grow and blossom into more independence. Spenser is completely capable of flourishing. That is what he is here to do – to thrive even though appearances would have you believe otherwise.

His energetic collage – the energy strands that make him who he is in this lifetime – arrived to flourish in resistance. This is his heart's desire. All of which you speak of are things he can care for if he is allowed, and will do with ease.

Now for your second question; how do you trust that he

will be cared for when you see things in his life that concern you?

You stop and feel the resistance. Allow yourself time and space to be with these energies and balance them. Only get involved when you've completed balancing the energies, because imbalanced energies will cause ripples that impede his growth. You have done a beautiful job, which you came here to do, and now it is time for you to trust and let go. Now that is your job.

Beth: Let me see if I'm clear. Spenser came to this life to experience his challenges and thrive in spite of them, and I am getting in the way of his attaining fullness by casting a net of caring over him. Is that accurate?

God: Yes, but it is not that simple. He has come to experience flourishing in resistance. He does find safety in your net of caring, but it does not serve him fully.

Beth: Why does he need to experience this "flourishing in resistance?"

God: Without resistance there can be no ease, because one only exists with the other. In other lifetimes, with other energetic combinations, Spenser has experienced little resistance. Flourishing in resistance means living fully and expressing fully, while the opposite energies push against the ease.

As Spenser finds his way, has success, and builds confidence, the resistance dissipates, and then his life can be experienced fully. It is only in the realm of physical existence that this kind of blissful experience can be had. It is the homecoming he wants to experience, the bliss he knew as a nonphysical being that he wants to experience in this physical form. For him it will take this kind of resistance in order to experience that.

Beth: But to me, he looks uncomfortable and unsatisfied, rather than blissful. I only want what is best for him, so how can I support him?

God: Support him with your clear energetic presence and vision. You will know by how you feel. If you feel discomfort or tension within you, this is not supportive. When you feel joyful, happy, and peaceful, and are enjoying deep interactions with him, this is supportive. And of course you still may offer physical support as long as you're paying attention to your feeling state.

Beth: I'd like to be specific. For example, do I make phone calls regarding the leaky roof?

God: You are there to hold the space, you are there to ask questions, you are there to balance your energies so that he can mingle with them and feel the strength from them. Energy is the issue. Do you make phone calls with balanced or imbalanced energies? This is the question to ask yourself.

Beth: I worry about what might happen in the future, and try to manage problems before they turn into a mess.

God: Yes, things may turn into a mess and there may be things for you to do later. But there may not be. You cannot know. Your stress is caused by trying to manage things that haven't happened. And then the fear energies become imbalanced. This is when you are to pay attention to your energy, not to details of the situation.

Beth: So when I see a leaky roof and I worry that he will get sick, what exactly do I do in that moment?

God: You stop and get very present in the moment of the now. All else will fade. Allow thoughts to arise. These thoughts will carry you to energetic imbalances that need attending to. As the thoughts arise, the way to balance them will arise with them. If the balancing method does not come clearly, ask for it. Then do what has come to you to do.

There is no predetermined formula, no menu of holistic techniques. It is a moment by moment exercise and that is the joy of life. It is only then that life is truly experienced, in each moment. There is always an obvious next step as long as you are present in that moment of now. The next step will present itself to you.

Beth: Thank you.

I remembered all the times that I dealt with Spenser's issues from a place of upset, worry, or frustration. When he was 8 years old he was diagnosed as being developmentally delayed, or what used to known as "mentally retarded." I was stunned the first time a doctor used those words in relation to Spenser, and when that wore off I was devastated, scared and confused. It didn't seem accurate, because Spenser never fit clearly into this diagnosis. He was capable of doing things a developmentally delayed child should not have been able to do. Yes, he has short-term memory retrieval problems and cognitive reasoning challenges and so has trouble putting long-term plans together. But in my experience, when he's motivated by a strong desire, he can do almost anything.

For instance, a few years ago he wanted to ride in a limousine to a high school dance. He asked me if I would pay for it, and I told him no, but I'd be happy to drive him. He wouldn't let it go, and so I said that if he could figure out how to pay for and put it all together then he could go to the dance in the limousine.

So he did the research, talked to his friends' parents about sharing the costs, and with almost no help from me besides depositing the checks, he went to his dance with his friends in a shiny white stretch limousine. Knowing what he's capable of, I now get frustrated when he's not more proactive about his health and well-being, such as in this current apart-ment situation. Why am I taking care of things that he could probably do himself?

As I thought about this contrast, I realized that it's as if old movies that are stored in my body start playing out before I notice them. My frustration and worry is an old habit that pops up and then floats away like thoughts in a good medi-tation; it doesn't have the same hold on me as it used to. I don't relate to these fleeting emotions as the "truth" anymore. They are truly "energy in motion" and as long as I don't try to hold on to them, or make them mean anything, they leave as quickly as they come.

How could I possibly know what should be important to Spenser? We are different people; we've come into this life with different desires and wanting to experience different things. What constitutes a happy life to me obviously isn't the same for him, and why should it be?

After that day I gave him more space to figure out what was important to him, and asked more questions about what he wanted. I slowed down and waited before I jumped in to fix things for him. Now when he calls me and I ask him how his day was, and he tells me it was great because he watched three movies and picked up a pizza, instead of interrogating him about the details, I take a deep breath and simply ask if he's paying attention to his budget. If he says yes, I believe him. If he tells me he's happy, I believe him. This new rela-tionship is more peaceful and fun, filled with laughter and acceptance.

CHAPTER 26
The Shift

"Your sacred space is where you can find yourself again and again..."
- Joseph Campbell

LET IT SHINE

WE'D SPENT A LITTLE OVER MONTH at the vacation rental taking it easy, and now it was time to ramp up our energies for the big move into our new home. We hired movers, got the huge container with our furniture delivered, unpacked and set up our household. The beauty and peacefulness of living in Encinitas faded into the hectic reality of moving.

Beth: I'm really going to enjoy it here.

God: You do not like it already?

Beth: Well, with all the unpacking and arranging it's hard to stop long enough to enjoy it.

God: Dear one, do not miss the moments of your life.

Beth: OK, let me reword this – I love it here!

God: Good, and notice that sometimes you limit your enthusiasm. You think it is not there, but if you look, it is right under the surface. Always, always unearth your enthusiasm.

232

Let it shine. It is what creates the life you want.

Beth: Is there truth to the old "fake it till you make it" saying? If you're not feeling the enthusiasm, is it best to just fake it?

God: You are not really faking it. When you focus on your enthusiasm, even if it is a tiny little speck of your existence, you can then grow it out to be the major part of your awareness. So rather than "fake it till you make it," you focus on your enthusiasm, find it, and grow it.

Beth: What would you say to people who cannot even find a speck of enthusiasm?

God: I would say, stop focusing on what you do not enjoy and turn your attention to those things you do enjoy, even if it is a very small thing, such as the taste of a ripe peach. This is not fantasy, this is not faking it, this is not a farce. This is finding the essence of who you truly are and bringing that reality to light. Even when you touch it for a moment, you feel the truth. Find what is good in your life; it is full of gifts for you to discover and enjoy.

DIRECT CONNECTION

Inevitably, my circle of friends and family became aware of the unusual states I was experiencing. Some were curious, others skeptical, and some thought that I might be a conduit for them to experience, by proxy, my support and connection to oneness with All That Is. For instance, my friend Pamela wanted me to talk to God about her painful, on-again, off-again love relationship. I also wondered how much of my inner and outer journey would be best to share with people.

What would these conversations become, and how could they be useful to others?

Beth: God, people are becoming interested in what is happening to me. How much of our conversations am I to share?

God: I would like to speak clearly on this. The most important thing people should know is that they can experience all these things as well – and they can speak with me directly. When they understand that they are able to have a direct connection to All That Is and learn to trust that what is coming through them is their highest truth, then their messages will be received fully. They will most easily understand these concepts and feel the whole truth of them by direct contact.

As you continue your journey, your walk towards the future, your words will act as signposts for others, but not as their ultimate guide. Let them know that if they truly speak with me through their vessels – their bodies and hearts – they will get the answers that are most important to them. They will understand that they are me, and that we are all together. They will no longer feel alone.

Then they can enjoy creating their lives spontaneously, feeling the bliss you have felt. The purpose of embodied existence is to fully enjoy this plane. You are not meant to let the mind, what you call the ego, grab the reins of this life. Now is the time for the shift to a new way of being. For it to happen quickly and spontaneously, more of you need to start talking to me: God, All That Is, the universe, your higher self, or whatever name resonates most for each of you. Please, share these words as often as you can. Share through your actions, share in your conversations with other. This is the ultimate truth, the truth that everyone needs to hear.

CREATING PEACE

My friend Pamela was going through a very painful time. She and her partner Brian loved each other very much, but it seemed as if their relationship was doomed to fail. They were like oil and water. She loved holidays and birthdays; he didn't care to celebrate. She loved to decorate and have parties, but he liked to keep to himself. Pamela valued family and togetherness. She had made it clear from the beginning that she wanted a full, committed relationship. But Brian, having had many painful breakups, wanted something more casual, with independence and freedom. Now she had ended it for the third time, and was at her wit's end.

Beth: Pamela wants me to ask you some questions for her. Would that be in her highest good?

God: She can ask directly. The answers then would be more in tune with who she is and what she is able to hear. And as always, I am willing to answer as you ask.

Beth: We both understand that. And yet she still wants me to do the asking. The question is, how can she move through this transition with Brian in the most peaceful way?

God: The issue is not the transition, the issue is peace. There are many areas of Pamela's life that are not peaceful. She is shifting into a new world of perception, shifting from struggle into the joy that she and all others are looking for. So she is to focus on joy. As she lives in alignment with her truth, life will shift and peace will come.

Beth: Then what does she do with the pain she feels?

God: There is a difference between pain and suffering. This type of suffering is a creation of the mind – an emotion created by thoughts around past and future events that are not happening as we wish. As she focuses in each moment there is no suffering. There is only energy to move – stagnant energy caused by the emotions, which are created by thoughts. This energy can feel physically painful at times, but it is only when meaning is attached to this physical pain that suffering begins.

Beth: Are you saying to ignore the thinking that causes the suffering, or to ignore the pain?

God: The goal is not to rid yourself of pain or even suffering, but to create peace. Always notice what is there; do not ignore it. Be with, celebrate, or deal with the present moment as your heart knows to do. This is the truth of how it all works. Every moment is now. The now is your life to be celebrated.

Beth: She wants to know if it can be beneficial to "be with" the pain and suffering, to experience it fully.

God: Pamela is making choices that take her to places she needs to go. This is not good or bad, and there is no reason for her to feel sad or guilty. But when she does have painful feelings that cause her suffering, she can bridge the gap with the truth that she finds in her heart.

Sometimes though – because many of you believe life is hard and only hard work will get to you where you want to go – people must fully experience suffering to arrive at a place of no suffering. Sometimes people need to experience all that there is to experience in order to choose what feels better. But that is not required. There is always a choice – a choice between suffering and peace. When you choose suffering, it is not a problem. It is neither good nor bad; it is simply a day of peace that you are missing. So choose wisely.

Beth: What can she do in the moments that she feels pain to shift to peace?

God: It is in choosing peace, committing to peace, that she will find peace. She truly does know what to do. So I will say this to you, Pamela: you get to choose, and you know this. The choice of suffering or peace is yours. I am always here with you, you are never alone. Your point of peace is knowing that we are together, that you are cared for and loved. Your practice is to know the one that you are, not the one you think you are. Not your future or past. The one you have been looking for is here, in this point of presence. Be with me here and you will know the peace that you are looking for. It is always available to you. It is not fake; it is the one truth.

You are never alone; you are always one with All That Is. Feel the truth in these words. Do they resonate with you as you read this? Sit with this feeling and let the energy move through you, and then in each moment choose your next step. Not next week, not next year, not tomorrow, not in an hour, but right now. Feel the energy of us – take a step, feel the energy of us, then take another step, and this will lead you to where you want to go – the home filled with love – filled with peace – filled with care– filled with the energy of wholeness that you are.

CHAPTER 27

Surrender, Surrender, Surrender

"Always say "yes" to the present moment. What could be more futile, more insane, than to create inner resistance to what already is? What could be more insane than to oppose life itself, which is now and always now? Surrender to what is. Say "yes" to life – and see how life suddenly starts working for you rather than against you."

- Eckhart Tolle

THE SEARCH

AFTER A COUPLE OF WEEKS we were settled in to our new home in Encinitas. It was like living in my own fairytale; this lifestyle had everything I've ever wanted; in fact, it was better than I had imagined. I wake up every morning and turn over to see the ocean, and at night, I watch the moon in the dark sky radiate its silvery gold reflection on the water as it sinks toward the horizon.

We often eat on our deck, with a view of the endless blue water and the crows playing in the eucalyptus trees. The air smells of salt and cools our skin with moisture from the sea. The spacious master bathroom is a wonderful place for my

238

bath meditations. The oval tub has a wide shelf for my candles, crystals, and essential oils. I look out my office window to see a peaceful, tree-lined street.

Many days we walk across the railroad tracks to the quaint downtown area to eat lunch. Then we stroll to the beach with a warm cup of coffee to sit and watch the surf for a while. Sometimes we wander the flowering gardens of the Self Realization Fellowship on the cliffs overlooking the ocean. We are very happy here.

Our new town has a thriving new age community, so we asked Polly if she could recommend a yoga studio within walking distance. She said, "I can recommend one, but it's not that close."

I told her thanks, but that we were hoping to not to have to drive everywhere. She said, OK, you just try all the yoga studios within walking distance and when you're done, try the Soul of Yoga. I promise you'll never go anywhere else."

I laughed and said, "Okay, we'll try your yoga studio, but I am still going to try all others as well.

Neill and I went online and discovered that Encinitas had more yoga studios per capita than just about anywhere else in the world. We made a list of the closest ones and started taking classes.

We tried anahata yoga, hot yoga, vinyasa, restorative, and kundalini yoga. At each studio we enjoyed the people and the classes, but none seemed like the perfect fit. Finally we took Polly's advice and went to the Soul of Yoga. Tom Kelly and his wife Trisha had started the studio in their home over ten years ago. Now they've relocated to a big, beautiful and serene space. We wanted not only a yoga studio, but a community, and as soon as we walked in we felt at home.

On this Sunday morning there must have been over fifty people in the large room. Colorful yoga mats were laid out across the hardwood floor. A large, elegant oil painting of Krishna, with Radha leaning her head against his shoulder, adorned the front wall, and there wasn't a mirror in sight. I looked around and wondered where we would find room for our mats, but before the thought could fully form in my mind someone tapped my shoulder and said, "Let's find you a spot."

I turned around and saw a woman in her fifties with long blonde hair and a warm smile on her face. She led us into the sea of people and without a word they began moving their mats to make room for us. As I laid out my mat and got a bolster I felt the room humming with a happy and vibrant energy.

Up front, Tom rang his Tibetan bowl and the room became quiet. I was taken aback by how much he looked like my father. Probably in his late fifties, Tom had the same small frame and athletic build, the same shaped face and identical nose. They both had intense eyes and a big presence. It was strange sitting down to do yoga with my dead father's doppelganger!

Tom's playful and almost childlike presence could be seen in his broad smile. This was a very different kind of yoga class than I had ever experienced. He talked A LOT, and it was as though he was channeling some higher power. He talked about God, Krishna, Source and Jesus Christ. He made up sayings like "Relax your jaw and you will be in awe," "Don't be shy to sigh," and "Don't forget to open your joyful presence." He told us that ADD means Attention Divinely Directed, and FAITH means Full Attention in the Heart.

Coming from his mouth, the silly sayings became profound truths.

And yes, he did also teach yoga, but as he gave directions he said to pay more attention to the energy moving through your body than the accuracy of the pose. This is where I belong, I thought.

As the class continued, Tom's explicit spiritual language surprised me, because the other yoga studios I'd been to did not talk much about this. I realized that you CAN say the word God and talk about spirit, and people will show up. This room was now packed with over fifty people and they seemed hungry for this kind of spiritual food.

I felt inspired and hopeful, because when I got that message in the bath to get out in the world and be an example of embodied spirit, I didn't know how that would happen. I guessed it would be through our seminars and workshops, but when Neill and I conducted our seminars we always made it a point to not use spiritual language so we didn't turn people off. But after all my changes, I knew I couldn't teach anything now without including a spiritual aspect.

At the same time, I didn't have a spiritual background or even the language to talk about it in the traditional sense. Yes I had all these experiences, but I didn't feel comfortable discussing them. I still didn't want to alienate people or have them think I was crazy.

But Tom spoke very explicitly about these things. Maybe that was because before Tom and Trisha got married, he had been a monk at the Self-Realization Fellowship for thirty years, and he was so practiced in spiritual language that it now came naturally to him. In any case, it was just what I needed to hear.

That day I joyfully left the class, having found a new yoga studio AND a spiritual community. I especially realized that people were craving connection to their source, wanting to live knowingly as spiritual beings. The more I listened to others talk openly about these things, the more comfortable I became talking about them, and the more open I was to the full range of what this life had in store for me. I was so grateful for finding my incredible new home and to be living in Encinitas. Finding The Soul of Yoga was icing on the cake.

CRY FREELY WITHOUT CENSORING

Beth: The new yoga studio is wonderful; I can be in touch with All That Is very easily there. Yesterday a strong energy was running through me, and I found myself crying, as I so often do these days. Can you explain this to me?

God: Yes. When you are in touch with me/us, you know the truth of our oneness. You cry with joy because you recognize the truth of who you are.

Beth: What does the crying do?

God: The crying releases energies that hold you – what you think is you – together. It is a way to open, to expand into All That Is. The tears also come with delight of All That Is, as a joyous, blissful state envelops you. And it is also a collage of all emotions rolled into one. When the tears come, let them flow. Do not stay all wrapped up, but unroll, relax and let it flow. This is the practice.

Beth: In class, I had the urge to cry freely without censoring. But I didn't want to disturb the others.

God: Censoring keeps you bottled up and prevents the

energy from moving smoothly. Slow down, be patient, and allow. You are going through many changes and as you shift you are able to hold more energy. The energy in your system needs to move for the shift to happen easily, and yoga is wonderful for that. Just relax and enjoy the ride.

Beth: I am so grateful and happy to be in this new house, with this new yoga studio. These spaces enrich me so. Thank you, thank you, for all your support.

God: Dear one, you are so welcome. Gratitude is what moves things forward. Gratitude and love have led you to this place. Always, always ask for what it is that you want.

NO QUESTION IN HER MIND

Just as Polly predicted, we found a home at the Soul. I took four or five yoga classes a week. Besides Tom, I got to know Trisha, his wife and the cofounder. She was an extraordinary woman – beautiful, grounded and confident, yet at the same time she was very playful and loved interacting with everyone as she taught.

One of her classes was called Metaphysics and Masters, where she would focus on a particular spiritual teacher each time. We learned about their history and teachings, and she would read their quotations.

Like Tom, she spoke about spirituality with conviction. One day she talked about reincarnation as if there was no question in her mind that it was real. I wondered how she could speak so knowingly about things that can't be proven. I had a sense that reincarnation was true, but I wasn't sure about the details. What was the truth?

Beth: Is it true that there are multiple lifetimes, and that we reincarnate?

God: Not as you know it.

Beth: Please explain.

God: There is energy that expresses from All That Is into form, but it is not the exact same energy every time.

Beth: Can you give me an example?

God: You came and are expressing in this form you call Beth. The energy that is you has been before, but not only this energy and not all this energy. You will come again – but not all of you, and there will be some different energies that come as well.

Beth: Are you saying that the energy that makes up me is a composite of energies from many people from different lifetimes?

God: Yes. I am saying that the "you" in this lifetime is not the exact same group of energies that you will be in other lifetimes. The energies recombine to express a new being.

Beth: So there could be many lifetimes, but each one is a combination of different people from different lives?

God: There are not separate lives; there is only one, expressing simultaneously. This might seem confusing to you until you feel the truth of it for yourself.

Beth: I'd like to explore my previous beliefs. Here is the condensed version of what I thought about reincarnation:

1. My "soul" passes from one lifetime to another.
2. There might be a group of souls that move from lifetime to lifetime together.
3. There is something called Karma, or lessons, that move with each individual soul.

Let's start with number one. Do I have a soul?

God: What you call your soul is the connection and merging into form of All That Is.

Beth: Does All That Is merge all at once into each embodied expression of life?

God: Yes, in a way.

Beth: How can so many expressions happen all at once?

God: Time is not linear as you know it; multiple lines of time can happen all at once.

Beth: Can I really ever understand this with my mind?

God: It is good that you ask, because it will bring more understanding to the world. And you will understand what you are able to hear each time you ask. True understanding can only be felt, not in the mind but in the body.

Beth: My mind feels tired now. But I understand this at some level, and I feel the truth of it.

God: You are here to express the inexpressible. Rest now, and integrate what you've learned. Don't push so hard; there is more than enough time.

THE ARCHETYPAL ENERGIES WITHIN US

I thought about what it might mean to be a collection of energies rather than just this one exact "me" reincarnating over and over again.

I had heard about the concept of archetypal energies and wondered if that was what God was talking about. The idea of archetypes goes back to the time of Plato. It is said that archetypal patterns were imprinted on the soul at the time of birth, and these patterns play out during one's lifetime.

There are also modern philosophers and writers that talk

about archetypes and how they play a role in our lives. For example, an idea widely attributed on the Internet to Carl Jung is that a human being is inwardly whole, but that most of us have lost touch with important parts of ourselves, and that archetypes are energies of the collective unconscious and are at work in each of our lives.

Well, what if they aren't just working in our lives, but they are actually part of us – a part of who we are. I wondered if this was true, and how would we know which archetypal energies were part of us? My mind wandered back to when I was a child and first heard about Abraham Lincoln. I was obsessed by stories of his life, the Civil War, and his desire to abolish slavery. I read everything that I could get my hands on about him, despite my dyslexia.

I also had a particular fascination with John F. Kennedy, Martin Luther King, and Mother Teresa, as so many others do. I wondered what, if any, connection there was between the idea of archetypes and coming into this life as a combination of past life energies. What if there was something you admired about someone, and that the energy was alive and flourishing in you, or even wanting to express itself in you? Are these the strands of energy that made up our present incarnation?

This all seemed important, but incomplete. Then one day during a bath I heard these words, "You're not expressing yourself fully, and it is time to do so." By now, I didn't need to write down all my active imagination conversations. I would just speak out loud as though God was there talking to me, though me.

So I asked, "What do you mean? And what would you like me to do about it?"

I heard back that I had strands of energy that have not yet been expressed, but were ready to emerge.

Then visual images of the people I admired streamed across my mind as if there was a movie projector in my head. And I heard, "These archetypal energies are within you but not expressing through you."

The film that was playing in my head slowed down, and Martin Luther King gradually became the only image. His great passion filled my body as though it was mine. I could feel a vibration welling up in me as if I were a bottle of champagne being shaken, my cork quivering and waiting to burst.

Then one by one I felt them. Mother Teresa's deep caring, warmth and love filled me. I could feel her heart in my heart, and the complete and unconditional love that she experienced as her daily companion. Kennedy's charisma and Lincoln's eloquence – one by one they came to me and showed me what quality of theirs wanted to be expressed through me. I could have stopped and called these visual images ridiculous, but then I would not have experienced this powerful transformation.

I was guided to bring these qualities into me. Each of these people stepped forward in my mind's eye and handed me a quality. With each precious gift tears would roll down my cheeks and drop in the water below.

Mother Theresa handed me her unconditional love and told me to place it in my heart and allow it to grow and blossom into a great wave of compassion that would ripple through the world. I took this love from her hands and brought it to my heart and with a whoosh it was drawn into me, as my breath was taken away and then given back.

Martin Luther King gave me his passion and asked me to place it in my third chakra right above my belly button, and Kennedy's magnetism went into my creative center – my second chakra.

Lastly came Lincoln. As he approached I could feel the

storm brewing, and then it was like a faucet turned on and I began to sob. At first I couldn't take what he was offering me. I felt so inadequate and unprepared. I was terrified to speak in front of people, so how could I possibly express his quality of eloquence?

Then a blanket of peace covered me and wrapped me in its gentle weave. I heard these words, "There is much you were meant to say and now is the time to say it. Surrender, surrender, surrender. You are up to this task. Express this quality fully and completely; take this gift now and bring truth to the world." Lincoln stretched out his arms to me and as he did I stretched mine out to him. He handed me his eloquence as if he were passing a torch so I could light this flame within me. As I took this gift in my hands I knew where to place it. My throat chakra began to tingle even before my hands reached it.

A vacuum seemed to form, pulling the quality into me like a magnet to its polar mate. Again I lost my breath, and I began to tingle all over and sank deeper into the bathtub until I was completely submerged. I stayed until every ounce of breath in me evaporated and then I shot out the water like a whale coming up for air. I knew something important just happened.

For the days and weeks to come I felt more connected, grounded and confident. I'm learning to follow the subtle clues and trust the urges that arise. There is so much more to reality than we see and hear with our physical eyes and ears. All the answers I seek are within me and all of the support I need is there as well.

The same is true for you. It doesn't matter whether or not you believe in reincarnation, or archetypal energies; are you fully expressing what you've come here to express?

CHAPTER 28

Flowing With the Rhythm of Life

"Life is a series of natural and spontaneous changes. Don't resist them - that only creates sorrow. Let reality be reality. Let things flow naturally forward in whatever way they like."

- Lao Tzu

ACT FROM LOVE

A LARGE POSTER OF DOLPHINS leaping in a turquoise ocean caught my attention at the yoga studio, and on a closer look, I saw that the poster was advertising a trip to Bimini to swim with dolphins, led by Tom and Trisha. A rush of energy shot through me and I immediately turned to Neill and said, "I've got to go on this trip."

It's long been a dream of mine to swim with these beautiful, playful and peaceful animals, and now here was a chance to not only do that, but to go with my own spiritual community. As usual, my mind took over and I started wondering whether it was the best use of my time and money.

Beth: I'm having a hard time deciding about this dolphin trip. We have some money in the bank, but we need to be mindful of where we spend it. Is this trip in my highest good and is it the best use of our money?

God: Money is energy, energy is flow, and flow leads to places, experiences, and people. Money allows you to see the flow of energy as a physical expression. It's like a catalyst that directs the flow in a particular direction. So to discuss money in the bank is to talk about an object with no value. Money only has value when you put it into motion.

So the value of money is in its motion. There will always be catalysts to start or direct the flow of energy, whether it's money or something else. Your question really is, will you be safe and cared for if you use this money now to start this flow. Is it not?

Beth: Yes, I have some concerns about the future. If I spend all this money, will there be enough to pay our expenses? It might not make sense for me to have these concerns after all I've experienced, but here they are. So yes, will I continue to be safe and cared for if I spend this money now?

God: Oh, dear one, you are going through a process. Please do not worry about the destination. Do not concern yourself with your continued patterns. They are coming up so that you may clear them, and as you do, you expand further and further into All That Is. If you follow your guidance, and you hold the space of all things possible, and if you keep the energy flowing, then you will always be safe and cared for.

As you know, words mean different things to different people. You must clearly define these words for yourself in order to support your process. What is it you mean by "safe and cared for?"

Beth: I mean, if I run out of money will you continue to care for me, and will I be able to maintain my peaceful state?

God: Pay attention – I want to clearly state this now. Notice that money is a hot button for you, you attach it to your safety and peace of mind. The only time you aren't able to maintain your peaceful state is when you bring thoughts about what might happen in the future into your present moment. Events surrounding money take you out of the present more quickly than most things.

This moment is your place of peace. This moment is your place of clarity. This moment, standing here and now, is the place where your joy and bliss comes from. Look around you right now, dear one, and see the beauty of this moment. There is nothing more than this, no truth other than this, nowhere else to be than here. Now you tell me; in this present moment, are you not cared for? Are you not at peace?

Beth: Yes, this moment is perfection. I see the vastness of the ocean and I feel the cool breeze on my skin. If I sit and just be here in this moment and think about nothing else, I am at peace.

But there are so many people that are not in a beautiful place, and that do not have warm clothes or a full stomach. What about them? How can they feel the joy and peace that I feel right now?

God: What creates joy and peace for you? Is it not that same as what creates joy and peace for all others? You are a defined individual, created here to express itself through the body. The others you speak of must find their happiness in their own moments of now.

As they feel into each individual moment, they will be able to move into a place of creation and find the peace that is heaven on earth.

Beth: But what if they don't have money to pay the rent, or any way to feed themselves? With empty stomachs, how can they feel peaceful, never mind joyful?

God: There are many around your world that live in conditions that you would consider dire, and they are more joyful than many who have much money. And there are also those who suffer. These things are not exactly what they appear to be, although when people feel hungry it is most definitely real in their experience. You are all here to experience different things in order to move to your next level of evolution. Each person perceives them in their own way. Some will experience their stomachs empty, some will experience pain, and some will be at peace and find joy in their lives even while they are experiencing situations that you would consider unbearable. In each moment you get to choose peace or suffering. If peace is chosen, there is always reason for joy.

I would like to offer a different way of looking at this.

If you consider the events around the world as necessary parts of the whole cycle of life, then you can hold the space of love that will allow it to transform more easily. This is how the world transforms and evolves. There is truth and there is love.

If everyone who is in a place of physical comfort holds the vibration of love, it allows the other ones to move out of discomfort more easily. It is an evolutionary process; no one needs to suffer. Remember, suffering is a manifestation of thought; suffering is not the truth.

Beth: What else I can do to support others who seem to be suffering, other than holding a space of love?

God: First, do not underestimate holding a pure state of love. And of course, do what you are moved to do in each moment. I caution you though; pay attention to the energy that motivates you. Notice your motivations, your intentions – those things that cause you to act. The energy will either lead you to something that supports evolution or detracts from it. There is no good or bad way; it is just a process, so do not distress yourself over it. As you get more and more conscious, these are the things to pay attention to.

Beth: Could you give me a specific example?

God: Yes. If you are in the present moment and you find yourself with someone who is hungry and you are drawn out of love to feed them, then feed them. If you are in the present moment and you are stimulated by something you observe or something that you hear and you are drawn out of love to do something about it, then do that. This supports the evolutionary process, and also enhances your own evolution.

But if you are only doing it out of some belief that you should, that you are obligated, or that you fear the consequences if you don't, then the "doing" is to be avoided. That kind of action does not support evolution.

Now let's talk about thought alone. If a thought comes to your mind, such as, "Oh, I feel so good, but what about the people who don't have this beautiful view, don't have money to pay their rent, or don't have food to eat. They must be suffering." Then you too begin to suffer. This serves no one.

It lowers the vibration of the planet and slows the movement towards evolution. When these thoughts come to mind, raise your vibration instead.

Beth: How do I raise my vibration?

God: See truth, and hold it in the arms of love. Send this creative energy of love out into the world towards all others who do not have the feelings of joy or bliss that you have. Send that joy to them and see it enveloping them. It is most important to keep your vibration as high as you can, because when the opportunity arises, you can serve no one unless your vibration is high.

Before, we talked about money as a catalyst for moving energy. Always ask yourself, "How do I want to move the flow of energy? Am I moving it in a direction that all will enjoy, or in a direction that no one will enjoy?" Your job is to create love and light in your life. Be happy, dear one, for this will create the most joy for others.

If you pay attention to each moment, you will know if it is your time to act, because you will be doing it before you even notice. If you have missed the moment and are not sure, then stop, become peaceful, and ask if it is time to act. If the answer is yes, move forward into that action. Do not try to look ahead, because you never know where those actions may lead! Even actions that seem to lead away from what you want may lead to a glorious place for you and others. Follow your guidance, dear one, always follow your guidance.

Beth: I want to make sure I understand. When I see what looks like suffering in the moment, and I am drawn to do something by love, then that is the time to act. Is that correct?

God: Yes, very good.

Beth: How do I know if I'm drawn to act from love?

God: Love does not come with fear; it travels alone. You will feel some connection, and then you will be acting. This is being drawn by love.

Beth: Would you give me an example?

God: If you are on a street corner and see someone sitting against a building with tattered clothing, asking for money, examine your reaction. If you first feel a sense of connection but it quickly becomes intertwined with concern, worry or sadness, then this is muddled energy. It would be best to wait and clear the energy first, by getting back to the pure connection and love. Only then act.

This is a practice that does not come easily for the majority of you. You are conditioned to protect yourselves, so that in the same instant that you connect, you become separated. More specifically, in that split second that you have an urge to give money or do something to help, you immediately start thinking. Your judgments, your opinions and your fears cloud your ability to perceive the truth.

When you notice yourself hesitating, practice discerning your first reaction. The very first reaction leads to love and guides your way. If it is gone, wait until you can get back to love.

REFLECTIONS IN THE WATER

It was decided: the trip was booked and we were going to Bimini to swim with the dolphins! So I started to practice imaginary snorkeling in the bathtub – dunking my head under the water and blowing out as though I was clearing my snorkel pipe. Water draws me like nothing else, and yet it has always scared me too. I love living by the water, sitting by the water, and listening to the water. I love all things watery, even washing dishes and letting the warm glistening liquid run over my hands. But for some reason I have difficulty getting in deep water, especially cold deep water. But I wasn't going to let this fear stop me from realizing my dream.

I noticed that when I held my breath under the water I felt panicked, so I used Psych-K and did a balance. I sat with my eyes closed my hands and feet crossed, and said, "I feel comfortable and safe in the water." As I repeated this phrase over and over, I felt a rush of emotions: first tension, then fear, and then tears flooded my eyes.

In my mind's eye I saw a rushing river in front of me, and a person tumbling down head over heels with their arms flailing, hitting the rocks along the way. I realized that the person was me, desperately trying to get my head above the water enough to get a breath of air! In that moment I knew I was about to die painfully in this river. My heart raced so fast I thought it would explode and I felt the air being sucked from my lungs.

And then I was thrown back into the present moment. I opened my eyes and realized that I must have just experienced a scene from a past life. It was a real memory – I had been in that water – but never in this lifetime. It was as if I had been thrown back in my body seconds before I died in that river. *That's it,* I thought; *that was the root of this fear.* I couldn't leave myself in that overwhelmed state, so I relaxed until I could re-imagine the event to help transform the experience.

I closed my eyes and put myself back in the vision of that turbulent river. Again I felt the water flow past me, and a balance came to mind, "I flow naturally with the rhythm of the water." I repeated it over and over until I imagined myself flowing in harmony with the water. I now easily bypassed the rocks and moved gracefully through the water. Then I saw myself emerge from the water and walk onto the shore.

I was momentarily relieved, but the vision wasn't through with me yet. The ground beneath me began to move like a rolling earthquake, and as my feet hit the ground my body was unsteady and shaking. I realized that my fear of the water was affecting my day-to-day life. I needed to balance for more than just my fear of the water. I was not flowing with life – the gentle rhythm and subtle movement of my own life. So my next balance became, "I flow easily with the rhythm and movement of my life. I repeated this until I felt more stable and present. I slowly opened my eyes and knew something important had shifted in me.

The water had more to teach me. Even before I left for Bimini, it was helping me to understand myself better and I knew that it wasn't going to end there. It was clear to me now that this trip was meant to be – that it would be the most mystical, magical transforming adventure of my life.

CHAPTER 29
It All Became So Clear

"For each of us, then, the challenge and opportunity is to cherish all life as the gift it is, envision it whole, seek to know it truly, and undertake – with our minds, hearts and hands – to restore its abundance. It is said that where there's life there's hope, and so no place can inspire us with more hopefulness than that great, life-making sea – that singular, wondrous ocean covering the blue planet."

- Carl Safina

WHAT FELT LIKE FOREVER

THE LARGE CATAMARAN SAILED far out in the magnificent turquoise ocean on our first day of the dolphin trip. We were 24 in all, including the crew. Early on we stopped and got in the water to practice using our snorkels and fins. I don't swim very well and so before I got in the water I grabbed one of the brightly colored noodles that lay at the back of the boat. I managed the snorkel properly, but the fins had a mind of their own; the front of me swam one way while the fins pulled me like a rubber band in the other direction. After some practice, we all got back in the boat and we sailed on in search of dolphins.

Everyone was eager to see them; that's why we were here, of course. We'd been warned we might not see any today, so we all tried to relax and enjoy the sights: the ocean in blended shades of azure and bright turquoise, the distant green jewel that was the island of Bimini, and the large school of flying fish that overtook our boat and then raced on ahead.

I felt a bit of anxiety brewing under the surface. I was drawn to the water, but only marginally enjoyed being on a boat. However, the incredible beauty and the thought of seeing dolphins overcame my tension.

I sat down and hung my feet over the bow. The air was crisp and the ocean warm as bathwater. Suddenly I heard one of the crew yell, and we all looked in the direction he was pointing, where a dolphin leaped out of the water and then splashed back in. "Get your gear on!" the crewmembers yelled.

Everybody rushed over to their gear and started frantically pulling on their wet suits and fins, and hanging their snorkel gear around their necks. I wasn't going to miss this, despite my misgivings, so I did as everyone else and got ready to go. There were only a couple of dolphins so everybody hurried to get into the water before they swam away. Finally it was my turn.

The rest were already swimming out from the boat following the dolphins. I jumped into the water and put my head down as I was taught, knowing that I would breathe through the pipe. I inhaled, only to discover that in the excitement my mouthpiece was still hanging from my neck and not in my mouth, and because of my eagerness I had also forgotten to get a noodle. What seemed like a gallon of water came rushing down my throat.

I couldn't breathe, and began to panic as my lungs constricted and my heart raced. I frantically looked around for someone to help me but there was no one in sight. The waves splashed over my head and stung my eyes. I started choking and coughing, and as I tried to breathe, more water rushed in. No one saw me flailing and sinking into the water. The memory of drowning that I'd had in the bathtub before I left home popped into my head. Was this it? Had I come to Bimini to die again, another painful death in the water? NO! I thought, and with a blast of adrenaline I pushed my head above water and screamed, "HELP!"

Then I remembered the balance I did that day in the bathtub: I flow naturally with the rhythm of the water. *You've got to be kidding,* I thought myself, *I'm dying here.* But just as those words scrolled through my mind I was lifted out of the water. It was Sukuma, and she looked like an angel, with the sun at her back creating a halo of light around her. I continued to cough, but she wrapped her arms around me, and soon I was able to relax and breathe naturally. She led me back to the boat and helped me on board. I've been adventurous my whole life, but never before had I been so terrified that I was about to die.

I probably wasn't in the water very long, although it felt like forever. But why did this happen? I was so clearly guided go on this trip to Bimini, and now, shaken from this experience, I wondered why I had come. The rest of the day I barely got in the water, and when I did, I made sure I was close to one of the crewmembers.

RELAX

The next day on the way out we once again stopped for some snorkeling practice in shallow water. I wanted so much to manage these fins, to make them push me where I want them to go. I was a bit jealous, watching everyone else swimming, having fun, and exploring the water with ease. I sat on the boat thinking about my experience in the water yesterday and wondering if I should just stay put and watch the dolphins from this safe haven.

But I hadn't come all this way just to have a boating experience, I was sure of that. I couldn't let my fear of the water stop me. If I could just get the hang of these fins and the snorkeling thing I'd understand why I was here.

I looked around to find someone in the crew who would help me learn the ins and outs of snorkeling. I saw Sukuma, the dear soul who helped me the day before, but she was busy helping others. Then I saw her husband Nipun in the water and wondered if he would teach me.

So I put on my gear and edged my way to the back of the boat, and gently sank into the water. There he was, as if waiting for me. I said to him, "I wonder if you would spend some time letting me watch how you move your legs so I can understand how to do it."

"Well, what I would like you to do," he said, "is nothing."

"What?"

"That's right, nothing. Do you know how to float?" he asked.

"Yes, that I can do!" I smiled at him, relieved he asked me to do something I could actually do.

"Okay then, I want you to float face down in the water, breathing only through your snorkel gear. Don't move your legs or your arms or even your head. Just float. Keep this up until you're completely relaxed, and then and only then get up."

So I put my snorkel in my mouth, made sure my mask was on correctly, and I lay face down in the water. I almost panicked because I felt as if I couldn't breathe, but I soon realized that the snorkel was in my mouth and I was breathing fine. I took slow deep breaths, and with each breath I asked a different part of my body to relax. Consciously breathing, consciously relaxing.

For the first time I noticed all the beautiful creatures below me: fish with blue and yellow stripes, coral that looked like a brain, tiny little fish scooting in and out between the rocks. There was a whole world down here, that just moments before I was unable to see. Then I tensed up as my insecurity returned. I reminded myself to relax again. The feelings of calm and tension moved through me in alternating waves.

This went on for what seemed like hours. Finally only the peace remained, the deepest peace I'd ever felt. And as I sank into this physical peace, new sensations were available to me. Each ripple of the water moved through me as if it was inside my skin rather than outside, easy and flowing. The sun shining through the water created rainbows that shimmered on the rocks and danced on the fish. I didn't just see these things, but actually felt them in my body. I just wanted to stay in this glorious, extraordinary state forever, but I knew Nipun was waiting, so I decided to see what else he had in store for me.

As I poked my head up from the water he was waiting there patiently, as if he had never moved. I looked at him and smiled and all he said was, "Now it's time to move your legs." He asked me to go under the water and watch him. As he swam, my legs seemed to just start moving. It was like a miracle; the day before I couldn't navigate through the water at all, but now I was moving skillfully.

As the day went on, I only had to remember the feeling of relaxation and it came back to me. Relax, relax, relax. This became my mantra. Now more than a mental concept, it had become a physical experience, an expression of who I truly am.

Later that day, Nipun asked me how I was, and how I enjoyed the swim. At that moment my gratitude for his kindness, patience and caring brought me to tears. I had experienced a kind of freedom that I had never known – in or out of the water. All I could do is smile and cry. And seeing me, tears came to Nipun's eyes as well. It was the most amazing day. In that genuine state of full body/mind relaxation came everything: all that there is and all that I could ever want.

RECEIVE

Early the next morning before we were to leave on our dolphin excursion, I was exploring the compound when I heard the song Ong Namo, by Snatam Kaur, the music I listen to daily at home during my morning meditations. I felt compelled to follow it, pulled as if a rope was tied around my waist. Up the stairs I went until I saw everyone in the meditation room. People sat in a circle of chairs, and in the center were four yoga mats with someone lying down on each one. I entered the room and realized they were doing some sort of a healing circle. I squatted down to sit behind the chairs. Then I saw Tricia, my yoga teacher, pointing to the chair inside the circle. I sat as requested and began participating in the healing.

Within five minutes, I felt a tap on my shoulder, and Tricia whispered in my ear, "Just receive." She now pointed to one of the empty mats in the center of the circle.

As I lay down in the center, I kept hearing her words over and over in my head – just receive, just receive, just receive. It brought back yesterday's mantra – relax, relax, relax. As my body and mind released their tension, tears came. This sort of thing wasn't unfamiliar to me; sometimes I cried in yoga class. But this seemed different, as though I was releasing another internal fear that I'd only just discovered. I've committed to being an open channel and so I just let it flow. Then the tears subsided I went back in my chair.

When Tricia completed the circle she said, "If anyone needs an extra hug before we leave, come and stand on the blue mat." I felt compelled to follow my inner guide and stand on that blue mat.

One by one people came up and embraced me, and then began to embrace each other. As the circle of embrace grew the energy grew stronger, until it was palpable. I cried again, feeling the same profound sense of comfort as when my mother held me in her lap as a child. Others began to cry as well and I sensed that they felt that same feeling of comfort, warmth and safety. I stood in the center of this loving circle and felt so grateful. But every moment has to come to an end and I opened my mouth and said, "Okay I'm hot. Let me out!"

Everybody laughed and let go. Tricia remarked about the energy that still lingered in the room, saying that this is the energy of the New Age, of the feminine, of the mother. I loved the synergy of the moment, and I left that room with a new mantra. The words "relax and receive" rang in my ears.

Relax and receive, and all will be yours.

THE MESSAGE

Now all the pieces were falling into place. This was our last day here, the day I encountered the old spotted dolphin that I told you about in the beginning of the book. She had a message for me, for us… do you remember?

I was back on the deck of the catamaran, in this turquoise blue ocean. I had just met the magnificent old dolphin, who had sonared me and touched me so deeply with her presence. Here I was, sitting, and under my closed eyelids I saw the little blue dots reappear that I had seen just hours before during my massage. Now I recognized them as bubbles. I stayed open, watching the bubbles move around, change shape and create patterns.

Out from the middle of these bubbles in my mind's eye swam the same old spotted dolphin. Once again she came to me, eye to eye, as though she wanted to say something. I sensed the dolphin was sending me a message. I knew something important was about to happen. I held very still and opened my mind to hers. And then the message came.

She said, "If you just learn to love each other, we will be fine." Streams of thoughts flowed through my head… if we just love each other we don't have to worry about the dolphins, if we just love each other we don't have to worry about saving the forests, cleaning up the oceans, feeding the hungry, helping the poor. If we just love each other everything will be taken care of. It will all be fine. In that moment it became so clear.

If we loved each other – truly loved each other – instead of trying to get more and more for ourselves out of greed, fear and a belief in the illusion of separation, we would care and we would share. Because if we loved each other, how could we possibly let anyone go hungry, how could we destroy the forests and the oceans that sustain us, feed us, and nurture us? A few salty teardrops ran down the sides of my cheeks, as I watched the old spotted dolphin swim away.

I sat there in the darkness of my closed eyes, and I began to feel the absence of the love that she spoke of. A movie started running in my mind. I saw all the times that I could have loved more, been love more, opened my heart and given more instead of the holding back my love the way I had. More and more tears began to flow.

Intense images flashed through my mind's eye. Images of people I didn't know and didn't recognize. But I didn't just see them, I felt them. I felt their sadness, anger, frustration and pain. I sobbed more intensely. Other members of the boat came to sit by me. One woman began to reassure me that everything was all right, and I told her, "No, I can't stop crying. I must cry for all the people who believe they are un-loved. For the people who were afraid to love as much as they wanted to." I understood somehow that all their pain could have been alleviated with more openness, more caring, and more love. I also realized that I was not just crying for their sadness, I was somehow helping to clear the energy of sadness that was stuck in their bodies.

My crying went on for some time and then all at once I began to laugh. It started out softly, and then got louder and louder. I cackled like the crazy people you'd see in an insane asylum in the movies. I was aware that the energy created by laughter was the same exact energy as when I cried.

There was no difference. Angry, sad, happy, glad, it was all the same; it was all energy. The laughter and the tears were clearing that same painful energy. Then I got scared.

I seemed to be watching myself from outside my body. There I was, laughing hysterically. Was I insane? I tried to stop laughing but I couldn't, and I became more frightened. I saw my yoga teacher Tricia sitting on the deck a few feet from me. I've got to get over there, I told myself. I tried to move, and at first nothing happened. Then I tried again, it took every ounce of my strength to move my body. Finally I reached her, grabbed her knee, and squeezed. With an enormous sense of relief I looked at her and managed to say, "Please tell me I'm not going crazy."

She looked me right in the eyes, and with this beautiful combination of confidence and compassion said, "Breathe – you knew this was coming – just breathe."

Those words stopped me in my tracks. Recently I had told Tricia that I was ready to stop resisting – stop doubting – and start following my guidance. I told her that I was committed to work through my fear and walk the path I was meant to walk.

Relax and receive. That's how I've been able to receive, perceive and experience everything that has happened to me these past years. The more I was able to let go of my preconceived ideas about what was possible, what was real and who I thought I was, the more I was able to relax and receive what was there for me in the moment – the wild, special, and extraordinary things that I never would have experienced unless I was open to them.

In that moment I managed to stop laughing and start

breathing. A tremendous amount of energy was running through my body, and I was very cold, so I headed to the back of the boat to get warm. I didn't have my sea legs and everyone began to reach up to hold my hand as I swayed by. It was a beautiful sight, this sea of loving hands waiting to support me. I felt a sweet sense of love for each person whose hand I touched, and I leaned over and hugged each of them in turn. The words from the dolphin, "If we just love each other, everything will be fine," kept running through my head.

I do love them – I really do love them, I thought. Right then I committed to express my love whenever I felt it and stop holding back this precious commodity. If we just love each other, everything else will work itself out!

CHAPTER 30
Great Change Coming

"The greatest fear in the world is of the opinions of others. And the moment you are unafraid of the crowd you are no longer a sheep, you become a lion. A great roar arises in your heart, the roar of freedom."
~ *Osho*

NOT AS EASY AS I THOUGHT IT WOULD BE

ON THE PLANE RIDE HOME I kept pinching myself; it had all felt like one of those Technicolor dreams. But I was awake, and it had really happened to me.

I tried to remember and take in everything that I had learned in Bimini – what the water had taught me, especially all the physical ways I've learned to relax and receive. I had been getting this same message in many forms over the last few years, and this trip was the culmination of this body, mind, and spiritual message. When I am able to truly relax my mind and feel into my life, I can receive and perceive things that weren't available to me before. When I can trust, be open, and allow my inner guidance to lead, such wonderful miraculous opportunities are available to me.

269

The events of the last week and the words from the old dolphin – if we just love each other everything else will work itself out – kept whirling through my head. But what would this mean to me in my day-to-day life? I thought about the commitment I made to be more loving, and my heart over-flowed with compassion.

But how would I integrate this commitment into my life? What would it look like to be more loving? I already did what most people do: I help friends and family when I'm asked, and I tell those closest to me that I love them.

As I pondered this, I realized that the question was already being answered in my life. I knew I was meant to go beyond the typical ways people express their love. In fact, I already showed my love in a non-typical way, with my tithing practice – a tangible expression of my love and appreciation. For example, Neill and I had sent an extra hundred dollars to each crew member of the Bimini trip in gratitude, because they had contributed so much to the deep learning and epiphanies I had experienced. And we received back the most beautiful letters of gratitude; they were shocked by our gift. They were used to receiving tips, but never this kind of tribute for just being who they were.

Each time I gave money to someone because I felt touched, moved and inspired, there was a palpable exchange of love between us. It was more than an emotion: this kind of love, as God said, is the energy of creative expression itself, and within this tithing practice money became the physical expression of that love. That makes sense if you believe that love is energy, and money just one vehicle to transport that energy.

However, most people don't see money as energy, but as a means to get what they want. And if you don't have enough of it, you suffer. Money has so long been associated with the idea of scarcity and imbued with fear that its exchange rarely feels loving. Gifts of money are often wrapped in fear, so that they are not much of a gift to anyone. This can happen when people give money as a way of control or a power play, or to buy someone's love when they fear that they won't be loved any other way. Money can also be spent or given irresponsibly, leaving the giver and the receiver less than satisfied.

I learned a lesson about this when I was ten years old, getting ready to attend a family wedding. My mother and I looked through my closet to find something for me to wear, but there were only hand-me-downs from my cousins, some clothes my mother had made, and items from the thrift store. I complained that I didn't want to wear these; I wanted a new dress for the wedding. I wasn't aware that my father overheard our conversation.

Later that night my dad came into my room and quietly told me he was going to take me out to buy me a new dress and even get my hair done. I could hardly sleep because I was so excited. In the morning he took me out for breakfast, took me shopping for a new dress and shoes, and got my hair done at a local salon. I felt like a princess and couldn't wait to show my mother how the blue dress sparkled as I spun around, and how my new shoes snapped at the ankle instead of having one of those elastic straps.

As soon as we pulled up to our building I jumped out of the cab, went up the elevator and ran to the door. My mother opened it and stepped out, glaring at my father. She looked right through me as though I wasn't even there. Before my father was able to get out of the elevator she exploded with anger. "How dare you spend money on her when there isn't enough money to pay the rent?" she screamed.

My heart sank; I felt as scared and embarrassed as if I had stolen the money from her purse. I ran into my room, jumped on my bed and sobbed. A few minutes later my mother came in the room and told me she wasn't upset with me, that it was all my father's fault and I wasn't to concern myself about it. I got to keep the dress and the shoes, but somehow they now felt almost dirty and uncomfortable to wear.

When my mother yelled at my father, telling him he shouldn't have spent the money, I made it mean that he shouldn't have spent it on me. I understand now that in those moments I turned the sweet expression of love from my father into a belief that there wasn't enough to go around, and that I wasn't important enough to deserve having these scarce resources spent on me.

Of course I know now that my mother was simply scared and trying to protect us – she wanted my father to understand how worried she was. But for me, I now connected money to fear and scarcity, and my self-worth to money. My mother was so caught up in this fear and the mentality of scarcity that it prevented her from seeing my excitement or realizing how her words and actions might affect me. Any love that was possible in that moment was replaced by fear.

This belief stayed with me well into my adult life. In relationships, if someone was willing to spend money on me, it felt good and meant I was precious and worthy. If they weren't, it reinforced the belief that I wasn't good enough and not worth giving to. This belief also informed my choices about what I was willing to buy for myself, or spend on nurturing myself. If a purchase was for business, or if I had an obvious practical need for it, I would buy it. For example, I would get a massage if I was in physical pain, but not just because it felt good. If I couldn't come up with a logical reason for buying something, I would either find it used, cheaper, or stop myself from buying it altogether. In other words, I didn't just spend money on myself for pleasure.

This has been shifting for me over the last fifteen years. I've learned to treat myself well. I get massages for pleasure and buy beautiful things for my home to create beauty in my physical surroundings. I thought I had come to completely love and appreciate myself during the last four years, but there are multiple layers to everything. We are very complex beings – ever changing and ever-growing – and I found hidden remnants of the old beliefs about my own worth.

As I continued to explore being more loving and giving, it came to me through God that giving to myself in the same way that I give to others would be essential to my ability to give and receive love fully. So as I did with others, I watched for times when I was inspired by my own actions, moved by my caring, and touched by my own beauty and grace. Only when I was able to give to myself as I gave to others would the beautiful flower of love fully blossom in my life.

It was harder for me to spot these things in my own life, but when I looked, they were everywhere. I followed my guidance when I was scared, I took time for myself when there was "work to do," and I expressed my deep caring for people in many ways. Each time I found something, I tithed to myself and collected the money in a separate bank account. I was guided to spend the money on things that would allow me to feel precious and loved, but not to make any purchase until I felt the same exchange of love with myself that I did when I gave to others.

This wasn't as easy as I thought it would be, so the money sat in the bank for a very long time. The hardest part wasn't giving myself money, it was spending it. Maybe it was because the bit of extra money we got from selling the house was dwindling and there were bills to pay. When I gave money to someone else it was just gone, and the beauty of the moment overshadowed any fear of not having enough to meet our own needs. But when giving to myself, the fear was front and center. What if I bought something for myself and then needed the money for something "important"? What if Neill had some reaction about me spending money frivolously? This practice was about having more faith in love than fear.

One day I was in a little store near my house and I saw a beautiful long crocheted silvery-gray tunic. It was just the kind of thing I liked, unusual because of its asymmetrical design. This might be a perfect piece to tithe to myself, but the price tag said $325. That's ridiculous, I thought, and walked out of the store.

But then I stopped and confronted my beliefs. Am I worthy of this physical expression of love? I went back to the store three times before I was willing to buy this top. I remembered God's instructions: I was to get present to what touched, moved and inspired me, just as I do when I give to someone else.

Right before paying for it, I stood quietly and pretended I was handing myself this beautifully wrapped gift, and I told myself how inspired I was by my courage, how proud I was of me, how touched I was by the deep caring I saw in myself, and how moved I was by my commitment to my spiritual growth. I was giving myself something much bigger than this $325 piece of clothing. It symbolized that I was giving me back my self-worth.

How often do we love and appreciate ourselves enough to stop, acknowledge and honor ourselves in some way? And how often do we refrain from expressing love and caring for ourselves, or anyone else for that matter, because of some kind of fear?

I remembered the vision I had on the boat of all the people around the world that didn't feel loved, and a deep sadness came over me. How can that flower of love blossom through all this fear and the beliefs that we are not good enough and that there's not enough to go around? Is it possible to reverse this mentality of fear and scarcity?

You Are Not Alone

Beth: Is it possible for us to overcome fear and really love each other? Fear is so prevalent that it seems as if it's in the air we breathe. How do we get past it?

God: Fear is in the air and has been for very long time. It is in the air you breathe, the cells of your body, and even saturated in the food you eat. Fear has come to be a master of your reality. Yes, it is possible to change this, but the essence of fear needs to be shifted in order to breathe the air of peace. Once there is inner peace, love cannot help but be expressed.

There is great change coming. This environment of fear has caused the withholding of love in many areas. Not just between parents and children, or lovers – this withholding also causes wars and environmental disasters.

You and many others on this planet at this time are becoming conscious of the destructive nature of fear. As more of you turn your attention towards peace in your hearts and the expression of love, you are creating a polarity – an opposing energy – that can easily manage the fear energy that surrounds you. Because this fear and the people who perpetuate it are not separate from you, you can change the course of this fearful energy. As you maintain balance – the balance between truth and love – fear is no more.

You are not alone; there are a myriad of others who are at this time experiencing what you are experiencing. They are waking up from an old outmoded dream and creating a new one. This process will be experienced as a shock to some, but many feel it coming.

Are you ready to be completely awake? Are you ready to see the old dream for what it is? Now can be your time. Open your eyes as I speak through you. Wake up into the new dream, a dream that you have all dreamed many times before. You know this dream well – it is your heart's desire. There is no one on this planet that does not dream this dream. In some it is not as obvious as it is in others, but if you examine closely the desire for power, prestige, control, and also material items, within it there is the same dream at its core for each and every one.

The dream is to experience the gift of this glorious reality, to feel what there is to feel, to see the truth of all there is to see, to hear the gifts there are to hear, and to speak and interact with the other players in ways that bring joy and love energy to all.

These are the gifts that you have at your fingertips; these gifts only require that you open your eyes and see them. Open your eyes, and know that I am here as you, you are here as me, there is no separation.

Let me speak through you with confidence and clarity,

and you will realize that we are not separate. I/you/we are not separate from what you hear, what you see, and what you feel.

The birds that sit in a tree and tweet their musical song are of the same energy and essence you are. All that is different is the expression. Continue to lift your gaze from the old dream and see all that there is to see – not from the mind, but from the eyes that were given to you; feel all that there is to feel, not from the mind but from your body; hear all that was that there is to hear, not from the mind but from your ears.

And pay close attention to this next part, dear one: say all that is meant to be said, not from the mind but from the heart that was given to you.

Know that you are one with All That Is. As you move through this existence, you are experiencing the dream you have always dreamt. What you have always wanted is here, not in some distance place. It can't be reached through struggle or striving; all there is to do is to open your eyes, wake up, and experience the dream that is meant to be.

So yes, you can get past the fear. The process has begun. Keep allowing, keep believing in what you experience, claim those experiences as your truth and always remember that you are not alone. There is no separation – we are ONE.

Wake up and dream the new dream!

Beth: Wow, I don't have much to say after that.

God: Good. Don't talk about it; don't think about it. Just experience it.

WILL I BE REJECTED?

For quite a while I allowed what God said to wash through me and as I did, a tangible discomfort emerged.

Beth: I'm feeling uncomfortable. I have experienced the oneness you talk about, but as we speak it seems as if you and I are separate, so saying we are ONE feels very odd.

God: What feels odd about it?

Beth: Saying that there is no separation between us is like saying that this information is coming from me and not you. I'm reluctant to take responsibility for it because I don't know if it is true. All I know is it's coming out of my mouth.

God: What is truth, dear one?

Beth: Truth is something that can be proven in some way.

God: Proven to whom?

Beth: Proven to others. I don't want people to think I'm crazy or arrogant. Of course, saying I'm talking to you in the first place could certainly seem crazy.

And yet, I'm not sure it needs to be proven to anyone else, because our conversations mean so much to me. I'm confused.

God: Your confusion is a distraction that veils the truth. Confusion is only the mind getting in the way of what you know when you feel it. There is no confusion when you use the gifts you were meant to use. It is joyful to watch your re-integration.

Go deeper! Stop for a moment, feel into it, and tell me what it is you are truly concerned about.

Beth: Will I be rejected? It's so painful to think about, and it seems so silly to even say. But yet there it is.

God: There is nothing silly that you could say, dear one.

These are the roots you must unearth – the ones that hold you in this space and time. These thoughts, these beliefs that keep you clinging to old fears must be brought to the surface so that your feeling self can know them for what they really are.

They stem from the tenderness within you, from the loving and caring you. Will you be rejected? Rejection is impossible; there can be no rejection because you are one with All That Is. Take a moment and feel into what I have said.

Beth: When I just stop and feel, just literally feel without thought, there is no confusion because there's no thought.

God: Yes, exactly. And now how do you feel about this idea of needing to prove what is coming through you?

Beth: There's nothing to do, because there's no one here in this moment to prove anything to.

God: Yes. If you feel into in each moment of the now, there is only contentment.

CHAPTER 31
Build Something New

"Few are willing to brave the disappointment of their fellows, the censure of their colleagues, the wrath of their society. Moral courage is a rarer commodity than bravery in battle or great intelligence. Yet it is the one essential, vital quality for those who seek to change the world that yields most painfully to change. Each time a person stands up for an idea, or acts to improve the lot of others, or strikes out against injustice, (s)he sends forth a tiny to ripple of hope, and crossing each other from a million different centers of energy and daring, those ripples build a current that can sweep down the mightiest walls of oppression and resistance."

- Robert F. Kennedy

PRIMAL FEAR

GOD'S WORDS RANG THROUGH MY HEAD: "Are you ready to be completely awake?" After that conversation I realized two things. The first was that I still had a lot of energetic clearing to do. God's question had stimulated a ripple of deep primal fear in me, the same as I'd felt when I thought I was drowning in the water in Bimini.

But I wasn't in danger of dying now. This fear was about what might happen if I were rejected. If I were completely awake to who I am and what I've come here to do, I might have to stand apart from the crowd. I might have to say things that others don't want to hear, or do unusual things that might be scary for others to see.

But this fear didn't make sense. I thought I was ready; I knew that I was protected and cared for; I knew that I was part of All That Is, and that nothing, not even death, would alter this truth.

This fear was ancient and tribal, as if I could be cast out into the wilderness to fend for myself or die. It went deeper than my mind; it touched the deepest core of my physical being. It was as if my very cells held eons of fearful memories. I've heard about cellular memory – the theory that memories are stored in all the cells of the human body – memories from this life, or even past lives.

I was so confused and afraid. How could I feel this profound peace, and even experience a oneness with God, and at the same time care so much about what other people thought of me? But now I realized that being liked, respected, and cared about was so important to me because the threat of not having it triggered primordial fears.

Was I ready to be completely awake? I didn't know, but I did know that even cellular memory was just stagnant, blocked energy that needed to move.

To clear the energetic blocks, I used the modalities that I knew, including Reiki, Psych-K, and the Hawaiian energy clearing method Ho'oponopono, as well as other techniques that I had learned from God.

As I delved into the cellular memories, I often found

myself out in the cold. When I let myself be guided by past experiences or concerns about the future, it's like throwing myself out into a frigid lonely wilderness to fend for myself or die. When any part of me is disconnected from God, it is like being out in a desolate landscape, lost and alone. It was time to find my way home.

The other thing I learned was that my practice of spontaneous giving was very important to this process. My early childhood experiences had created a skewed relationship with money that had molded my life. Now I know that money is simply energy in a physical form, and the tithing practice allows me to experience money in a whole new way. Money can create a profound connection between people instead of a separation. Tenderness can be exchanged, instead of callousness. Money can express love, and even more than that, this practice can help heal a deep cultural wound that has been festering for so long, and needs attention, now more than ever. And tithing can heal my personal money wound as well.

So in the days and weeks to come I cleared a great deal of stagnant energy at a cellular level – releasing the primal fear that had such a hold on me for so long and that kept me from relaxing and receiving everything available to me. I also continued to give money to people, enjoying the sweetness of the connection, and sensing that this practice would play an even larger role in my evolution.

A VISION FOR THE FUTURE

One morning I woke up with the old agitation nagging at me. I knew it was time to get quiet, present and connected.

But woven into the agitation was a thread of anticipation that I couldn't explain. My bathing ceremony always got to the root of these feelings, and so before I even got my coffee I began to run my bath. As the hot water filled the tub the bubbling of excitement in me grew.

I began the bath in the usual way, with bath salts, aromatherapy, lighting the candles, and finally sinking into the hot water. My mind quieted down as my body melted like chocolate in a warm pot. As I relaxed, my mind drifted in and out of everyday reality. One moment I was aware of my physical surroundings – the bath and the water around me – and the next I was floating somewhere in a dark sparkly mist. The more I released my concerns, the longer I stayed floating freely outside my normal reality.

Something began to appear in front of me. I couldn't make it out at first; it was being created right before my very eyes. Then it came into focus as a visual image that I recognized – a dilapidated old machine. Its blackened metal surface was corroded and worn and it had three smokestacks running across the top, spewing out black smoke.

In front of this old machine was a large vault filled with gold bars – thousands and thousands of gold bars stacked one on top of another. There were dozens of little old men crouched outside the vault door, peering over their hands with their elbows nestled on their knees. All you could see of their faces were their fat, droopy cheeks and little beady black eyes darting back and forth. They seemed worried and looked as though they were guarding the vault to make sure no one stole the gold.

Another image began to form to the right of the machine. It started with a slight circular motion and then began moving faster and faster, around and around, until it looked like a shiny sideways golden tornado. I tensed up, and then took a deep breath, hoping the images wouldn't disappear. The tornado began to suck the air from the scene, but it wasn't the air that it wanted, it was the gold bars.

Then the gold bars started lifting up and floating from the vault – right over the heads of the little scared men trying to guard them – into this funnel-shaped object. I looked over at the old men, but they didn't seem to notice what was happening. As the gold bars continued their exodus from the vault, the tornado's form began to change and the spinning motion slowed down to a rhythmic roll and a peaceful hum.

From within the tornado, I sensed these words. "Stop trying to fix this broken machine, and build something new. You do not need to tear the old one down – build the new as the old continues to run."

As these words came to me I felt an intense energy surge like lightning through my body, along with a combination of fear and anticipation. I begin to shake, and as my body lay twitching in the water I realized what I was seeing. The dilapidated old machine was our financial system and the tornado was like a whirlwind of possibility – what we could create if we chose to. If we build something more wonderful than the outmoded machine that exists now, our money will flow to it naturally and without conflict.

But what in the world did it have to do with me?

And then I heard, "You can help change the way money is perceived and used on this planet."

"Why are you talking to me about this?" I said out loud, as if someone was standing there. I don't have a degree in economics; I barely graduated high school, so this had to be a mistake. And then a rush of ideas started pouring through me as if a fire hose was turned on.

It seemed to be some kind of a plan, but the thoughts came so quickly I struggled to hold onto them. I yelled out from the bathtub, "Neill, help! Come quickly! Please get a pen and write this down."

He ran in with the pen and paper in his hand. "What, what do you want me to write?" he asked anxiously.

I recounted what I heard:

There is a new type of economy coming, where money isn't held onto so tightly, where it is shared and allowed it to flow. In this new system all people in the world are encouraged and supported to identify and experience their ideal lifestyle – a lifestyle that is nurturing to them and that can be sustained. Each person's chosen lifestyle will be different. There will be no judgment of what is chosen, just a celebration of the choosing. This change will not happen overnight, and not all people will believe it is possible. But as the movement grows and is incorporated by some, the light of possibility will be seen, and then more will join. As more people choose what is possible for them, creativity flourishes freely and innovation supports the process. As more and more people are touched by the freedom to choose, they will eagerly contribute to the shift that is happening and enjoy the gift that their contribution can bring.

In this new system, when people have achieved their ideal lifestyle and can maintain it, they will freely and without hesitation commit to giving 50% of their excess income back into the flow. But this release – this giving back – will not be one of desperation – not to fix what is broken, not out of obligation or duty. They will do this spontaneously, giving back into the flow to any person, business or organization that supports the giver in feeling touched, moved or inspired. It will flow from them as a joyful act that gives equally to giver and receiver. Until the time that they are fully living this ideal lifestyle, they will happily commit to giving 10% to support the shift that is happening in this way.

As these words came out of my mouth I remembered my tithing practice. I remembered all the joy that I felt as I gave money in this way. When I saw acts of kindness or love, how my heart expanded. When I gave people money and expressed my gratitude for their kindness, how their faces lit up and tears came to their eyes. I imagined how this world would change if thousands and thousands of people spent their days focused on things that move and inspire them, instead of what's wrong and what's not working.

I realized that my vision was a possible future plan for changing the way money is perceived and used on this planet. And it makes sense, because we couldn't help but change the world if we used the energy of money in this way. Imagine how satisfying it would be if every dollar exchanged was given or received with gratitude and love and appreciation.

I thanked Neill for writing this all down and as he left the room a jumble of questions filled my mind. Why just fifty percent, why not one hundred percent of everything over and above the ideal lifestyle? I mean why do we need more than what would fulfill us and give us joy?

And the answer came.

"You are not ready for that. Fifty percent is an incremental step to experience the fulfillment this brings. That will allow you to maintain and trust this practice."

Why me? I thought. There are others more qualified than me to do this work.

"Why you? You are uniquely qualified. Stop comparing yourself to others. You are ready to hold the energy of this vision, you are ready to commit to this practice, and you are ready to share it with others. This is all that is needed."

But I have so many questions; I need to understand this better in order to act.

And the answer came, "You understand as much as you need to now. The rest of your questions will be satisfied when you need the answers."

CHAPTER 32

Follow Your Leadings

"To be beautiful means to be yourself. You don't need to be accepted by others. You need to accept yourself."

- Thich Nhat Hanh

THE ROOT OF ALL EVIL

THE NOTION THAT I WAS TO HELP change the way we perceive and use money on this planet blew my mind. For days after my last experience in the bath, I didn't know what to do. God had said I would get the answers when I needed them, but whenever I thought about the vision of the dirty old machine and the golden tornado, my mind reeled with questions.

Beth: Why me? And what do I do with this vision?

God: You allow it to integrate. You allow it to mature within you like a seed being planted in rich soil; allow the sun and rain to nurture it until it shoots its young tender head up to meet you.

Beth: That's all very poetic, but again, why did I receive this message? You say I'm uniquely qualified, but there are others so much more qualified. Please explain.

God: First of all, do not devalue poetry. You and your life are poetry.

And do not hurry these words that come through you – feel them and enjoy them. Allow them to work their magic in you. There is loveliness and grace in you and all around you that could be sung in song, sculpted in stone and written in beautiful words. Receive the beauty in your life; do not limit it with haste. This is true for everyone else as well.

But back to your question. You received this message because you are open, prepared and available to receive it. But "Why you" is not the most important issue to be discussed. A better question to ask is, "Why do you compare yourself to others?" This propensity towards comparison is a hazardous one.

It's often said that money is the root of all evil. The evil is not rooted in the money itself, because money is just energy. But when fearful people are hoarding or distributing this energy, it becomes infused with fear and generates consequences that are interpreted as evil. So you see, it is not money or the love of money that is the root of all evil, but it is fear-based habits. Painful comparison is one such habit.

Comparison can create a deep deadly root that you must be wary of – one that keeps you stuck in pain and despair. The propensity to compare yourselves to others is interwoven in your culture and causes you to believe that there is a better or worse way to be, better and worse things to have or own, better and worse ways to live your lives. Comparing yourselves in this way leaves you either vying for position or allowing others – or your perception of them – to influence your lives. You see, each of you has your own divine gifts, your own divine wants and desires, and your own divine experiences that can lead you to the best place for you.

What if you experienced your vision without comparison? What if you had no ability to compare yourself to others in a painful way?

Beth: Before I answer that question, I want to understand more clearly about comparison. You say comparison creates big problems, but don't we have to compare things to one another in order to discern what we like and what we don't like, what feels good and what doesn't? Don't we need to see contrast in order to experience one thing as different from another?

God: Yes, of course. This brings us back to your main mode of discernment. When you use your physical mind to discern two experiences, everything, including contrast, is experienced defensively. When you are in defensive mode you look for the things that will protect you, and this often means that you look outside yourself, at others. Do they look better off, safer, happier, or freer? You can't really know that they are better off, but you often use this information as your guide to safety and happiness. This tendency makes you believe that if you are not doing, saying, and acting as they are, then you will be in jeopardy. If you are not as wealthy, educated, thin, or athletic as they are, you are "less than" and therefore do not feel safe.

Your physical mind is designed to protect you by looking for threats to your safety. When something different is perceived than what it has known, the mind interprets this as danger. But if there is no actual danger in your physical reality, this is very stressful and confusing. It can be internally painful because you are, in a way, at war with your higher knowing.

But, when you discern from your sensing self – your higher mind – and there is no physical danger at hand, there is no need to become protective and your physical mind does not need to get involved. From this place, contrast does not elicit the need for painful comparison. You can sense what there is for you there; you can be drawn to or repelled without inventing a meaning that causes you pain. You just experience truth. Is this clear?

Beth: Can you give me a specific example?

God: Let's use this one. Because you are now so open to your divine energies you received a vision of a new possibility. You still retain some of your thought habits, so your physical mind perceived this vision as a threat because it is very different than anything the mind has known. It compared the new vision with what's been possible in your life up until this point. Because this looks so different, your physical mind became defensive and looked for a way to wipe out this threat. So it brought up comparisons.

It told you things such as: "this is ridiculous; you have no training or education; there are people who are better than you; don't make a fool of yourself; people will think you're crazy, etc." Up until now, these thoughts have done a good job keeping you in your place. Don't make waves; don't cause a fuss. Most of the time you didn't even know a war was brewing under the surface of your consciousness.

Because your higher mind is always aware, if only subconsciously, of your connection to all possibilities – a painful struggle ensues. This struggle manifests first as an inner war, and then it turns outward.

This conflict manifests itself inwardly in you as tiredness, sadness, and confusion. For other people it could show itself as severe energy loss, depression, eating disorders, addictions of all sorts, or mental illness.

Turned outwards, comparison manifests itself in you and the majority of others as jealousy, lying to protect yourself, and some degree of stinginess.

For some, this external manifestation of comparison expresses itself to extremes. Jealousy turns into fierce compassionless competition. Lying becomes so constant and ingrained that it is hardly noticed. The stinginess that comes from the belief in separation, loneliness and lack turns to greed and winning at all cost. This is why you see your financial structures, governmental structures, and societal structures crumbling around you now.

There is a longing in all of you who live on this planet at this time to grow, expand, and become fully realized. There is a collective restlessness – can you feel it? This longing is to go beyond what you have known before, to explore new and far-reaching possibilities. But first this habitual nature must be confronted. And here we can begin with the insidious nature of comparison.

So I ask you these questions again. What would happen if the vision that came through you were not met with comparison? What if you had no ability to compare yourself to others in a painful way?

Beth: Then it would be just a possibility to explore. I might trust that it was an important message for me. I might be excited about the adventure.

God: Yes. If your higher mind was in its rightful position as decision-maker and the one who discerns, and your physical mind took care of your physical needs and the basic things that it does so well, then you would be able to respond more accurately and appropriately to the multitude of choices and options that come your way.

You would not need to compare yourself with anyone else. There would be no need for jealousy and no need to be stingy, for you would know beyond a shadow of a doubt that you are deeply loved and cared for. You would know that what comes through you is for you and you could relax into that knowing and move as you are guided to move. There would be no confusion, no doubt, only you flowing with the energy of life.

Beth: Now I understand about comparison and how destructive it is. How do I become less habituated and let my higher mind take over in these situations?

God: You are well on your way. Continue to notice these habitual protection mechanisms. The transformation happens when you slow down enough to notice when they have engaged. It is the unconscious behaviors that run rampant – unseen and uncontrolled.

Beth: That is very helpful. And what do I do about this vision that came through me?

God: Allow the mystery to work its way through you and integrate. Allow it to mature within you and pay attention to what you are drawn to. You will notice opportunities for learning and integration weave their way into your life. Follow your leadings and examine when you encounter resistance. Continue to clear stagnant energy, and expand into more and more of who you are. Begin to see your whole life as the great and wonderful journey it is. Enjoy it, love it and share it.

After this conversation I was able to notice what we had talked about. I didn't have to look too long to find these painful comparisons. Even with all the personal growth work

I had done, I noticed them everywhere. For example, I compared myself to others based on Facebook comments. Or when someone told me about a book they were reading, I compared this book to that one. I was shocked by how often this happened and how these comparisons led to negative thoughts about myself: Was I good enough? She writes better than I do. He's so much smarter than I am. Who's going to care what I have to say? On and on, I saw myself make one heartbreaking comparison after another.

I now see how these kinds of habits could be considered the root of all evil. I looked back in my life and saw the jealousy, stinginess, and the lies I told in order to make myself feel better or look better. But now I was able to shift my focus very quickly and allow the energy to move through me before it stagnated. To do this, I used the question God asked me. What if I couldn't compare myself in this way or to this person?

This helped with the doubt that kept cropping up in relation to my vision. In the weeks to come I allowed the vision to work through me. In my meditations I would sense things to do in relation to it and would do them. I stayed connected to God and did as I was guided. Some of the tasks made sense in relation to the vision, such as creating a new business entity that would help entrepreneurs make more money, and also inspire them to give money away. Some of them didn't seem to relate, such as being guided to create an online event where I would interview dozens of famous people from different walks of life. But when I asked about the random nature of these tasks, God assured me that these pieces would eventually come together. Then something unexpected happened.

CHAPTER 33

Seeds of Transformation

You suppose you are the trouble
But you are the cure
You suppose that you are the lock on the door
But you are the key that opens it
It's too bad that you want to be someone else
You don't see your own face, your own beauty
Yet, no face is more beautiful than yours.
~ Rumi

A PROFOUND REALIZATION

IT WAS AS IF SOMEONE SLAMMED on the brakes, and everything came to a crashing halt. My baths were just ordinary baths, my meditations were short, and my conversations with God were as casual as having a chat with an old friend I saw once in a while for coffee.

My confusion and frustration grew, and then I remembered the story of the bamboo tree: A farmer had a beautiful little bamboo seed and expected a big healthy plant. He took the seed and planted it, watered it, and fertilized it, but after the first year, nothing happened! The second year came and went, and then the third, but still there was nothing to show for all his care and attention to the little seed. After the fourth year when there was still no sign of his little tree sprouting from the ground, he became very frustrated and almost gave up.

When the fifth year came, he continued to water and fertilize the seed, almost out of habit. Then much to his surprise, the Chinese bamboo tree sprouted and grew to over 80 feet in just one growing season.

Despite how it appeared on the surface, things hadn't come to a stop for me. I just needed time for this new growth to expand within me until it was ready to show itself in my life. I did my best to relax about my vision and trust that when it was time to do something, I'd know it.

Then one day I was drawn like a magnet to a new Jean Houston virtual seminar called Awakening to Your Life's Purpose. But I was already leading a purposeful life, and lately, I'd also made it a point to limit my input from other people so that what was coming through me for this book was as clean as possible. So I questioned whether or not to take this course.

Don't get me wrong; I knew Jean Houston could teach me a thing or two, or ten! She was one of the original gurus of the human potential movement. She's started wisdom schools, worked with political leaders and the United Nations, written a vast number of books, and has shepherded thousands of people around the world to develop in ways they never thought possible.

Even though I've learned to follow my guidance, the $500 fee seemed like too much. My money issues were a work in

progress; it was still challenging to trust my guidance in relation to spending money. This was an opportunity to ask
myself if this was true guidance, or if I was just attracted to
this shiny object.

After much uncertainty, I stopped, quieted down, listened, and felt. The answer was a clear YES, so I registered for
the seven-week course. Since Jean was a master I appeased my
doubt by telling myself, if nothing else, I'd learn something
from her teaching style.

Jean was an engaging storyteller and I found it easy and
enjoyable to listen to her. Each week she wove colorful stories
to illustrate her teaching points, and she'd lead us in unusual
meditations, exercises, and assignments. Some were storytelling exercises; others promoted imagination, and some were
to stimulate the etheric body. I enjoyed the class, but I still
wondered what the point was, for me.

Week four was called Discovering the Nature of Your
Own Mythic Life and Aligning with Your Destiny. Jean began the session by saying, "Beneath the soil of your everyday
world lies vast root systems of the once-was and the what-
could-be." She remarked that story is the juice through which
consciousness and culture move. I wished I had her talent for
writing such beautiful words! What fun it could be making
up stories about imagined places and people. But that wasn't
one of my talents.

She went on to say that our lives are our stories. If we view
our life as inconsequential, the deep meaning and purpose
can be lost, but if we can see our life as a larger picture, one
with epic meaning, we can easily find the motivation and
drive to be more fully engaged.

She told us how human consciousness is contained in our

cultural myths, and these myths have been told so often, over vast time spans and diverse cultures, that they become part of our psyche. We are so drawn to and compelled by these stories because we recognize they can provide answers to deep longings and unanswered questions in our current lives. Then Jean quoted Joseph Campbell: "The symbols of mythology are not manufactured; they cannot be ordered, invented, or permanently suppressed. They are spontaneous productions of the psyche, and each bears within it, undamaged, the germ power of its source. It has always been the prime function of mythology and ritual to supply the symbols that carry the human spirit forward."

You may be familiar with the work of Joseph Campbell and his ideas about the hero's and the heroine's journey. Jean broke down the story of the Wizard of Oz for us using the heroine's journey model. Dorothy comes from a normal and almost dismal life in Kansas where she is sad, misunderstood and longing for so much more. She journeys to the magical and colorful world of Oz where she meets new friends, engages with new enemies and has many adventures. She discovers new possibilities for her life, only to learn that everything she always wanted was hers for the taking if only she could find her way back home. And then she learns that she had the power to get there all along. In the story, when Glinda the good witch is asked why she hadn't told Dorothy earlier that she had the power to get home, Glinda said, "If I had told her, she wouldn't have believed me. She had to learn it through her own efforts."

This is all very interesting, I thought to myself, but how does this apply to my life?

"Nobody escapes from myth," Jean says. "Myth is at the

very heart and soul of every human being. Each of us can use myth to brighten and energize our present lives. We are all Dorothy, longing for the deeper realities that live within us."

When I heard those words I felt a combination of hesitation and excitement. I certainly had longed for and now was experiencing deeper realities, and I knew they all lived within me. Were there more to come?

Then Jean asked us to do an exercise to uncover what she called our "woundings." She said that our woundings can be the seeds of transformation. We were to list all of the painful and awful things that have happened to us throughout our lives – physical illness, accidents, and disease; violations such as rape, child abuse, torture, and robbery; losses that could include jobs, relationships, self-esteem, sanity or financial security; and other forms of suffering that go past what we thought we could bear. Yet these same products of pain could be vehicles for transformation. When we can allow our woundings to become sacred and are willing for them to be a channel through us, a new story can emerge. We can stop repeating the same old story over and over and are able to explore the deeper implications – the hidden story within the wounding.

Then Jean suggested that we reinvent the circumstances of our wounding as a mythic adventure – into, through and beyond the wounding to the point of noble rebirth and empowerment, even though in reality this may not have happened. She told us to start the story by saying, "Once upon a time…"

I agreed with this premise of uncovering and exploring that which was not conscious; certainly, all the personal clearing work I've done has been extremely transformative. But my life was pretty blessed compared to some of the horrific things that happen to other people. I've never experienced physical abuse or life-threatening illness. I had eccentric but loving parents, plenty to eat, and always had a warm and comfortable place to live.

What could have happened in my life that surpassed what I thought I could bear? Then I remembered that God had said that I was uniquely qualified and prepared to receive the vision about transforming the way we perceive and use money. Issues around money had certainly affected me. As I grew up, lack of money was a painful subject between my parents, and the backlash from this had been key to my forming the belief that I wasn't worthy of receiving love or money. So I could use my experiences and beliefs around money as my wounding for this exercise.

But I felt a strange resistance. My mind started racing away, and then I heard a voice in my head say, stop knowing everything; quiet down and go deeper. In the calmness of my mind, like a miner digging for gold, I spotted the glint of a new idea out of the corner of my awareness. What was that? I thought as it dashed again out of sight. Then pictures of my life began to assemble themselves in my awareness. All those times that I was taken to the psychologist – why was I there? Because I was making things up and my imagination was running away with me. I remember being told repeatedly that my experiences – things I felt, saw and knew in my heart were real – weren't real at all. They were just my imagination and couldn't be trusted. If I couldn't prove it in some tangible way, it wasn't real. And if I continued down that road then I would be considered crazy.

Here it was; I'd found my gold! I'd uncovered the wounding that could resurrect my life – I found, as Jean put it, the God-seed waiting to emerge. It was sitting right in front of me, all covered with dirt and forgotten. As I rubbed and dusted off this nugget, its gold was revealed.

In that moment I knew that my deepest wounding was that my imagination had been stunted and not allowed to flourish. God had told me that imagination was the beginning of all creation. If I continued to doubt my own reality, and if I kept comparing my experiences to those of others, then I would never be fully awake to what life has in store for me.

Without my imagination fully intact I could not reach my highest potential – I would never realize my complete and total connection to God. Now the doubt and confusion that had gnawed at me made sense. If I didn't believe my imagination was something to honor and trust, how could I accept the vision – or any of my other experiences – as real, meaningful and important?

With this realization, I sat down and wrote my mythic adventure.

IN HER LIGHT

Once upon a time there was a kingdom of darkness shrouded in a great lie. The king, who had ruled over this land for as long as anyone could remember, had convinced his subjects that light was their enemy. He told them that darkness was the only thing that would keep them safe, and that he was the only one who knew how to keep the light from hurting them. He showed them horrible images of what would happen if they left the darkness and ventured into the light. He told them repulsive stories about the gruesome light monsters that lurk just outside the walls of their kingdom.

His subjects were so terrified that they would do anything, give him anything, and believe anything he said in order to stay safe. By means of a sinister enchantment, he'd surrounded the kingdom on all sides with a barrier of darkness that allowed no light or anything else to enter.

Over the countless years of darkness, the people had developed catlike eyes that could see in the dark. They huddled in corners telling half-forgotten stories of the unfortunate ones who'd been thrown out into the light, and how their tortured cries struck fear into the hearts of anyone who heard them! Eventually their voices faded, and they were never seen or heard from again.

Within this unhappy kingdom, a child was born who was imbued with the most beautiful light. It shimmered like a little star within her. Initially the little girl's parents were delighted with her softly glowing beauty. How unique and precious she was! But as she grew, she shined ever brighter, and her parents started to worry, as well they might. She was so strange, so different than the other children, and soon she started to attract attention. You see, it had been so long since anyone had seen the light that they didn't even know what it was or what it might look like. Yet something drew them to her. She seemed unnaturally beautiful, and she radiated a warmth that attracted them like a magnet. But in this kingdom, it was not good to be different, and her parents were afraid that she would be ostracized or worse. She might even be thrown out into the light to be hideously burned, or devoured by the sharp-toothed monsters that the king had so graphically described.

At first the parents kept their fears from the little girl, but as she grew the light grew within her. When she went about her daily chores, she would daydream, and the light would take her to a beautiful place – an enchanted land with all the colors of the rainbow, inhabited by joyful and kind beings. She noticed that she could see so clearly, and felt in her heart as though she was being transformed in some strange way each and every time she came to this magical place. Her daydreams filled her with joy and fresh delight, and she began to wonder what might really lie beyond the edges of the kingdom. She dreamed that she might one day live in her magical world.

Late in the evenings, back in the dreariness of her home, she told her parents about this other realm where things were different, where people were happy and loving, where they were not afraid. She tried to describe the unusual creatures and fantastically shaped plants, but she would struggle to find the words, because nothing like them existed in the dark world. And color! How do you describe color to someone who's never seen it? Each time she talked about her adventures her light flared vividly and her parents became more alarmed. If they had ever seen the light, they'd long ago hidden the memories, even from themselves. But they knew that their child was treading on very dangerous ground.

Her parents didn't know what to do about her, so they brought her to be examined by the wise men of the dark kingdom. The men peered at her, poked at her, prodded her, and asked a lot of questions, and so she told them about her nightly visits to the other realm. They told her she was imagining things, and that she was going mad, and that the light was working its evil ways on her. She was scolded, threatened, and told never to talk about these things again else she be banished from the kingdom and sent out to die in the scorching light. They arranged for spies to keep an eye on her.

The king's men delivered her back to her parents with

some stern warnings. Now terrified, her parents covered her with black clothing and tried to hide her from the world. But her light continued to shine and it seeped through the dark garments that she wore, no matter how many layers they wrapped her in. Their neighbors began to whisper whenever they saw her, and former friends stopped coming to their door. The spies reported these events to the king.

Out of desperation her parents locked her in a tiny pitch-black box with sides that closed in on themselves. Each time they saw the light brightening within her, they tightened the sides of the box so the light could be wrung out of her like a dirty dishrag. The girl was afraid she would never see her beautiful world again. She furiously fought the sides of the box tightening around her. But there were two of them and only one of her, and they were big and she was small, and eventually she weakened, and then gave up fighting altogether. With each turn of the wheel she watched her beautiful world fade away and along with it, her hopes and dreams withered as well. Finally, when the light disappeared completely from her eyes, her parents celebrated and opened the door and allowed her to leave. She took a step out and fell onto the floor, looking like nothing more than a shadow of her former self. She lay there, unable to move, for hours. Finally she got up and crawled to her bed.

Slowly, slowly, she regained her strength and began moving about in the dark world again. She was so grateful for her freedom that she didn't remember being tortured or how wonderful the light had made her feel. Now, she only felt relief. Her parents made her promise to love the darkness and hate the light forever more. She would be dim and normal, just like everybody else.

She wandered around the kingdom drained, confused,

and broken, flinching away from the dark barriers that kept out the light. No one – not even the girl – could see her light now. It flickered so faintly inside that it could be blown out like a candle with one halfhearted breath. She tried to be dutiful, to be satisfied with subtle differences in the hues of black and gray, with darkness. But sometimes she would catch a glimpse of the faintest of color, or meet someone whose eyes hinted at the knowledge of the brighter world. And she would remember. A little hope stirred in her at those times.

Years passed, and each time she was reminded of the light, she felt her light grow a little stronger in her soul. And so at night in her dreams she secretly began to travel again to that wonderful world of light, seeing the happy people, marveling at the strange animals and green plants, and feeling the delight she knew those many years ago. And with each trip, her light intensified.

This terrified the girl because now she was old enough to understand the danger she was in, and so she tried to hide her light by wrapping herself in layers and layers of black cloth. But she could no longer contain it, and the light kept seeping out until one day her worst fear was realized. The king's spies had brought him the news that her light was shining once again. He was furious, and he gathered his subjects in the town square where he yelled and threatened and worked them into a frenzy of fear. They marched to her home and dragged her out as her parents watched in horror. They stripped off her layers of black clothing until her brilliance was revealed. And then the king decreed that she be banished – cast from the safe and familiar darkness into the blazing light and the horrors beyond the kingdom.

A few men carried her to edge of town, where the magic barrier was like a bank of dense fog, and tossed her through it like a bag of garbage. Her shock was so extreme that she mercifully fell unconscious before the deed was done.

Soon after being thrown out into the light she began to wake up. From beneath her closed eyelids she remembered what had happened and realized she must now be in the light. She tightened her eyelids down as the horrific stories and images she'd been bombarded with throughout her life came back to her. She lay there, naked and frozen with fear, and her mind began to race with ways to protect herself from the light monsters. After some time she realized she was still alive and nothing bad seemed to be happening; on the contrary, she felt a pleasant tingling sensation on her skin that seemed to liven her whole body. She slowly opened her eyes, and found herself lying on a patch soft green grass. In front of her, very quiet and still, stood three silvery white unicorns.

Now that her eyes were open the smallest of the unicorns moved towards her, bent down, and nuzzled his soft velvet nose in the nape of her neck. She began to cry as a very familiar, warm and comforting feeling enveloped her. Looking around she noticed everything was bright and beautiful, with magnificent colors that she had only seen in her dreams. Leaves shimmered with gold and silver edges from a light that spanned as far she could see.

Just then the other unicorns moved towards her. One draped a soft cloak around her that allowed her light to glow through the loose fabric. Another started moving down a path bordered with flowers, then turned his head and looked back at her, clearly expecting her to follow. They guided her gently toward a large golden tower in the distance. She saw that the other people on the path had their own inner light, which shimmered in an aura around their bodies, each one a unique blend of color and intensity. Within a few moments she and the unicorns were at the gates of the tower. As they approached, the large, twisted, wrought iron gates opened as if by magic. They entered through the gates into a large, beautifully appointed courtyard containing seven throne-like chairs.

As the unicorns guided her past each throne, it lit up and sparkled. The first throne shimmered with a powerful ruby red tone. It was embedded with garnets and obsidian stones. The girl noticed that she now felt grounded, steady, and had a strange sense of belonging. The next throne was orange; it sparkled and glowed as they approached. It was covered with carnelian, agate and tiger's eye. Waves of insight and inspiration washed over her as they walked by. The third throne was yellow and covered with shiny topaz stones. It stood proud and tall, and she felt her own power bubbling within. As she came within reach of the fourth throne she began to feel a warmth rise up from the center of her being that dropped her to her knees. The green throne, glowing with jade and emeralds, pulsed as the girl began crying with joy from a love she had never felt before. After a few moments the largest of the unicorns nudged her with his nose and moved her towards the fifth throne. It was adorned with sapphires and lapis lazuli, but the throne's blue light was dim, unlike the bright essence of the others. The unicorns all stopped and kneeled down on one leg in front of the fifth throne, inviting her to sit. Just as she sat down, her shoulders felt heavy and her throat began to vibrate. The feeling intensified until she had to press her hands to her head just to keep it steady.

With difficulty, she uttered the words "What's going on?" And just then a large glowing figure floated in from the opposite side of the courtyard. Within its light, a physical form was faintly visible, but she couldn't tell if it was a man, woman or something else entirely. Yet she felt that it was a friend, one that she could completely trust. Somehow she knew this with every cell in her being.

Her whole body began to vibrate, and she heard a low and familiar sound come from everywhere and nowhere at the same time. "Ooommm, ooommm."

"I know that sound," she said.

And now the glowing figure spoke to her. Not in words, but as though she felt the words in her heart. It said, "Yes, of course you do. Om is the sound of all creation; it is the sound of you. The sound of All That Is.

"Where am I, and who are you?" the girl asked.

"You are where all creation begins, and I am you and you are me."

"What do you mean, you are me and I am you?"

"Can you not feel me?" the glowing figure said. "Can you not hear me without words?"

The light being moved closer, until the girl was completely enveloped in it, and said, "Your understanding comes from feeling the truth, not knowing it with your mind. Trust me... trust me... trust me."

As the words entered her awareness, she melted into a pool of knowing. The girl felt so alive and so blissful that her own heart's glow expanded to meet it until she and the light were One.

"Please tell me why I am here," she said.

"You are here to remember, replenish yourself, and return to the dark kingdom. You are an illuminated one, and not the only one. There are many of you hiding in the darkness. It is time to shine, to bring light to the shadows and joy back to your fearful hearts.

"But when my light began to shine I was cast out. How can I go back?"

The glowing figure glided back, and its light expanded

until it reached as far as she could see. Now the girl looked around in amazement. There were purple mountains, green valleys, golden deserts, turquoise waters, sienna towns and silver cities, and the azure sky was filled with white clouds edged with gold. And all of this was lit with perfect brilliance.

The girl swept her gaze over the row of chairs she'd passed earlier, and saw that now her own blue chair was glowing as bright as the rest. She would speak her truth with a strong and clear voice. She turned to see the last two chairs, which were indigo and purple, sparkling with azurite and amethyst. She suddenly knew that she was wise beyond measure, and felt her connection to All That Is. At that moment the light of all the chairs seemed to enter her and merge with her own.

The figure said, "This is your birthright. Do not crouch in a corner, hiding under dark clothing, waiting to be found out. Stand tall, let your light shine fully, and tell your story boldly without fear. For I am more real than any harm that could come to you. Each word you utter will cast particles of truth into the darkness and allow the light to return. Your truth will give permission for others who are hiding to speak their truth as well. Trust me, trust me, trust me, for I am with you and will be with you always. You have now been restored to your full glory. Go home, and let your words be the beacon of light."

As the light being spoke these last words, the girl found herself alone back in the field where she had woken up. She was dressed in bright shimmery clothing, and her whole body was tingling. She saw the edge of darkness in front of her like a wall of thick black smoke, and she walked towards it with some hesitation and fear.

But she knew she wasn't alone, for she felt herself now connected to the being of light. Its strength and courage were now within her. She stepped into the darkness and her light beamed out in front, showing the way.

At first, only a few people dared come close enough to listen to her tales of magical creatures and far-off lands. But as she wandered around the kingdom, the word spread, and more and more people stopped and listened, mesmerized by her stories. Her words ignited a spark of light within them and some began to faintly glow. Soon she was attracting crowds.

And with each story told, more light returned to the dark land. Trees grew, flowers bloomed, and the tales of her adventures spread far and wide. Some of the oldest countrymen began to remember a time when light shone in them as well, and they told their own stories to everyone they met. The girl also met young people with an inner glow like her own, and they cast off their dark wrappings and allowed themselves to shine. And so, in this way, the light spread throughout the kingdom.

Of course the king soon heard tales that the maiden had returned, and how she was bringing new light to the land. He became furious, and he worried that if the light reached him he would be seen for who he was – a weak, frightened little man whose only form of control was to keep the people scared.

He began a new fear campaign, circulated more horrible images, and told even more hideous stories than he had before. But something was changing; everyone could feel it. The people were not so quick to believe the scary images and stories as before. They gathered in groups and told their own empowered stories of a better world, and the light grew brighter until they could only see the beauty all around them.

But the story doesn't end here, for we too live in a land of untold wonder, only ever limited by shallow imagination and unquestioned fear. As for the little girl, she grew into a beautifully confident woman. She continued telling her stories and helping others to see the light. Together they created communities of people who were inspired and dedicated to shining the light of awareness all across the land.

THE UNENDING

Writing this story touched me deeply. It flowed out so quickly, coming from a place hidden deep within. And now it was time to complete the exercise. Jean told us to dance our myth to some powerful and meaningful music. She said that this would allow the myth to become fully embodied in our physical reality and could lead to profound new realizations.

So I put on music and began to dance my mythical adventure into life. I swirled and jumped as I was born filled with light. I shook with fear as my light was noticed. I got on my knees and rolled on the floor as I was tortured in the box and drained of my light. I ran and hid as I was hunted and cast from my community. I fell to the ground and lay still, frozen with fear, and then rolled and stretched, basking in the warm golden light.

I danced and I danced. I danced until I cried, I cried until I laughed, and I laughed until I remembered – remembered who I AM.

THE NEW BEGINNING

What about you? Do you remember who you really are? To some degree, I believe that we've all had our imaginations stunted. It makes perfect sense. In this culture, and many others, if something can't be proved scientifically, it's considered fantasy and looked at with great skepticism – with the exception, of course, of the major religions and their faith-based beliefs.

So what happens when we experience grace, but it's outside the realm of what we've been taught, and outside the realm of organized religion? What do we do when extraordinary things happen to us that can't be explained with the mind, and can't be proven in traditional ways?

When these things began to occur in my life, I sought out the support of healers and shamans. I began to meditate, do yoga, and connect with my internal guidance system by having conversations with God and then trusting and following the guidance I received. I also used the tools I had learned during years of personal growth work to keep me centered, grounded and clear. And now I will also cultivate my imagination, and encourage imagination in others.

I've come to realize that whether we know it or not, most of us have hidden our true selves behind the arbitrary rules and standards of others, and we've connected money with our self-worth to some degree. We hide out of fear that who we really are is not enough, and that if others find out about our inadequacies, we'll be banished from our communities, lose friends, and be lost and alone.

There is an ancient story ingrained in our cells – that our safety comes from staying connected to the tribe and having something of value to offer. In its truest sense, it's a beautiful and valuable myth, for staying connected to the tribe is the truth of our oneness, and our value is the experience that our individual expression brings to the whole. But these ideas have become skewed over time, and often our value has come to mean how many titles we acquire, the positions we hold, and how much money we have.

It's no wonder that so many of us work too hard at un-fulfilling jobs, chasing money and acceptance. And it's why most of us feel a low-grade tension all the time. We hide who we are for fear that we don't live up to some narrow cultural standard.

This journey back to myself has brought me to a place of peace and joy far beyond what I thought was possible. And to paraphrase Yogi Bhajan – I am not telling you that I am awake, and I'm not telling you that I'm not awake. All I'm telling you is where my peace and joy comes from.

So when you experience the unexplainable, don't dismiss it as your wild imagination, Go with it, invite it in and let it expand in you. When you experience grace, don't shoo it away and pretend it never happened, but instead trust your-self, feel into it more deeply, and allow it to have its way with you.

There is a great awakening coming; maybe you can feel it. The time of cowering in dark corners trying to escape notice is coming to an end. The time of trying to fit into the crowd is over. This journey back to myself has brought me to un-expected places. Many of them were uncomfortable at first, and some of them seemed to go nowhere, but when I follow my own guidance and remain unattached to the outcome of my actions I am fulfilled – peace and joy are my day-to-day experience.

I've embarked on new adventures and am now traveling in uncharted terrain. But this is all leading me to a very fa-miliar place, to my deepest desire – to help create a world that works for everyone.

To support this intention, I'm writing this book, and I'm committed to its wide distribution, yet I remain unattached to that outcome. I want to inspire others to tell their own journeys of awakening. Much like the character in my mythical adventure, I will tell my wild stories to those who will listen, hoping to stimulate the remembrance of the light within each of you.

I've also created a whole new business entity as a platform for continuing my mythic adventure, which you can learn more about on my website at BethBanning.com. So many of us are chasing this elusive idea of success but we haven't a clue what that really means. Many of us have lots of "stuff, " but not enough meaning or fulfillment in our lives. I'm supporting awakening entrepreneurs to create fresh and more holistic kinds of business that will contribute to a new and more sustainable economy and culture. To that end, I'm asking them questions such as, "What is 'enough' for you? What would give you the deepest satisfaction? What creates wonder and delight in your life? How can a for-profit business be something that not only contributes to your personal joy, but also helps create a sustainable future for everyone?"

I'm also in the process of creating an event called Awaken into Action – Changing the World One Dream at a Time. This initiative will bring world leaders from diverse backgrounds together to support and encourage everyday people to think bigger, act more boldly, and contribute to the world in a much broader way than they ever thought possible. My partners and I have already enrolled over two-dozen well-known world leaders in this project. By the time you're reading this the event will have launched. I've also been guided to create other communities in which to support change through websites such as IAmCommittedToChange.com and YourConversationsWithGod.com.

If you have been touched, moved or inspired by this book, then I invite you to come play with me so we can allow our journeys to unfold together. As I continue along my path, there seems to be no end to the possibilities for living my life more and more fully as an expression of who I truly am. On a regular basis I discover new ways to engage with others so that we can cultivate our imaginations together. As these opportunities continue to evolve I will be updating the websites I listed above with information about various ways that you can get involved.

I don't know how these things will turn out, and that's not the point – there is no perfect experience waiting at the end of this road that I'm traveling. The point isn't for me to get somewhere and to only experience "good" things on the way. The point, my friends, is to create my life as I go. And to live, in-love and in-joy – no matter what that life brings.

In many ways, I am no different than you. Our lives may not seem the same, but we all have old, outdated stories to uncover, tell, and transform, so that our bright inner light can be fully revealed. Those old stories are just myths that need to be updated and allowed to change with the times.

Your story will be different than mine, but only you can be the perfect author of your own transformation. My wish for you is that you remember and allow yourself to once again experience the extraordinary, unseen and unquantifiable realities that are available to you. My hope is that you cultivate your imagination and develop your intuition, and that you trust and let it guide you. My desire is to "hold" you in love as you express yourself fully and experience the peace and joy that I have come to know as my day-to-day experience.

What I know in every cell of my being is that you have so much to offer, that you are valuable beyond measure and that you are loved more than life itself.

Live in freedom and joy!

REFERENCES

CHAPTER 1
Williamson, Marianne. A Return to Love: Reflections on the Principles of "A Course in Miracles." New York: HarperCollins, 1992.

CHAPTER 3
Zukav, Gary. The Seat of the Soul. New York: (Fireside) Simon & Schuster, 1989.

CHAPTER 4
Johnson, Ranae. The Rapid Eye Technology Institute. http://rapideyetechnology.com. 2014.
Jalal al-Din Rumi. "Out Beyond Ideas." The Essential Rumi. Trans. Coleman Barks. New York: HarperCollins, 1995.
Rosenberg, Marshall. Nonviolent Communication: A Language of Compassion. Encinitas, CA: PuddleDancer Press, 1999.

CHAPTER 5
Ruiz, Miguel Angel. The Four Agreements: A Practical Guide to Personal Freedom. San Rafael, CA: Amber-Allen, 1997.

CHAPTER 6
William, Robert. Psych-K Centre International. https://www.psych-k.com/. 2014.

CHAPTER 8
Bach, Dale. Intuitive Counselor: Body Mind and Spirit. http://www.reikiraptures.com/. 2014.

CHAPTER 9
As Above - So Below: An Introduction to Fractal Evolution. Lipton,

Bruce. http://www.brucelipton.com/store/products/above-so-below-dvd. 2013. DVD.

Lipton, Bruce. The Biology of Belief: Unleashing the Power of Consciousness, Matter and Miracles. Carlsbad, CA: Hay House, 2005.

CHAPTER 10

Animal Totems. http://www.linsdomain.com/totems.htm. 2014.

Introduction to Animal Totems: Life Totem Animals. http://soul-psychics.com/blog/introduction-to-animal-totems-life-totem-animals/. 2012.

CHAPTER 13

Conscious TV. http://www.conscious.tv/. 2012.

Muktananda, Swami. Play of Consciousness. 3rd ed. Fallbook, NY: SYDA Foundation, 1971.

CHAPTER 15

Kelley, Tim. True Purpose Institute. http://truepurposeinstitute.com/our-purpose. 2014.

Jung, Carl. Ed. Joan Chodorow. Jung on Active Imagination. Princeton, NJ: Princeton University Press, 1997.

CHAPTER 17

Gaines, Edwene. The Four Spiritual Laws of Prosperity: A Simple Guide to Unlimited Abundance. Emmaus, PA: Rodale, 2005.

CHAPTER 27

Jung, Carl. As quoted on many websites online, none of which list the source.

CHAPTER 33

Houston, Jean. Awakening to Your Life's Purpose. http://evolvingwisdom.com/jeanhouston/yourlifepurpose/digital-course. 2014.

Campbell, Joseph. Hero With a Thousand Faces. Princeton, NJ: Princeton University Press (Bollingen Foundation, Inc.), 1949

The Wizard of Oz. Dir. Victor Fleming. Warner Brothers. 1939. Film.

(Originally a book by Baum, L. Frank. The Wonderful Wizard of Oz. George M. Hill Co., 1900.)

TRUSTED ADVISOR DIALOGUE PROCESS

I found so much benefit from the active imagination process presented throughout this book that I want to share it with you.

If you ever wished you had a trusted advisor who had the answers you needed when you needed them, then the good news is that you already do. All you need to do is cultivate a relationship with your own divine source.

Here's the process:

Find a quiet space where you won't be disturbed.

Name your trusted advisor. For me it's God, for you it's whatever feels right, just figure out what you'll call this trusted advisor. (Read more about naming your trusted advisor starting on page 138.)

Get into a meditative state. Quiet your mind by focusing your attention on your breath for a minute or so.

Then begin a dialogue that goes something like this.

Beth: (Ask a question.)

God: (Write down whatever response or answer that comes. Do this without hesitation or second guessing, just let it flow.)

(You can see an example of how I started my own dialogue process with my trusted advisor starting on page 143.)

Stay relaxed and keep asking all the questions that occur to you, and don't hesitate to ask any skeptical or doubtful questions you might have about this process. Your trusted advisor will answer them as well, and if you receive an answer that is not satisfying, then ask a question about that answer.

Have fun with this! About 80 percent of all people who try this process find it valuable and often quite profound. If you do this process with an open mind and an open heart I promise you will get the answers to important questions that you may have been struggling with. And why wait? Start right now.

Your Trusted Advisor (TA)
Dialogue Process

[ ]: _____
Your name   _____

[ ]: _____
TA's Name   _____

[ ]: _____
Your name   _____

[ ]: _____
TA's Name   _____

[ ]: _____
Your name   _____

[ ]: _____
TA's Name   _____

[ ]: _____
Your name   _____

[ ]: _____
TA's Name   _____

[ ]: _____
Your name   _____

[ ]: _____
TA's Name   _____

[ ]: _____
Your name   _____

[ ]: _____
TA's Name   _____

(Continue on an additional piece of paper if necessary.)

If you would like more information, and a downloadable version on this process I have one available on my website. You can find it by visiting BethBanning.com/resources/

Also, if you have enjoyed this book and see how if more people had this information and got in touch with their own internal guidance it would help create a world that works for everyone then please leave a review and your comments at as many of these places as you you're willing.

Amazon review link: http://amzn.to/1nugDMc

GoodReads review link: bit.ly/gr-ibg

My Website: http://bit.ly/ibg-reflect

ADDITIONAL RESOURCES

30 Days of Free "With Love, God" Texts

We all need love and inspiration in our lives; little reminders that we're not alone and we're always cared for. How much the better when we can add a little fun into the mix.

That's why my team of human angels and I have created the "With Love, God" text project. Just the funny little profound tidbits of wisdom and humor you need to hear delivered right to your phone every day. When you sign-up to receive your 30 days of free love note texts from God you will get that little dose of lovin' you've been craving.

To start receiving your free love texts for 30 days, either text the code "god30" to 96000, sign up online by copying this address into your browser, "bit.ly/godtexts", or scan this QR code:

Trusted Advisor Dialogue Process

If you've enjoyed the dialogues in this book and would like to experience this for yourself, please download the Trusted Advisor Dialogue Process from my website. You can find it by visiting: BethBanning.com/resources/

Other Books from the Author
Meditation Resources

Meditation has become a cornerstone for the ongoing expansion of my awareness and my continuing connection with my higher source of knowing.

If you've ever wanted to explore meditation I've created a free down-loadable resource document called, *101 Ways to Meditate*. This has a plethora of meditation options to investigate. Visit BethBanning.com/resources/ to get this free gift from me to you. I'm confident you'll find great value in it.

I've also authored several meditation eBooks you can find by searching Amazon.com for: ***The Meditation for Life Series***

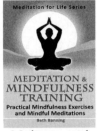

Meditation and
Mindfulness Training

Meditation for
Beginners

Meditation to Awaken
your Kundilini Life Force

Relationship and Communication Resources

As you read in this book, Neill and I have been teaching relationship and communication workshops for many years, the basis of which plays a vital part in my continuing expansion of awareness and connection with God. To discover more about our work please visit, FocusedAttention. com, or explore the three relationship eBooks we've authored that you can find by searching Amazon.com for: ***The Marriage Guide Series***

The Secrets to a
Happy Marriage

How to Rekindle an
Unhappy Marriage

Relationship Tips for a
Happy Marriage

Other Ways to Stay Connected Through Social Media

I am quite active on social media, sharing a theme of the week related to many spiritual, personal growth, and social issues. Please join me online so we can stay connected.

Facebook: www.facebook.com/BethBanning
Twitter: www.twitter.com/BethBanning
Pinterest: www.pinterest.com/BethBBanning
Google+: bit.ly/gplusbeth

ABOUT THE AUTHOR

 BETH BANNING is a best-selling author, inspirational speaker, and spiritual catalyst who lives in California with her husband, their cat, and their six pound poodle. She was born in New York City and from a very young age could sense the feelings of people around her, felt kundalini energy running through her body, and experienced other unusual events that she didn't understand. The well-meaning adults in her life told her she was depressed and that these experiences were just her imagination. Growing up in this cloud of ignorance and disbelief these gifts were buried and unable to flourish, and so she was left confused and lonely.

As a young adult she recognized the same sense of confusion and loneliness in others and became passionate about helping people better understand themselves and those around them. Later in life she took this passion into her work with her husband Neill and co-founded Focused Attention, Inc. She has written numerous books, co-created the Pathway to Personal Freedom, and the Art of Conscious Connection Seminar Series.

After many years of integrating this consciousness shifting work into her own life and teaching it to others, she experienced a profound reconnection with God that turned her life upside down. This radically changed the way she perceives the world and functions in it. Beth now lives her life guided by her inner source of divine wisdom. She is committed to helping others discover this for themselves and fully experience the essence of who they truly are.